Principled Persuasion

Influence with Integrity
Sell with Standards

Marlene Caroselli, Ed.D.

**A CENTER FOR PROFESSIONAL
DEVELOPMENT BOOK
Published by CPD Press**

Published by the Center for Professional Development
324 Latona Road, Suite 1600
Rochester, New York 14626

D1508792

Dr. Caroselli is available for conferences, keynotes, and training programs. You can reach her at:

Center for Professional Development
324 Latona Road - Suite 1600
Rochester, NY 14626-2714
(716) 227-6512; fax: (716) 227-6191
mccpd@aol.com

To order additional copies, contact Total Information Books:
1-800-876-4636

ISBN 0-922411-07-7

First printing, January 1999

Dedicated to
an extraordinary proofreader
and exemplary friend:

Amelia Barclay, CPS,
former president of PSI©

Foreword

~~~~~~~~~~~~~~~~~~~~~~~~~~

Leadership for the 21st century will rely on a different means of direction than the command and control techniques of the past. As our organizations become flatter, employees more educated, and information so available that no one person can possibly know everything, the leader will rely on influence to guide the organization and the activities of employees. Moreover, as employees become less loyal to organizations and more loyal to their own skills and careers, influence will need to be in accord with an acceptable set of values.

Principled Persuasion is a book about this kind of leadership and the ability to influence with integrity. Isn't that what is expected from leaders? If the answer is yes, then here is the secret: influencing with integrity is everyone's business!

When one thinks of great leaders, the first recollection is more likely about the emotions the leaders generated than the actions completed. Words like "charismatic," "inspirational," and "courageous" come to mind. The influence of such leaders seems almost magical. The truth is that these great leaders had two things going for them. First, each had a belief about which that leader felt strongly. Second, each was able to convey that belief with simplicity and passion. The good news is that you and I can learn to do the same.

Principled Persuasion begins by asking us to question not only what we believe in but challenging us to consider how firmly we hold those beliefs. It asks hard questions that require uniquely personal answers. These answers put us in touch with the first thing that great and ethical leaders have, a sense of integrity. The second thing *Principled Persuasion* does is to provide us with clear examples of the ways in which we can use our influence skills more effectively--influence skills that we must use and can practice countless times a day.

Leadership brings with it responsibility. When we choose to influence with integrity, we become part of a trusting relationship. It is within this relationship, when we act in accordance with our integrity, that we grow in spirit and add value to the lives of those around us.

John V. Stephano, Senior Associate
VIMA International, Inc.

Table of Contents

~~~~~~~~~~~~~~~

Chapter 1
Introduction

~~~~~~~~~~~~~~~

A Question of Choices

It's easy to influence. It's much harder to influence
with integrity. Whether you persuade for a living or you
simply "sell" your ideas in the normal course of learning and
living and working, you have already discovered influence
techniques that work. Persuaders, in effect, are sellers. And
vice versa. If you merely wish to improve the influence
techniques that help you persuade others to your point of
view, you can find numerous guidelines and primers and
recommendations. The rule books for principled persuasion,
though, are few and far between. And the books for
powerful, principled persuasion are fewer still.

Part of the difficulty lies in the many possible
definitions of key words, like "integrity." Is it, as the
dictionary denotes, a question of honesty? Is it a matter of

sincerity or of uprightness, as the dictionary also suggests? Would you perhaps equate integrity with sound moral principles? If so, what exactly are those principles?

Some people regard integrity as the decision to live according to the Golden Rule: "Do unto others as you would have them do unto you." Is this your belief as well? And what if you were seeking to measure your degree of integrity as well as define it? Would you assess your actions as ethical ones if they brought improvement to existing situations? If not, what gauge would you use? The choices for determining what integrity means are multiple and mingled-- they overlap with many other factors.

In the simplest sense, "integrity" means living according to specified values. But, of course, simplicity is usually deceptively complex. Living by specified values involves complex ramifications and interpretations. The definition of integrity that we endorse has ever-widening circles. The more integrity you demonstrate, the more widespread the benefits to others.

In other words, when you act with integrity, you are widening the sphere of influence, you are using power tools to achieve powerful benefits for those who "buy" your concepts or your commodities. If your actions are taken for your own advantage exclusively, you are following a narrow moral code, one that places your needs above all others. You no doubt operate within the letter of the law but perhaps not within the spirit of the unwritten laws that govern our behavior as human beings. If your actions are self-serving, you are not concerned with serving others. Consequently, your ethical influence is limited.

On the other hand, when your actions benefit other people, you are operating from a higher-level moral code; you are living by and influencing others with generally accepted principles of correctness rather than your own interpretation of specific rules. In later chapters, you'll have a chance to learn more about widening both your perspective and your approaches to ethical influence.

Unlike morality--which implies a codified sense of ethics, an acknowledged system to which many people subscribe--integrity is an individual consideration. Consequently, achieving clarity on integrity is much harder than achieving clarity on influence. But once you have made the choices that lead to clarity, you can consciously take ethical actions--actions that reflect the principles by which you wish to live. Having grasped what integrity is, you'll proceed to use it in your efforts to influence others in honorable ways.

Remember, though, the second sentence in this Introduction: "It's much harder to influence with integrity." Don't think that once you have managed to define "integrity," the definition will last a lifetime. Integrity, in truth, is a slow-moving target. Think about it. Over the years, haven't you shifted some of your views, in keeping with Emerson's insistence that "a foolish consistency is the hobgoblin of little minds"? Some of those views probably involved the definition of what it means to act with integrity.

The events or encounters that occur even after you have finally defined integrity to your satisfaction keep the target in a state of slow flux. These occurrences may be significant enough to force you to re-think your definition. You may have determined your personal set of principles, but when those principles are put to the test, you may find they are not steadfast after all. Or, you may find that your principles do not apply to other people. Or, that certain factors cause a given principle to recede in importance. You may even modify your definition to include certain behaviors that gained greater significance in your life. Having been betrayed by a friend or an employer, for example, you may now decide that keeping one's word is a critical aspect of integrity.

Psychologists have a name for these below-the-surface rumblings in our mental terrain: "cognitive dissonance." In other words, you may have determined for yourself what actions fall within the acceptable realm as far as integrity is concerned. To be sure, it is important to make these determinations. Otherwise, you may find yourself in a state of emotional disequilibrium. But then you receive information that upsets what you've come to believe is true. You are thrown off balance, so to speak by the information that runs contrary to the belief system you've established. Your ethical "wholeness" now has a now has a crack in it.

To illustrate, let's assume you have placed various individuals in either the acceptable or the non-acceptable area on the integrity spectrum, on the basis of their actions. Then you learn that someone you regard as a person of high moral character has done something you consider unethical. You actually have several options available to you in order to change your mental "dissonance" to "consonance." You can refuse to believe the story you are hearing, thus maintaining the image you have of this person. Or, you can relax your standards, perhaps even redefining what integrity means to you, in order to keep this person's behavior within the realm of acceptability. Finally, you could decide to shift your opinion of this individual from the high end of your integrity scale to the lower end. But, resolution of some kind is necessary. Otherwise, you will continue to experience psychological discomfort.

Let's look at another example. If you were asked what core values you abide by, would you be able to express them without hesitation? Many people would find this question a challenging one, to be sure. Having lived through recent eras such as the Me Generation, the Greed-Is-Good Era, and a Scandal-in-Government era, you may find yourself wondering more than ever before how steady your moral compass really is. When you read that approval ratings for dishonest politicians continue to soar or that stock prices continue to climb despite charges of unethical practices against corporate leaders, you may even wonder if the integrity-component of the leadership personality is as important as you've always thought it was.

Current events force us to grapple with questions just like these. We choose our leaders in part because we believe them to be men and women who act with integrity, which in the eyes of many is an integral aspect of leadership. When we learn they are alleged to have done things we regard as unethical, perhaps even immoral, we have to make some tough choices. Do we still support such individuals? Do we revamp our opinions of them? Do we widen the borders surrounding appropriate behaviors? Do we remove certain actions from our previous definition, regarding them as unimportant after all? Do we decide that the person can still be an effective/successful leader despite his transgressions, because the economy is strong and/or because the nation is at peace?

Our basic moral foundation was formed early in our childhood. But experience and events cause it to undergo periodic revisions. Think of the childhood and young-adult experiences that shaped your ethical view of the world. Would you want your children growing up with the moral outlook that you depended on to guide your actions? In what ways has your belief system changed to accommodate today's world? Once you entered the world of work, did you find a fit between your beliefs and the culture in which you work? Depending on your answers to these and other questions, you make choices--important choices--about the way you choose to live and work. The choices bring you closer and closer to the target that represents your ethical core.

The choices, as we've mentioned, cannot be made collectively. Yes, you may be swayed by the results of polls, you may engage in discussions of these issues, you may read how others are leaning. But in the end, you must decide for yourself what constitutes integrity. The decisions are seldom simple and almost never quick. But they must be made. Otherwise, you find yourself floundering in a sea of decisions each time a new scenario presents itself. You probably know some metaphoric boats that have capsized or sunk because there were cracks in the hull. In reference to the integrity of boats and individuals alike, the literal definition of "wholeness" or "soundness" is a good one to use.

It is our hope that by reading *Principled Persuasion*, you will gain a deeper understanding of what it means to act with integrity in general and to influence with integrity in particular. That understanding will enable you to know when you are acting honorably and when you are not. It will also enable you to continually add to your range of ethical behaviors. A fuller comprehension of the ways in which we ethically persuade and scrupulously sell may even impact others in their efforts to do the same.

Principled Persuasion is designed to assist you in making the choices that lead to a clear understanding of what integrity means to *you*. A simple example may help illustrate the choices and the personalized nature of them. First, though, decide if you think lying is wrong. Then consider the following situation and decide if the woman involved influenced with integrity, even though she lied as she did so.

A perfectly healthy woman is dining in a restaurant with signs on the wall that clearly state "No smoking permitted." She sees a rather surly looking man blatantly light up a cigarette. There is no waiter or waitress nearby and so the woman approaches the man. She does not wish to start an argument, she does not wish to be rude, but she does want to influence him to put out the cigarette. Fearing that a simple request--"Could you please not smoke?"--will yield an antagonistic response--"Make me!"--she decides to tell a white lie: "I suffer from bronchial emphysema and the cigarette smoke causes me to gasp for air. Would you mind not smoking in here?"

It works. The man immediately crushes the cigarette and even apologizes to the woman. Would you have taken a similar influencing course, given these circumstances? Was the woman dishonest and thus lacking integrity as she influenced the man? Or, was she successful in her influence objective: getting him to stop without causing an unpleasant exchange?

As you read through the positive elements associated with influence--integrity, leadership, trust, appropriateness, style, impact, vision, visibility, and values--you will be acquiring ammunition to steady your aim as you focus on that ever-moving target known as your ethical core. In the final chapter, you'll find discussions of the less-positive elements of influence, namely manipulation and Machiavellianism. Situations such as the telling of white lies will be further examined there.

You'll find many questions in both the positive-element chapters and in the final chapter as well. Sometimes the answers will be provided. Occasionally, you'll be asked to find answers on your own, for in the exploration of ideas we eventually come to terms with our views.

As we've noted, choosing an operational definition of "integrity" is a personal matter. By contrast, when we work collaboratively and collectively, it's fairly easy to establish standards to govern us. As team members, for example, we have groundrules that promote ethical treatment of one another. As organizations, we have mission, vision, and values statements that guide our operations. As members of one religious group or another, we have holy books and golden rules that encourage ethical practices. As members of a reading community, we are able to purchase books that encourage us to adopt specific behaviors. While we can, as a society, as a nation, as a member of one group or another, establish agreed-upon principles that overarch our collective behaviors, it is much more challenging to know and articulate our own core values.

In addition to the questions regarding integrity, you'll also find questions such as these regarding influence: What does it take for you to be influenced? How do you feel when someone has influenced you unethically? What led you to believe it was unfair or unethical? Do we have a right to influence those who hold onto their viewpoints as firmly as we hold on to our own? What role does "manipulation" play in ethical influencing?

Think of what life would be like if integrity did not govern the actions of those with whom you come in contact, especially those attempting to influence you. Speculate for a few moments about the results of a world in which ethical questions had not been answered, had not, perhaps, even been asked. Consider the products you buy, the services you receive, the work that you do, the community in which you live--if there were no moral premise governing decisions, the world would be in a sorry state indeed. Perhaps the best business-related commentary is the one expressed by Peter Drucker, often referred to as the Father of Modern Management Science: "Moral vision and commitment to social values are the foundation of enduring business success."

Answering these and related questions requires effort. Is the effort-investment worth the return? We believe it is. Expending the time and energy to explore the issues surrounding integrity results in the formation of those sound moral principles that serve as a base of operations. Without this foundation, we lack the higher purpose that makes us feel good about what we do--as individuals, as corporate citizens, as citizens of even larger communities. As you study the questions and answers associated with influence and integrity, you'll be adding to your store of knowledge. And, the greater the array of choices on the shelves of that store, the more carefully and correctly you can select the ones allowing you to influence with integrity.

You Cannot *Not* Influence

This book is broadly focused on improving the ways in which we influence. There is a more narrow focus, too, one that is equally important: improving the ways we *ethically* influence. Each day, we hear of situations that are easy to identify as unethical, immoral, or illegal. Such situations require little thought or effort from us, in terms of separating right from wrong. Actions involving murder or theft or abuse or drug activity, for most of us, fall clearly in the "wrong" end of the ethical spectrum. But when we influence others, there are multiple shades of gray associated with our actions.

Because you are influencing all day long, you may not be paying attention to the ways in which you exert influence over others. But in truth, you cannot *not* influence. Everything about you influences others, whether or not you are aware of the impact you are having. The way you dress, the way you organize your workspace, the way you speak, the way you decorate your home, the way you drive and the car you drive--all of these and more send out messages that influence others--negatively, minimally, optimally, or ideally. That influence may be intended or inadvertent, effective or ineffective, correct or incorrect, positive or negative, driven by ethics or by self-aggrandizement. But you are indeed sending out non-verbal messages all of the time. Consequently, you influence the way others think and act, based on their perceptions of both your message and your motivations.

The most effective influencers use a honed, not a haphazard, approach to interpersonal interactions. They weigh the possible outcomes of the words they've chosen to speak and the actions they've decided to undertake. You may be starting to equate such deliberation with manipulation. Realize there *are* some parallels. We'll explore them in greater depth in subsequent chapters. Those who "sell" with standards know that "object language" can easily influence the impression others have of you, may even be a factor in their decision to hire you or to do business with you. Do decisions to put your best foot forward mean you are behaving improperly? Absolutely not. They simply mean you are doing all you can to influence the outcomes you believe are directly advantageous to you and indirectly advantageous to others.

If you've ever watched a courtroom drama or served on a jury yourself, you know that lawyers make special efforts to relate to the jury. They may speak in a certain way, cite particular references, dress in a deliberate fashion, carry a certain kind of briefcase. Would you regard their efforts as dishonest manipulation or deliberate influence? You must judge for yourself, of course. But if such actions were immoral, then salespeople, leaders, ministers, managers, teachers, attorneys, and a host of others--including those who spruce up their home before selling it--would be guilty of unethical influence.

Effective influencers are multi-lingual: they use the language of objects and a variety of other languages to lead others to think or act in a certain way. As long as the purpose behind their use of those languages is an ethical purpose, designed to benefit someone or something beyond the influencer, then the influencers are acting with integrity. To effectively employ body language and paralanguage and silence and neurolinguistics and proxemics (the use of space) is to understand that different folks need different strokes. Your ability to use a wide range of tools is a tribute to your understanding of human dynamics.

Leading by Influence not Authority

Influencing with integrity, not surprisingly, means exerting positive leadership, effecting positive change. In fact, author Kenneth Blanchard observes the key to successful leadership today is influence, not authority. If you wish to lead others, you can no longer depend exclusively on the power of your position. Your authority, such as it is, carries less weight today than it did in times past. Because the Quality movement emphasizes empowered behavior and because flattened organizations spell leadership opportunities for everyone, you are probably eager to learn how to lead by influence--no matter what degree of authority you have in the organization or in the other structures in which you participate.

Realize the initial reaction to many of your leadership proposals will be a healthy skepticism. Most people are slow to change. They have adopted an "if-it-ain't-broke-don't-fix-it" attitude. Thus, to be effective, you must withstand and overcome the reluctance that is the usual response to a leader's initial suggestion. You and your ideas must be strong enough to withstand a range of negative reactions-- from apathy at one end to complete refusal at the other. Influencing with integrity may mean overcoming objections, or igniting passions, or changing minds. It may be convincing through information, or persuading through personality, or swaying through strategic alliances. No matter what means or combination of means you use, the purpose behind your efforts must be an ethical one--to effect positive change for both yourself and others.

If your efforts are less than admirable, others will sooner or later learn of the unethical stance you have taken. Not only do you stand to harm your reputation but you may harm your career as well. Every action you take has consequences--positive or negative, sooner or later. Sometimes you will not learn of the ripple effect you have created until long after you have spoken or acted. Whenever you set out to influence, you will be tossing words onto smooth surfaces of paper, computer screens, or minds. There is no telling how far your influence may extend, no foreseeing how wide your audience may become. If only for this reason, integrity should guide all your influence actions. And the more tools you have at your disposal, the more effective your influence can be. Those who are limited to the metaphoric hammer view every influence-situation as a nail. The more effective influencers, though, have acquired several different integrity-tools and several different influence techniques.

The former CEO of Ford Motor Company, Don Petersen, once observed that results depend on relationships. You may be able to maintain relationships for a while by operating in a less-than-scrupulous manner. You may be able to cover truth up for a time. Before long, though, it is destined to emerge. Because it is impossible to hide duplicitous behavior forever, someone is bound to uncover your ulterior motives. And when that happens, the consequences are usually dire. If you are interested in results, you need good relationships. And to sustain those relationships, you need to influence with integrity, to take a standards-driven approach.

Drucker reminds us that leaders know how to ask questions--the right questions. As a leader of others, you will willingly explore the many questions associated with influence--many to be found in this book, others that will occur to you as you execute your leadership plans. Among the concepts to be probed as you build mutually influential relationships is awareness: do you know when you are acting with integrity? What leads you to your conviction that your actions are proper? On what bases do others view your actions? How can you expand your influence without lessening the ethical component of it? Ideally, by the time you have completed *Principled Persuasion* and have given serious thought to the questions and activities, you will have developed:

- your own definition of "integrity"
- your own philosophy for integrating integrity into your influence endeavors, and
- your own practical approach for operating from an ethical stance whenever you seek to influence others.

Organization of the Book

In Chapter 2, "Influence and Integrity," the basic foundation is laid for deciding what constitutes influence and what constitutes integrity. Because integrity affects every other element of influence, we begin with definitions of both words. You'll learn about the Return on Influence Factor and the pPp Plan. And, the Circle of Influence will help you gain an in-depth perspective by affording you the opportunity to develop the various skills that comprise that circle.

"Influence and Leadership" are examined in Chapter 3, and concrete examples are provided, showing how leaders use language in their influence efforts. In addition, the dangers of being in the influence-spotlight are studied. So, too, is the temptation, while in that spotlight, to weasel out of the glare. (We strongly urge other means.) The chapter concludes with a comprehensive study of ways to make your writing style more influential.

In Chapter 4, the emphasis is on "Influence and Trust." The importance of this component of influence is demonstrated in discussions that focus on earning and giving trust, particularly when we, as individuals and teams, work to make a difference. Of particular interest for business influences is the connection between trust and empowerment explored here.

The "nanosecond nineties" yield to the culture of chaos predicted for the millennium. As corporate, societal, and communications structures are revamped, certain things remain constant. Among them is the importance of treating one another and the environment itself with respect. This aspect of influencing with integrity is examined in "Influence and Appropriateness," the title of Chapter 5. You'll learn about being politically correct. You also learn about using truth honestly, honorably, and using it within a results-driven framework. The context of influence, whether it is a one-on-one setting or an electronic exchange, is enhanced by messages that reflect both efficiency and sensitivity.

Impeached governor of Arizona, Evan Meacham, once told reporters that if he had to do it all over again, he would pay as much attention to style as he did to substance. In Chapter 6, "Influence and Style," you see how style impacts substance and vice versa. You really can say anything you wish to say and have others not only accept your point but be willing to act upon it--provided you have used the right style.

You'll enjoy making the hard-to-swallow easy-to-digest as you work your way though Chapter 7, "Influence and Impact." Here you'll find user-friendly but nonetheless powerful techniques for diplomatic influences. You'll discover effective strategies for delivering truth and will learn when to sugar-coat and when not to.

Chapter 8 takes a hard look at "Influence and Manipulation." You may be surprised to find yourself giving new attention to old definitions. The Influence Continuum will help you determine correct courses of action, as will other "integrity gauges." The ROR-Shock Model will facilitate the transition from reality-based openness to the actualization of your ideas. The questions raised in this chapter are important ones for anyone who worries about "right" crossing over to "wrong."

What value do you bring to the work you do? Typically, your expertise lends value to the processes in which you engage. Frequently overlooked, however, are the values that create a moral infrastructure for the working environment. Chapter 9 considers "Influence and Values" that both employers and employees are seeking. This section also pinpoints the values by which effective teams operate.

Vision has been defined as "the art of seeing the invisible." As you work to make the ideal vision real, you will be gaining visibility yourself. Chapter 10, with its attention to "Influence, Vision, and Visibility," looks to long-term outcomes. It discusses the entrepreneurial spirit and the self-promotion and idea-promotion necessary for realizing long-range plans.

To test your "What-would-you-do?" skills, you can work on the case studies found in the Appendix. Based on real-world examples, they allow you to compare your likely course of action to the actual outcome and also to the recommendations from a panel of experts.

Finally, you will find numerous authors referenced throughout the book. The Bibliography cites their works, which provide a wealth of additional material, directly and indirectly on the topic of ethically selling your ideas, your products, your services, your self.

Organization of the Chapters

Each chapter begins with an Overview, which presents a construct for the general concepts introduced. The chapters then move to examinations of specific elements of influence. Historical and contemporary examples and exemplars are featured, along with quotations, anecdotes, and statistics to illustrate the points made. At the end of the chapters, a Preview is provided. It points the way to what you will encounter in the upcoming chapter.

Additionally, each chapter contains an interview with an outstanding exemplar of influence and/or integrity. Their comments are used to illustrate key elements of the chapter. A summary is presented at the end of each chapter in the form of a specific listing of "Do's and Don't's" and "Will's and Won't's." (At a recent conference in Washington, D.C., I was fortunate enough to obtain mini-interviews with a number of well-known Americans. Their thoughts on influence, scattered throughout the book, appear like the following.)

Gay Talese, Author:

"Influence is an ongoing use of those values that are most enduring. Most of the values that comprise ethical influence originate in the home and thus reflect the totality of experience."

Included in the Do's and Don't's are recommendations for you to pursue in order to enhance your influence-skills. The Will's and Won't's represent guidelines for future eventualities likely to ensue from the "will's," or professional pledges you make to yourself.

You'll also find, sprinkled throughout the chapters, exercises that invite you to interact with the material. These exercises sometimes appear in the form of questions. Other times, they may be quizzes, self-assessments, or requests for you to explore a given idea further. (Many of the activities ask you to assess your workplace. If you are a full-time student who is not currently working, simply ask a friend or family member for information.) Don't hesitate to interact with the learning. Be encouraged by two thoughts:

1) The more you learn, the more you'll earn.
2) Confucian wisdom: "I hear and I forget. I see and I learn. I do and I remember."

Take advantage of these learning opportunities. (You'll find them represented by a check mark inside a box: ☑.) Take the time to explore these challenges and to learn more about yourself and your style of influencing in the process.

A final note: references to both genders are made chapter by chapter, using first the male pronouns, and then, in the next chapter, the female pronouns.

Results Depend on Relationships

Every action in which we engage has consequences, many of which are unanticipated, some of which are unanticipate-able. When we toss words onto smooth surfaces of paper, computer screens, or receptive minds, there is no telling how wide the ripples might be, no foreseeing how wide our influence. And so, it behooves us to operate with integrity, to seek many-layered benefits, to ensure that an ethical outcome is designed for every step of the journeys we propose others take with us.

As businesspeople or students who will soon enter the business world, we recognize the merit in the assertion that results depend on relationships. We may be able to maintain those relationships for a while in an integrity-vacuum. We may be able to operate with less than full disclosure, we may be able to sell a shoddy product or disguise a true intent. Sooner or later, though, some of the people who cannot be fooled all of the time will see through the threadbare mantle of integrity, worn by unethical individuals in order to cloak ulterior motives. And when that happens, the consequences may easily doom the unscrupulous seller.

On a Personal Note

Several years ago, at the end of a ten-week program I conducted for Allied-Signal, an executive named Darius Irani approached me. He had attended the "Effective Business Writing" class and had heard me bring closure to the course, thank the participants for their time, and had watched me pack up my materials and get ready to leave the building.

He asked me to come to his office first. Without preamble, he began to chastise me. "In your business," he observed, "you need both excellence and hype. Your problem is that you have only excellence." He noted that I had been ready to leave without learning if the client wanted further training programs. He faulted me for doing nothing to further my own cause, to pave the way for future business, to assess client needs.

On the long freeway ride back to the office, I mulled over his words and realized how accurate they were. Proclaiming my own excellence was an uncomfortable feeling for me; it smacked of self-promotion and opportunistic, perhaps even manipulative, behavior. I've since come to realize that influencing others means giving them what they need to make informed choices. Hype should help the influencee. When it harms the influencee, hype becomes dishonest manipulation.

By reading *Principled Persuasion*, you are giving yourself several gifts:

- A refined ability to hype yourself and your ideas for the benefit of others
- Access to new knowledge
- Opportunities to explore ideas further
- The chance to meet, if only on paper, remarkable exemplars
- Checklists and guidelines to apply to improvement-efforts
- An investment in yourself.

It may be that author Charles Handy is correct in his prediction that tomorrow's employee will be a "portfolio person." In other words, the employee of the future will be one who contracts with various companies for the skills and competencies amassed in his private portfolio. If the prediction is correct, then developing your ability to influence with a fine sense of ethics will surely thicken your professional portfolio. And to paraphrase a popular bumper sticker, "The person with the fattest portfolio wins."

Chapter 2
Influence & Integrity

~~~~~~~~~~~~~~~

Overview   To help ensure common understanding of terms to be used throughout the book, we begin with definitions, acknowledging that influence has parallels to both leadership and manipulation. We move on to the pPp Plan, which, properly executed, will extend your influence through an assessment of purpose, the big picture, and the persons who will be impacted by your goal.

Additionally, by studying your Sphere of Influence, you can increase the Return on your Influence. And the Circle of Influence, with its components of integrity, negotiations, vision, political savvy, problem-solving, self-confidence, communications, and respect, should make you more adept at influencing with integrity by virtue of the practice it provides.

The chapter ends with Dr. Georgeanna Ahlfor's interview. She confirms the importance of communicating well with those we need to influence, whether for personal or professional reasons.

Definitions

An ancient Buddhist observation reminds us that "anything we do is everything we do." In the smallest gesture are reflections of attitudes, values, beliefs, philosophies. Connected to the ancient aphorism is this saying: "Character is what you do when no one is looking." A simple action can reveal the complexities of character that constitute your personality. To illustrate: you're alone in a restroom. You wash your hands and use a paper towel to dry them. You toss it into the wastepaper basket but it falls to the floor instead. No one is around. Do you pick it up?

Assume that you did pick it up. This small gesture reveals a number of things about you: Your concern for others, for the "environment," for orderliness, perhaps even the pride you take in cleaning up after yourself.

By extension, the whole realm of influence is tightly connected to character. The way you influence in the least significant matters is reflective of how you will influence in the most significant. To be sure, the purpose, persons, and big picture will change in various sets of circumstances, but the underlying approach remains the same. You either influence with integrity or you do not.

By "influence," we mean "employing both verbal and physical tools for getting others to do what we wish them to do." This definition parallels the definitions of leadership. It also bears a surprising resemblance to manipulation. Influence is actually a neutral term. Coupled with integrity, it falls at the positive end of the influence spectrum. Used for greedy or dishonorable purposes, influence belongs at the negative end.

Think of influence like a car. It could be driven in order to achieve positive outcomes--getting an expectant mother to the hospital in time for her baby to be delivered. That same car, though, driven irresponsibly or drunkenly, could cause the death of others. Influence, like a car, is what it is. *How* it is used--with positive or negative consequences --determines at which end of the ethical continuum the influence belongs.

While we will view "influence" as a verb, it can, of course, be used as a noun. We've opted for the verb form as it is more direct, contains more action. The noun implies less immediate or significant impact, but like the verb, it can apply to both people and things. Your life style, for example, might influence the type of home you own. Or, the biography of a great humanitarian might have a positive influence on your own philanthropic intentions.

Can you increase the number of tools in your persuasion portfolio? Of course you can. You can become quite masterful, in fact, by reading about these tools and practicing them frequently. (Keep in mind the Latin origin of the word: literally, "influence" means "flowing into." The ancient Romans believed an ethereal fluid or power flowed from the stars into people and that they were subsequently influenced to do things.)

The choice, however, of whether or not to incorporate integrity into the use of those tools is a choice only you can make. If you influence with integrity, you will evince ethical persuasions in everything you do--that is the premise of this book. And, of course, if you choose to enhance your powers of influence for purposes that smack of deception, then that too is your choice.

In defining the word "integrity," we turn once again to its Latin root. The word "integer" means, quite literally "not" *(in)* "touched" *(tangere)*. Thus, an integer is something complete unto itself, an entire or whole entity, as opposed to a fraction. From "integer" comes "integrity," a quality or state of being complete, unimpaired, untainted or sound. As used here, "integrity" will refer to "sound moral principles, uprightness, honesty, and sincerity."

Let's relate these definitions to circumstances you may have found yourself in recently. (Through such efforts, our understanding of concepts is deepened and thus, we are more likely to apply those concepts to future situations.)

☑ When was the last time you attempted to influence another person on an issue of some importance to you? Briefly describe that effort here.

_____

_____

_____

Keeping in mind that when we influence, we employ both verbal and physical tools to get others to do what we wish them to do, consider what evidence the other person had that you were acting with integrity. In other words, how did you demonstrate that your efforts were based on sound moral principles, uprightness, honesty, and/or sincerity?

_____

_____

_____

When is the last time you were influenced by another person, someone who was successful in getting you to do

what he thought should be done? Outline that experience
here.

_____

_____

_____

Did you trust that person? If so, what was the basis for that
trust?

_____

_____

_____

If you did not trust that person, what else persuaded you to
be influenced by him?

_____

_____

_____

Influence, we believe, is tightly tied to integrity. If
you wish to persuade others to your way of thinking and/or
acting, you will find the process made easier by their faith in
you. Of course, it is possible to persuade others to immoral
ends. Typically, though, that power is a short-lived power.
Yes, history has afforded men like Adolf Hitler and Charles
Manson some prominence for some period of time, but the

influence they had over their subjects is not the influence we will explore here.

Instead, we subscribe to theories, such as those espoused by psychologist Douglas McGregor, that assert most people want to do the right thing, want to work in efficient ways, want to help others move toward positive ends.

Multi-lingual Advantages

The quality guru, Dr. Joseph M. Juran, frequently noted that executives speak the language of money. And employees speak the language of things. If you wish to be effective, he would assert, if you wish to assume a leadership role, it is important for you to be "bi-lingual."

In truth, there are many languages to be spoken as we attempt to influence others. Our choices depend on what we think will be most effective in getting our message across. Ideally, we will think about ethical factors as well. If you are persuading without principles, you are selling your soul along with your mental or physical wares.

The most effective influencers are well-versed in the many ways to communicate. They select the language best suited for their audience, knowing that passion, principles, and/or products cannot be sold if you cannot reach the audience. It follows, then, that the more polyglot you are, the more "languages" you can speak, the better equipped you will be to meet people on both their literal and figurative terms. The following exercise will help you develop your multi-lingual skills and thus, your ability to target your influence efforts more exactly.

☑ You do not have complete control over every facet of your life. No one does. There is someone or perhaps several someones you would like to influence to do some things your way. It may be a supervisor or co-worker, a friend or family member, a neighbor or someone you know in a social or community setting. Tell exactly what you'd like to influence that person to do.

_____

_____

_____

Now consider the outcome you would like to see. How do you wish the other person to feel after hearing your "pitch"? Check every adjective from the following list that would apply in this situation.

☐	abundant	☐	accepting
☐	acclimated	☐	adamant
☐	bedazzled	☐	benefited
☐	blameless	☐	bonded
☐	cajoled	☐	calm
☐	capable	☐	championed
☐	challenged	☐	debriefed
☐	determined	☐	empathic
☐	enabled	☐	energized
☐	familiar	☐	fortunate
☐	guided	☐	identified
☐	informed	☐	inspired
☐	other _____		

Look at those adjectives you've checked. Which is likely to be the most potent of all for the influence situation you've just described? _____

Now, record what you would have to do and/or say to leave your influencee feeling the emotion you've described as most potent of all. _____

_____

_____

☑ As you make preparations for proposing your plan, think about the various languages you could use to communicate your ideas. A partial list is presented here. Feel free to add other types of language to the list, given the vantage point of your particular circumstances. Then select the language that would probably prove to be most persuasive with the person you hope to influence.

☐ the language of money
☐ the language of things
☐ the language of technology
☐ the language of business
☐ the language of teamwork
☐ the language of sports
☐ the language of politics
☐ the language of global economy
☐ the language of leadership
☐ the language of quality
☐ the language of innovation
☐ the language of _____

What specific words do you associate with the language you checked? Which of those are likely to have a positive impact on the person you hope to influence?

_____	_____
_____	_____
_____	_____
_____	_____

Case Study #1 in the Appendix will give you another chance to consider a given situation from several angles and to select the language that will probably be most easily understood by the person you are trying to influence.

Challenge Yourself

It's been said we should make no small plans for they have no power to stir the soul. On the other hand, Mother Teresa maintained that "we can do no great things--only small things with great love." Think now about a plan by which you hope to influence a number of others. The plan to exert influence and create mutual benefits may be small or large in scope, but it should be a plan that allows you to demonstrate your leadership capability and one that effects positive change.

Your proposal may be social in nature--make plans to take charge of the next Christmas party and to make it a truly memorable affair. It might be quality-oriented--form a team to benchmark how another organization performs the same processes in which you engage. It could even be professional--prepare a speech to deliver at a conference--or philanthropic--assemble a group to build Habitats for Humanity. You might prefer something related to employee concerns--develop a video that can be used during orientation for new employees. The possibilities are infinite.

Whatever your idea, approach it with confidence. Heed the words of Ralph Waldo Emerson: "Do not be too timid and squeamish about your actions. All life is an experiment."

☑ Capture here the main thrust of the project you hope will influence others to act in such a way that positive outcomes result.

_____

_____

_____

Read about the pPp Plan as follows. Then apply the purpose, big picture, and person questions to the plan you've outlined.

The Return on Influence

Purpose

To optimize the ROI Factor (Return on Influence), we need to incorporate many factors into our basic influencing style. Otherwise, we would be using only four cylinders when our influence-vehicle is actually equipped with eight. One method of optimizing the power being used on selling is the pPp Plan. It will enable you to give full consideration to the many factors that impact your ability to influence with integrity.

Chief among those factors is the purpose behind the decision to influence. As you consider rationale, you will simultaneously consider answers to questions like these:

- ☐ Whom do I want to influence?
- ☐ Why?
- ☐ What outcome do I intend to achieve?
- ☐ What influence techniques have worked for me in the past?
- ☐ What is likely to work under these current circumstances?
- ☐ How is this plan superior to others that are similar?
- ☐ What benefits will accrue, to whom, if this idea is implemented?

☐ What precedents could I cite to encourage adoption of this plan?

☐ To what extent will this project consume me? In other words, will I have time to see it through to completion?

☐ What indications have I had thus far that the idea is a feasible one?

☐ How much support do I have for this?

☐ How much homework have I done for this?

☐ Other _____

Which of these questions are most relevant to the project you've outlined? Check three of them off now. Then answer those three questions in relation to the influence project you've outlined.

1. _____
_____

2. _____
_____

3. _____
_____

Big Picture

In addition, the big picture must be taken into account. (It is represented by the capital or "big" P in the formula.) When we look beyond the tip of our nose, we contemplate the outcome or results in places beyond our immediate sphere of influence. Moving us from a limited perspective to a wider one will require extensive examination. Questions like these will help widen the angle of the lens through which you are viewing the situation.

- [ ] What is there to win if I am successful in this endeavor?
- [ ] What is there to lose?
- [ ] What might be a penalty associated with success?
- [ ] What might be a reward associated with failure?
- [ ] In hearing this plan, would someone who does not know me see the value or ethical principles behind it?
- [ ] How does it advance the organizational mission?
- [ ] How would it impact the bottom line?
- [ ] What does it make faster, cheaper, more efficient?
- [ ] How could it be replicated in other places?
- [ ] How much resistance will it generate?
- [ ] Other _____

Which of these questions are most relevant to the project you've outlined? Check three of them off now. Then answer those three questions in reference to the influence project you've outlined.

1. _____

_____

2. _____

_____

3. _____

_____

Persons

Having given some thought to intent, you can proceed to consider the individual(s) whom you hope to influence. As part of the preparation process, you need to spend time identifying both those who will support the plan you hope to initiate and those who may squelch its progress.

- ☐ What objections might the person I wish to influence raise?
- ☐ How will I respond to his objections?
- ☐ Who else might benefit by being included in my influencing endeavor?
- ☐ Who can I count on to support this plan?

☐ Who has done something similar in the past?

☐ How willing might he be to serve as a mentor on this project?

☐ Have I considered widening the audience that will hear this message? What are the pro's and con's of doing so?

☐ Who above me should be made aware of this message?

☐ Who should serve on my team?

☐ Who might benefit indirectly from this plan?

☐ Other _____

Which of these questions are most relevant to the project you've outlined? Check three of them off now. Then answer those three questions in reference to the influence project you've outlined.

1. _____

_____

2. _____

_____

3. _____

_____

If we fail to attend to the pPp questions, we will fail to achieve the fullest return on the investments we make-- investments of time, energy, and reputation. Not taking full advantage of the power we have means selling less or persuading less effectively than we are capable of doing. Yes, you should move ahead boldly, for if you always do what you've always done, you'll always be what you already are. Nonetheless, to move too quickly is to jeopardize success.

The Sphere of Influence

Another kind of deliberative thought can help assure success. Consider your "sphere of influence." Typically, the phrase refers to the range to which your influence extends. So in the conventional sense of the term, various individuals in various communities are willing to listen to your ideas and be influenced by them.

Graphically, your sphere of influence would be a concentric one, representing the numerous areas in which you can use your leadership skills to make a difference. If we were to sketch your sphere of influence, it might look like this, with the concentric rings showing the groups you are most likely to influence and/or the groups you most frequently influence:

Co-Workers   Strangers

Your
Influence

Friends & Family   Community

☑ Influence, as we use the term here, does not only mean getting your own way. Instead, it means a combination of persuasion and principles to achieve positive results for several individuals, yourself among them. When you "powersell" your ideas or your intent or your product, you are ideally combining influence with integrity. You are persuading others to understand and carry out your proposal because it has benefit for them as well as for yourself.

Influence is not about self-aggrandizement but rather about improving both self and situations. With this definition in mind, reflect on some of your recent influence efforts. Notice there are three parts to the following exercise:

Family/Friends, Community, and Strangers. For Community, think of neighbors, PTA, church groups, professional associations, etc. For Strangers, think of daily encounters, audience members, e-mail/correspondence, etc.

Beneath each category here, list two recent influence situations: note the person whom you attempted to influence, the reason or circumstances, and the degree to which your efforts succeeded. (Use a scale of 1 - 10, with 10 indicating total satisfaction with the encounter.)

Person	**Reason**	**Success Scale (1-10)**
Family/Friends		
_____	_____	_____
_____	_____	_____
Community		
_____	_____	_____
_____	_____	_____
Strangers		
_____	_____	_____
_____	_____	_____

☑   In reviewing these six exchanges, identify the one with the highest score and list here the reasons why it succeeded as it did. Make certain to note the "integrity" aspect--in other words, why might the other person have emerged from the encounter feeling satisfied? What may have caused your own satisfaction?

_____

_____

_____

_____

_____

_____

The Circle of Influence

Having examined the outer spheres of influence, let's turn now to the core of the spheres: your influence. The influence or power you possess to positively impact other people directly and other things indirectly (the environment, for example) is shown as a circle with many elements.

It's been said that on the most basic level, it all coheres. We'll briefly explore each of the segments in the circle of influence now, acknowledging they are truly integrated. The expertise you have in each of the parts contributes to your accomplishment in the total picture of able influence. A kind of internal synergy occurs each time you influence--you simultaneously develop particular skills and general skills at the same time. The following section explores the particular skills.

Integrity

According to Dr. M. Scott Peck in a *Bottom Line* interview (Volume 14, Number 14, July 30, 1993, page 1), it is a lack of civility in America that is the primary cause for "the breakdown in family life, unethical practices in business, selfishness, and dishonesty in politics." His definition of "civility" echoes what's been stated here. Peck asserts that personal well-being is inseparable from the well-being of various groups to which we belong.

☑ The following exercise is designed to stimulate thought and discussion regarding ethical issues. First, encircle T for "true" or F for "false" on the left-hand side. Your choice should reflect how you feel about each statement. Then, discuss the statements with at least five other people at work or at home or in a class. Use the column on the right to reflect how the majority of those people felt about the statements.

Individual   **Opinion of Others**

T F   T F
    1. I believe we are experiencing serious moral
       decay in this country.
T F   T F
    2. Because our political leaders have violated the
       public trust so often, it is little wonder the
       average citizen feels it is acceptable to lower
       his own standards.

T F   T F

    3. Young people today have as much integrity as
       any other generation has had.

T F   T F

    4. Business, in general, is concerned with profit,
       not people

T F   T F

    5. Religious faith is stronger today than at any
       other time in history.

Finally, compare your answers to the opinions of others. Do you think you hold a more optimistic or pessimistic ethical view than most others hold?

Negotiation

Life may not be fair, but chances are it is equally unfair. By that we mean you cannot expect to win all of the time....but you are not alone. No one else wins all of the time either. Influencing others toward the greater good demands great skill in a number of areas, including the negotiations arena. But as skillful as you are, you are not and never will be perfect. We can only hope to get better, to become more influential, to achieve greater gain for ourselves and others along the way.

☑ Read the following statements about the negotiating process. Then check off the one that has the most significance for you in terms of experiences you have had.

☐ "The hardest time to negotiate is *after* the contract is signed." (Gerard Nierenberg)

☐ "No is only the beginning to a possible Yes." (Judy Markey)

☐ "Train yourself to say in every one of your negotiations, 'If everything goes wrong, will my life end?'" (Herb Cohen)

☐ "Most people hate silence and will attempt to fill it with information--which is exactly what you want." (Fred Jandt and Paul Gillette)

☐ "Often just recognizing a tactic will neutralize it. Realizing, for example, that the other side is attacking you personally in order to impair your judgment may well frustrate the effort." (Roger Fisher and William Ury)

Why did you select the one you did? How does it relate to a recent experience? How does your negotiating skill (or lack of it) affect your ability to be influential?

_____

_____

Vision

Once again, we turn to an ancient language to obtain a deep understanding of current usage. "Vision" comes from the Latin word *videre*, meaning "to see." As you think about the future--for yourself, your family, your department, your organization, your professional/ community associations-- what is something you would like to see happen?

☑ Outline that future occurrence here.

_____

_____

_____

Next, think of what it will take to convert your vision from the ideal to a real state. Assume you had all the resources you need for this reality to come into being, what steps would you need to take, in what order, to influence others in order to make that vision a concrete reality? List the steps here.

1. _____
2. _____
3. _____
4. _____
5. _____
6. _____

Political Savvy; Teamwork

When Don Petersen, Ford Motor Company's former CEO, asserted that results depend on relationships, he was attesting to the importance of being able to get along with others in order to move them toward accomplishing a common goal. Getting along includes being politically astute as well as working cooperatively in a team setting. Both abilities, ideally, are used to pursue the goal.

You may prefer to avoid organizational politics, but to make a difference, to assume leadership, to use influence to effect improvements, you'll find politics an unavoidable aspect of being effective. We want to re-state an earlier caveat here. As you contemplate how best to get things done--whether or not you are in charge of those things--you may feel you are strategizing to the point of manipulation.

To make the distinction between the two realms clear, ask yourself this question: "If I succeed in having things turn out the way I wish them to, will others profit as much as I will?" If the answer is "no," chances are the effort is manipulative. However, if benefits will accrue to several people or to the organization itself, then your political maneuvering is designed, in all likelihood, to serve the common good. If such is the case, then you are using influence as we recommend it be used.

Being politically savvy can spell the difference between individual and team stalemates or success. In the following exercise, you'll find proposals from various members of a team. Check off the one strategy you feel will most influence the others to accept it.

☑ Tim, Sue, Chynna, and Whitney have been operating as a team for the last six months. They have worked out all the details for a benchmarking study they're ready to launch, pending approval from the Executive Committee. They are meeting one last time to plan how they'll make the presentation to the committee.

Tim: ☐ I think we should be planning a contingency strategy. There's a strong possibility, you know, that they won't fund this. So I propose that we continue meeting every month, revise our original proposal and keep on submitting it until they say, "Go for it."

Sue: ☐ I agree that we have a limited chance of gaining approval right now. But, if they do say no, then I think we should engage in some *informal* benchmarking. We can gather data and then if further or formal studies are warranted, we can resubmit our proposal, using the data we've gathered to validate our proposal.

Chynna: There seems to be some doubt about getting the approval we need to move forward. This is what I think we should do. Let's present our proposal as a modified pilot project. It will take less time for us to prepare it today if it's a modified version. But, more important, I think the Committee will be more willing to fund something that is limited in scope. If we can get approval on the sequential steps, one at a time, we are more likely to win them over than if we ask for the whole enchilada at once. Also, while the pilot study is going on, we can learn more about the Committee members to see what appeals we can make to them. We can determine what's in it for them.

Whitney: Ah, the old WIFM Factor. It does have some merit, finding out what they are interested in and making an appeal based on those interests. It has merit, but here's what I think we should do. Polish our presentation in the time we have left today. Make the presentation on Thursday, as planned. If it is rejected, ask them why. Then we can decide if we want to pursue fixing it up for re-submission.

Which plan did you select as the most feasible?_____

_____

Which plan would you say is the most political? _____

_____

Of all the people you know, who would you say is the most political? _____

_____

Ask that person which of the four options he would have chosen and why.

(By the way, sometimes when a team is experiencing gridlock, it helps to bring in an outside opinion to ease team members through the choice(s) to be made.)

Creativity; Problem-Solving

Problem-solving depends on both creative and analytical skills. Because different problems require different solutions, the best problem-solvers have trained themselves to be lateral in their thinking--that is, they can use the scientific approach when a problem calls for it or a more divergent style when required. Are you able to apply both types of thinking equally well? Try the following quiz to find out.

☑ There are no right or wrong answers here. The quiz is designed only to indicate your problem-solving inclinations. Circle True or False to the following questions to indicate if the statement is more like or unlike your typical behavior.

True   False

1. When directions are given to me, I tend to write them down (as opposed to visualizing what has to be done).

True   False

2. I prefer to read instruction manuals (rather than experiment on my own).

True   False

3. When I'm trying to remember someone, I can visualize their name more easily than their face.

True   False

4. I pride myself on being organized, good with numbers, and detail-oriented.

True   False

5. I prefer to work with and within a small corner of the big picture.

True   False

6. It is difficult for me to generate multiple solutions to a problem in a short period of time.

Score-interpretation appears later in this chapter.

Self-Confidence

A lack of faith in yourself or in the challenge you wish others to pursue can limit your power to influence. Although self-confidence is not easy to acquire, it can be increased with a steady program of incremental attempts to gain new experiences and profit from them.

☑ Following is a list of attributes/actions that self-confident people exhibit. Rank them in terms of their importance to you by giving the most important a (1) and the least important a (10).

Ranking	Trait
_____	Positive thinking
_____	Goal-setting
_____	Willingness to change
_____	Seeking of adventure
_____	Ability to remain optimistic in the face of adversity/rejection
_____	Continuous learning

_____   Steadfastness in pursuit of a
mission/achievement

_____   Energy

_____   Enjoyment of challenges

_____   Ability to overcome fear/stress

Now, make a copy of these ten traits (without the rankings). Show them to three people who know you well. Ask them to evaluate you by writing the number (1) beside the attribute they feel is most dominant in you and continuing until they have given a (10) to the trait you display least often. Compare their rankings to the way you see yourself and discuss with them any large discrepancies.

Communication

Legal superstar and author Gerry Spence claims "the best arguments dazzle with metaphor." Understanding metaphors, Aristotle asserted, "is the beginning of genius." What is this simple communication device and how should you use it?

To begin, the metaphor is a simple comparison between two things not usually compared. Leaders use metaphors frequently, for this simple verbal image enables others to visualize your hope in a simple, concrete way. You can use too many metaphors. You can even mix them inappropriately or choose ones that confuse. But, in those circumstances when you need the comprehension and concurrence of others in order to move your vision forward, nothing works quite as well as the metaphor.

[√]   Possible metaphors are listed in the following left-hand column. In the right-hand column, you'll find the actual things that could be represented by the metaphors. For every item on the right, draw a line to at least one comparison that could be used to express it metaphorically.

Metaphors	Items
A train	Your workplace
A rainbow	Your organization
Zero-gravity	Your social life
Baseball	A current problem you face
Magic tricks	Your job
A journey	Your team
Sewing	Relationship with your boss
A puzzle	Morale in your worksite
A jungle	Your family
A storm	Your future
A race	Expectations others have of you
Jazz	Communication styles
Farm equipment	Degree of empowerment

Select one of the above matches now and explain why you
selected this item to go with this metaphor. What particulars
do they have in common?

_____

Finally, think of how you could influence with integrity,
using this particular metaphor. Record your thoughts here.

_____

_____

_____

Respect

In reference to this topic, we've decided to share
some ideas with you anagramatically. That is, we've taken
each letter of the word and used it as the first letter of another
word related to respect and also related to influencing with
integrity. The word "respect" refers not only to our treatment
of others but also to the way we act in the various
environments we encounter on the influence journey.

RECOGNIZE   Recognition is the first step in influencing
others to think or act in a way you believe will have
better results than the current way of thinking or
acting. The word, of course, has multiple meanings
and multiple applications, but it includes recognizing
others have their own points of view and may wish

to retain them, no matter how well, intensely, or often you influence. Recognizing others also involves appreciating their capabilities and acknowledging them both publicly and privately.

ENCOURAGE   Respect involves accepting others where they are. Some may be far ahead of you, in their thinking, in their expertise. Others may need to be carefully guided along the influence path. Encouragement reflects concern for other people, which is synonymous with respect for other people.

STRETCH   To become masterful in influence attempts, you need to stretch the current boundaries of your comfort zone. And, as diplomatically as possible, you'll need to invite your prospective influencees to stretch as well, to envision what as yet cannot be seen. In so doing, you are implicitly commending their ability to become more than they currently are.

PLEASE   Being pleasant, creating pleasant surroundings is yet another way to demonstrate respect during the influence process. Think ahead to creature comforts--both physical and psychological-- as you welcome others into your realm of influence.

EXACT   Sometimes, in our eagerness to
demonstrate respect, we fail to make demands on
others, we hesitate to make them accountable for
their actions. "Exact," as used here, means to
develop responsibility in others, to make clear what
we are exacting or expecting from them. (The
adjective form of the word has significance as well.
Being exact implies we can measure the results of the
actions we have taken.)

COHERE   As an outstanding influencer, you will
seek to make sense out of chaos, to take the first step
in learning--a step described by educator John
Dewey as "confusion." You'll demonstrate respect
for the undertaking and respect for those undertaking
it by uniting disparate elements. As you do so, you'll
create an *esprit de corps* strong enough to withstand
the storms that lie ahead.

TOUCH   Influence is difference-making. It is
reaching out to touch others in emotional and
psychological ways. It is, as a civilian-astronaut once
said of teaching: a way to "touch the future." Before
beginning the implementation of an influence project,
you must know exactly whom and what you hope to
touch in order to make a difference.

Preview   Effective communication skills keep the wheel of influence turning. They infiltrate each section of the wheel and make the whole greater than the sum of its parts. Another aspect of communication, beyond those comprising the wheel, is explored in the next chapter, i.e., the actual words that stand for influential leadership. The chapter concludes with an interview of a businesswoman who literally lives by her words.

INTERVIEW

Dr. Georgeanna Ahlfors, President, WorkLIT Associates, Los Angeles, California

Our company is dedicated to providing skills, both literacy and lifelong learning skills, to working adults. My work consists, in part, in being able to influence others to see the importance of having such skills. One of the things that works well for me is accepting people for who they are and respecting them for their abilities. These abilities do not match my abilities, but they are no less valuable because of that. They may have poor communication skills, for example, but their mechanical abilities may far exceed my own. I don't view my workshop participants as people with a problem. Rather, I respect what they already know and encourage them to know more.

To reduce the artificial barriers that the letters "Dr." can sometimes produce, I make it very apparent, very early on, that my own background is a working-class background. I talk about coming from northern Minnesota, which is not exactly a prestigious location. I tell them both my parents spoke English as a second language and that my grandparents could only speak in their native tongue.

Another element that permits me to influence their attitudes toward further training is my lack of pretense. I

77

emphasize the idea of multiple intelligences, the research that divides cognition into eight areas. No one person excels in all eight, but we all excel in some. I admit that some of them have spatial reasoning intelligence that I envy because I have so little of it. Encouragement is part of the rapport-developing technique: I emphasize the pride they take in the work they do and the confidence that will grow as they learn more about how to learn.

With the executives who make decisions regarding the need to provide literacy training, I assure them first of all that the problem is not a critical one. Instead, I emphasize that a wide range of people can benefit from acquiring new learning tools. The focus of the training may be remedial for some but self-discovery for others. Most managers have positive relationships with their employees and they appreciate, I think, the acknowledgment that these talented workers may be technically proficient but may lack some learning skills that will facilitate acquiring new knowledge in the years ahead. None of us can afford to wait for knowledge to come to us and then hope we will be ready to accept it, to gain from it. To maximize efforts, we have to be active and pro-active in the learning process.

DO:

-- Realize that employing both verbal and physical tools for getting others to do what you want them to do is acceptable behavior.

-- Remember that the average person wants to do the right thing.

-- Regard life as a experiment.

-- Consider "civility" as the integration of personal well-being and other people's well-being.

-- Use your political savvy to get things done.

-- Recognize others if you are serious about respecting them.

-- Attempt to bring cohesion to seemingly disparate elements of a situation.

-- Respect what people already know.

-- Remove barriers that may stand between you and others.

-- Try to find common ground to stand on.

DON'T:

-- Confuse manipulative behavior with influencing for mutually beneficial purposes.

-- Forget to consider the feelings of your influencee.

-- Neglect the answers to numerous questions as you plan your influence strategy.

-- Overlook the need to achieve win/win outcomes in negotiating.
-- Rely exclusively on your most-favored cognitive style in order to solve problems.
-- Force others to think as you do. Encourage them instead to explore best options.
-- Hesitate to make demands--in the most tactful way possible.
-- Operate with pretense as your base.

YOU WILL:

-- Find others influenced by your every gesture. Act with integrity in every case.

-- Be more effective in your influencing efforts if you can speak multiple "languages."

-- Be able to improve the ROI via the pPp Plan.

-- Become more influential as you widen the spheres of influence.

-- Increase self-confidence if you stretch yourself incrementally.

-- Need to invite influencees to move beyond their comfort zones as well.

-- Touch others when you influence.

-- Help others to concentrate on your message if you can offer assurances first.

-- Often have to make the first move if you hope to persuade others.

-- Overcome resistance more easily if you can "emphasize the positives."

-- Lessen the severity of "bad news" if you can offer multiple perspectives regarding it.

YOU WON'T:

-- Be able to separate enduring values from life experience.

-- Grow unless you challenge yourself in big and/or small ways.

-- Be able to influence well without considering the many components of the Circle of Influence.

-- Be able to see the invisible without vision.

-- Communicate as clearly without metaphors as you will with them.

-- Maintain your influencee's interest very long without making exchanges pleasant.

Analysis of the Creativity Quiz on page 69. If you had three "True" answers and three "False" ones, then you probably do use both types of thinking skills equally well. A majority of "True" replies suggests a dependency on your analytical skills, whereas a majority of "False" answers implies a more creative bent.

Chapter 3
Influence & Leadership

~~~~~~~~~~~~~~~~

Overview   This chapter is jammed with examples of
how poorly chosen words can nullify both influence and
leadership efforts. The examples serve to remind us that
when we influence, we are leading; and that, as leaders, we
invite more scrutiny than we do as followers. Sometimes,
the glare of the spotlight may be so intense that we try to
remove ourselves from it by using "weasel" words. These
not only smack of dishonesty, but they usually evoke scorn.

By studying the writing styles of those leaders who
wield tremendous influence through public speaking, we can
learn what works and what doesn't. Chapter 3 analyzes the
styles of two American presidents and one presidential
contender. Attention is then paid to overcoming objections
and to incorporating the Indices of Excellence so your words

will remain memorable. Finally, Joe Gennaro illustrates the connections between good writing and career success.

Examples of Non-Influential Statements

To paraphrase the inimitable Yogi Berra, you can learn a lot just by studying. Contained within the speaking/ writing styles of the great communicators are innumerable tips that, properly analyzed, will afford tremendous insight into successful styles. And, conversely, by studying the mistakes made by less-than-great communicators we can also learn what works and what does not.

Here are examples of the latter: non-influential statements, uttered by "leaders" in one sense of the word only.

Asked about the Holocaust, Dan Quayle replied, "It was an obscene period in our nation's history." A reporter intervened, asking if Quayle meant something other than "our nation's." Mr. Quayle grasped the opening, explaining that he had meant to say "in this century's history."

He then elucidated further: "We all lived in this century--I didn't live in this century, in this century's history. We did not have, as a matter of fact, we fought, Hitlerism. The Holocaust is a critical point in history that we should as a nation understand."

Of course, when understanding of your essential point eludes your listening or reading audience, it is virtually impossible to influence them towards a course of action you've deemed worth pursuing. Other examples follow to show how incomprehension can negate leadership.

Secretary of State Alexander Haig was (correctly) quoted in his definition of diplomacy:

"The conduct of international affairs is essentially dialectic and you have a sine curve of attitudes. We felt there had to be some clearing of the air."

"Things happen more frequently in the future," Washington governor Booth Gardner declared, "than they do in the past."

A *Wall Street Journal* article (Lee Berton, "The Simple Truth of It Is That He Was Channeling Immanuel Kant," March 22, 1989, page 1) provides another illustration of the importance attached to using language that enlightens rather than language that leaves us in the dark.

Candido Mendes, a Brazilian political scientist, offered his views on global environmental problems, "The fiat of sustainability of [the report] asserts the necessary engineerings of totality built this first basic intertwining between development and environment in an at-random set of the inner dynamisms of those ecosystems, with no assessment of their self-closing, or disruption, or dependable reading of their effective interplay." (Reprinted by permission of *Wall Street Journal* © 1989, Dow Jones & Company, Inc. All Rights Reserved Worldwide)

In his defense, it is only fair to note that his remarks were not intended for a lay audience. So, when asked to "translate" for the non-scientific mind, Mendes gave this explanation, "It asks whether sustainability should be considered from an *a priori* or *ad hoc* approach."

Inadvertent insensitivity also negates whatever good intentions you may have had. What's worse, the more visible your position, the more likely you are to be publicly criticized for remarks that, on the surface at least, appear callous.

Gil Lewis, Speaker of the House for the Texas legislature, addressed a wheelchair-bound audience on Disability Day. He foolishly asked, "And now, will y'all stand and be recognized?"

Actress Joan Collins gave an interview that was not only politically incorrect but historically incorrect as well: "It's like the Roman Empire. Wasn't everybody running around just covered with syphilis? And then it was destroyed by the volcano?"

Francophiles, similarly, may easily take offense to the remarks of Prince Charles: "Life is not worth living unless you have a choice of all the gloriously unhygienic things which mankind--especially the French portion of it-- has lovingly created."

Of course, "weaseling" one's way out of difficulty not only doesn't work, it makes one's sins seem even more egregious.

When former New York City mayor David Dinkins was asked by reporters about his failure to pay taxes, he unsuccessfully attempted to create his own definition: "I haven't committed a crime. What I did was fail to comply with the law."

John Hogan, the Commonwealth Edison employee responsible for "news information," had to deal with charges by the Nuclear Regulatory Commission that two operators at a nuclear plant were found sleeping on the job. His reply: "It depends on your definition of 'asleep.' They were stretched out. They had their eyes closed. They were seated at their desks with their heads in a nodding position."

Our final category of non-exemplars centers on the danger of making too declarative a statement:

Admiral W. Leahy, in 1945, assured President Truman that "the atomic bomb will not go off. And I speak as an expert in explosives."

President Grover Cleveland assured the nation in 1905 that "sensible women will never want to vote."

Producer Irving Thalberg felt strongly that Clark Gable had no career in the movies: "You can't put this man in a picture. Look at his ears--like a bat!"

Forty years ago, the head of IBM, Thomas J. Watson, declared, "I think there is a world market for about five computers."

How Leaders Use Language to Influence

We've seen how *not* to influence:

-- By clouding rather than clarifying your point
-- By using language that floats above the heads of your audience
-- By being insensitive
-- By being inaccurate
-- By giving words your own definition so your errors seem less serious
-- By being too emphatic.

Now let's explore some of the successful verbal techniques used by influencers who are good at what they do. First, though, take this little quiz.

☑ Assume you are scheduled to deliver a short speech following the person who is now speaking. Which of the following persons do you think would be the toughest act to follow? Circle your answer.

a) Businesswoman Mary Kay Ash

b) Motivational speaker Les Brown

c) President Jimmy Carter

d) Comedian Jay Leno

e) Talk show hostess Rosie O'Donnell

f) Basketball coach Pat Riley

g) Movie star/AIDS activist Elizabeth Taylor

h) Businessman Tom Peters

i) Golfer Tiger Woods

Based on the selection you made, what does this person say or do that matters to his or her audience? Write two details here:

_____

_____

How could you use some element of influence employed by these individuals (or another effective influencer) in your next influence effort?

_____

_____

Use the list as a discussion prompt with those who are considered influential in your organization or community. Compile a list of the methods used by successful influencers.

At the end of three months, ask a friend or co-worker to be present at the next occasion when you are expected to influence others. Have your colleague evaluate your presentation on the basis of the effective attributes you have listed.

The individuals quoted below could easily be included in the cadre of successful influencers. Read these excerpts from speeches they have delivered. Then, examine the stylistic devices that were used.

Reverend Jesse Jackson

Jesse Jackson, more than 20 years ago, spoke to educators about the problems we face in the education of our children. Imagine yourself as a member of that audience. As you study his words, determine what phrasing impacts you and why.

"We are producing the most educated, articulate, and brilliant sidewalk superintendents the world has ever seen."

"The principal role of leadership is to keep hope alive. I don't think you've done very well in recent years."

"The time spent inside [the schoolhouse] doesn't lead up, it just leads out. And that's not good enough--not good enough for the children, not good enough for the teachers, and not good enough for the country."

☑ There are at least four elements here that will serve you well in your influence efforts. Can you identify three?

1. _____

2. _____

3. _____

His many years of ministry, coupled with his political aspirations and media opportunities, have made Reverend Jackson one of the most compelling of all speakers. Among the many verbal techniques he employs are the following.

1.   He is predictably unpredictable. He sets us up to expect one thing and then he suddenly switches the direction in which we have been moving. We see this in the words "We are producing the most educated, articulate, and brilliant...." To an audience of teachers, pride is no doubt beginning to swell. But the next phrase "sidewalk super-intendents" immediately pricks the inflating balloon of accomplishment.

2.   He employs catchy phrases, such as "sidewalk superintendents." Sound bites such as this one depend on alliteration, among other things.

3.   He uses simple words. It was Winston Churchill who noted that "big men use little words." In the first example from Jesse Jackson, there are 16 words, 11 of which are monosyllables. The second example has 20 words, 17 of which are monosyllables.

4.   He issues a challenge. The audience was no doubt sitting up and taking serious notice as he asserted, "I don't think you've done very well in recent years."

5.   He plays with words. "The time...doesn't lead up, it just leads out."

6.   He makes bold statements: "And that's not good enough.

7.   He uses parallel structure by repeating the phrases "not good enough for...."

President Bill Clinton

The first 1996 presidential debate, held in Hartford, Connecticut, began with the President speaking these words.

"I want to begin by saying again how much I respect Senator Dole and his record of public service, and how hard I will try to make this campaign and this debate one of ideas, not insults. Four years ago I ran for President at a time of high unemployment and rising frustration.

"Four years ago, you took me on faith. Now, there's a record."

☑   Do the same thing now. Study these four sentences and try to isolate elements that might influence voters to support the President and not his opponent.

1. _____

2. _____

3. _____

Clinton has garnered praise from a number of sources for his masterful use of language. See if your analysis of his words matches the analysis below.

1. Clinton's opening words constitute a very clever ploy. Not only does he appear gracious by expressing his admiration for the Bob Dole, but he also places the debate on "high moral ground." Should his opponent begin with attacks on Clinton's character, he will appear to be relying on insults and not ideas. Few would dare make themselves vulnerable in this way after what the President said about discussing ideas.

2. Clinton acknowledges there have been problems--high unemployment and rising frustration. Typically, disclosure helps create the sense that the influencer can be trusted. Of course, the implication is that the President inherited those problems but nonetheless he cuts to the quick by telling us what his focus has been.

3. Clinton juxtaposes long sentences with medium-length sentences, with short sentences.

4. He indirectly compliments the audience's good judgment in having taking him on faith.

5. He sets up a bi-polarity between faith and fact.

6. This bipolar structure permits him, in just a few sentences, to introduce the accomplishments of his first term in office.

President Ronald Reagan

Not surprisingly, we find the comparison to the earlier administration appearing in another inaugural address--that of Ronald Reagan.

"When I took this oath four years ago, I did so in a time of economic stress. Voices were raised saying that we had to look to our past for greatness and glory. But we, the present-day Americans, are not given to looking backward. In this blessed land, there is always a better tomorrow.

"Four years ago, I spoke to you of a new beginning and we have accomplished that. But in another sense, our new beginning is a continuation of that beginning created two centuries ago when, for the first time in history, government, the people said, was not our master, it is our servant; its only power will be that which we the people allow it to have. That system never failed us. But for a time, we failed the system."

√   Once again, you have an opportunity to analyze the words of a beloved leader and learn how he used language, in this case, to influence the American public to sustain the confidence and optimism he had generated in his first term.

1. _____

2. _____

3. _____

Perhaps more than any president in recent history, Ronald Reagan captured the hearts and minds of millions across the world. An examination of his linguistic style unearths several effective techniques.

1. Throughout his speeches are alliterative phrases, such as "greatness and glory" in this excerpt.

2. Reagan inspires by appealing to a national pride--"But we...are not given to looking backward."

3. He uses opposites, the past and the promise of a better tomorrow.

4. Given statistics about the number of people who have faith in a higher power, he bonds with the majority by using the word "blessed."

5. He personifies, making the government a "servant" and not a "master."

6. He uses turnaround phrases: "That system never failed us. But for a time, we failed the system."

√   Think of some message you will have to deliver in the near future, a message that you hope will influence another person(s) to take action you believe should be taken. Jot down what you plan to say.

_____

_____

_____

_____

_____

Now rework that message, using at least three of the
techniques described in these analyses. Label the three you
have selected as you incorporate them into your message of
influence.

_____

_____

_____

_____

_____

Overcoming Objections

To influence well, you must not only advance by
taking the offensive, but you must also be prepared to
defend your position when it comes under attack. When you
address an audience, you are pre-active: you inspire and
motivate and explore ideas prior to execution. You
encourage others to be pro-active and re-active. Some of the
reactions, though, may be critical. If that happens, you must
be non-defensive in your defense. Even if you suspect the
questions or comments fall into the heckling category, you
must maintain a professional stance as you reply. It is

altogether possible the questions are simply questions and not criticisms or indictments. Even if the responses to your proposal are vitriolic in nature, you must still respond from an information-sharing and not a sarcasm-venting position. The following tips, used alone or in combination, will assist you in dealing with objections to the proposals you make.

1. If possible, especially in a large group setting, restate the comment in a way that is less damaging to your position. For example, assume you are a manager asked by the company president to encourage empowerment among employees. You've called together the whole department and have made a convincing case, you feel, for the importance of empowered actions and the benefits that will accrue to individuals, teams, and to the organization itself.

Someone in the back of the room raises her hand and loudly declares, "This just sounds like another management ploy to get us to work harder without rewarding us for our efforts."

If you re-state her viewpoint verbatim you will be reinforcing its negativity. But, with a slight twist, you can still capture her concern and yet present it in a more positive light. Here's one thing you might say. (You will need to say it quickly before the person jumps up to contradict you.

Move right into the explanation of why the concern is unfounded.)

"Tamara is worried that empowerment could mean working harder without being rewarded for doing so. It's a legitimate concern, but let me tell you why it shouldn't worry you. First of all, empowerment is not mandatory. If you don't want to be empowered, no one will force you to be. Secondly, what often happens is that empowered employees can actually *reduce* their workload. For example, if you feel there is duplication in some of the record-keeping you have to do, you should be able to point this out to your supervisor and with her approval, eliminate the unnecessary paperwork."

2.   It often helps, when an objection is raised, to mentally convert that comment to a question so you can address it with reasons and not emotions. In a meeting, for example, you may be suggesting a particular course of action and the office curmudgeon might point out, "We tried that three years ago. It didn't work then and it won't work now."

By translating that comment to a question--"*Did* it fail three years ago?"--you can quickly marshal your thoughts in reply to that question. Consequently, you might reply along these lines: "No, it didn't really fail then. You might remember that Tonia Johnson had proposed this idea and had laid the initial groundwork for implementing it. Then, when she accepted the transfer to the European division, the whole project got put on a back burner because so much else was happening then. I think it merits examining it again. As a matter of fact, I just had an e-mail from Tonia. She's using these concepts over there in Germany and has had some impressive results."

3.   When appropriate, turn the objection around, if only to stall long enough to gather your thoughts. So if someone objects to a point you've made, firmly but diplomatically, you could challenge the person's assumption. Your turn-the-tables question might be, "Leslie, I appreciate your concern. I'm wondering if you've come across any data that would back it up."

If she says no, she is, in effect, weakening her own position. If she says yes, you can ask her to share the data she has acquired.

4.   Anticipate objections and have answers ready in advance. At least a week prior to meeting with those you need to influence, sit down with a trusted friend or colleague. State what you will say sentence by sentence, while sentence by sentence your partner offers an objection or negative comment for you to overcome. True, you cannot prepare for every possible eventuality, but having anticipated the worst and made provisions for it, you will definitely

pump up your self-confidence before and during the presentation.

5.   Involve others. Sometimes an objection is really the unmasking of a private fear or the seizing of an opportunity to grind an axe in public. In such cases, it may help to ask the other members of the audience how they feel about the objection. Chances are, few hands will go up in support of it, thus affording you the chance to minimize the negative impact of it. On the other hand, if you find there is serious resistance to your proposal, you will have to re-think its worth.

6.   Recognize that some issues are too broad to merit investigation at the present moment. While it is not likely, it is possible that you have overlooked a critical aspect that could impinge upon the success of your proposal. A statistically equipped opponent of the plan might attempt to sway others by citing figures you have not seen. Rather than allow such one-upsmanship to continue, assert that you need time to review the figures. Ask the person to meet with you at a later time, continue your presentation, and assure your audience you will update them on the information that has just recently come your way.

7.   Employ humor, even if it means repeating a memorized example. This Yogi Berra classic can be adapted, for example, to virtually any situation in which you are

coming under attack. Your reply to a criticism or objection might sound like this: "You comment reminds me of a conversation between Yogi Berra and Mrs. Berra. She came in the house one day and when he asked where she'd been, she replied, "I just went to see Dr. Zhivago."

Alarmed, Yogi demanded to know, 'What's wrong with you now?' Clearly, he knew the world of baseball but was not familiar with other forms of popular entertainment. Sometimes, because we are so consumed with the requirements of our own work, we don't have time to know what's happening in other worlds. My research on this proposal convinces me it's working out there and I'd appreciate the chance to share just a few more figures with you to illustrate how well I think it will work in here."

8.   Let the past prepare you for the future. On occasion, a member of your audience may get so carried away with her own war story that valuable time is wasted. (Additionally, such stories usually move an audience off the track and thus derail the persuasive points you may have made to this point.) If you have ever had that happen to you, you don't want it to happen again.

One method that invites input, but only the most succinct and relevant input, is a simple timing device that has a shrill sound. Announce before the question-and-answer period begins that you anticipate considerable input and so in fairness to all members, you will set your timer for exactly two minutes. And when it goes off, the person (who will not want to compete with such a sound) will be asked to sit down so the discussion can continue with other points of view.

9.   Don't overlook the power of anecdotes. You can weave them into your actual presentation and then again into your spontaneous remarks as you handle objections. The stories need not be funny or fabricated. In fact, the more poignant they are, they more they strike a common chord, the more likely are they to be remembered and you to be believed.

In a study conducted with MBA students (Martin, J., and Power, M., "Organizational Stories: More Vivid and Persuasive than Quantitative Data." In B. M. Staw [ed.] *Psychological Foundations of Organizational Behavior.* Glenview, Ill.: Scott, Foresman, 1982, pp. 161-168), researchers attempted to learn what information would be most influential in persuading people that a particular company was committed to avoiding downsizing of the workforce. Four information-sharing techniques were studied: telling a story, using statistics, using the story plus statistics, and sharing a policy statement the company had prepared.

Which technique do you think would be most effective? _____

Chances are, you listed the second one, the combination of story plus statistics. If indeed this was your selection, you did not guess correctly. The study found the MBA students who heard the story alone believed the company's claim more than did students in any of the other groups. (We actually recommend a combination as well, for facts can be very compelling in moving others toward your viewpoint.)

10.   Cite a higher authority or precedent. People are usually influenced by someone who is nationally recognized and respected. (Oprah speaks; the nation reads.) Save some of the power in your argumentative arsenal for the question-and-answer period, when you can overcome objections by referring to an endorsement by a well-respected figure ("Our CEO has asked me to share these details with you") or to a comparable project being successfully executed elsewhere.

11.   Leadership has been described as a liberation of competence. Recognize that objectors probably have a great deal of competence you can tap into in support of your project. When apathy reigns, you will not hear objections. By contrast, when people are concerned enough to discuss your plan, they are giving it some serious thought. It may be that a given objection impresses you with the depth or clarity it reflects. By extension, the objector is probably someone

who has given considerable thought to this whole arena and so would no doubt be a good person to have on your team (no matter how hostile her objection may seem at first).

12.   Go out on a verbal limb. If you are supremely confident about the worth of your idea, you can offer assurances that represent an iron-clad guarantee for your influencee. To illustrate, we know one consultant who is so confident of the merit of his seminars that he makes this proposal, "If the evaluations do not average 4.5 out of 5, then you do not have to pay me."

If you have too much to risk to make such an offer, however, you can go out on a different kind of verbal limb by stating an outrageous opinion instead of an outrageous offer. Tom Peters, for example, is known for such remarks: "Every organization should have at least one weirdo on staff." Or, "If you have gone a whole week without being disobedient, you are doing your organization and yourself a disservice." Of course, you can always make an informal promise such as, "If this doesn't work, I'll bring doughnuts to the staff meeting for a whole year!"

Writing Wrongs

In the preceding section, we analyzed ways to counter objections when you are on the spot. When you put

things in writing, of course, you have the advantage of time-
-time to plan what you will say on paper, time to revise, and
time for your influencees to mull over your presentation.

Of all the elements that constitute excellence in the
written word, clarity is no doubt the most important. One of
the most serious mistakes businesspeople make is writing to
impress and not to express. To illustrate, we know of an
attorney who informed a vendor, "When I juxtapose
empirical inefficiency with theoretical competence, inevitably
and invariably, empirical inefficiency prevails." Of course,
the whole point of the utterance may have been to
overwhelm the listener, in which case the lawyer succeeded.
But if clear expression was the purpose, the listener missed
the point entirely.

Can you quantify clarity? _____ It may surprise
you to learn that, in fact, you can! What follows are Ten
Indices of Excellence. Study these mechanical approaches to
good writing and then apply them to a recent communication
you wrote to influence others. Take the time to right the
"wrongs" you find. It's the best way to acquire new,
improved communication habits.

Index #1:   Average Sentence Length
Count how many words in each sentence from a
recent memo you wrote. Then divide that total by the number

of sentences. If you averaged more than 15 words per sentence, you are heading into the domain of dense writing. Obscurity and not clarity is the ruler of this domain.

Index #2: Variety in Sentence Length

If all your sentences were of approximately the same length, you would soon bore your audience. Boredom leads to disinterest and disinterest spells failure for the would-be influencer. There is an easy way to determine whether you have variety in your sentence length. You have already counted the number of words in your sentences. Now draw a bar chart showing at a glance what your sentences look like when measured in increments of five. If the chart has great variety, you are more likely to capture and maintain your reader's interest.

Once a month, do another graph from a randomly selected communication. Keep your graphs in a folder so you can tell at a glance if you are getting better. Do this until you have formed the habit of varying the length of your sentences.

Index #3: Variety in Your Paragraph Length

"Eyeballing" the size of your paragraphs is one way to measure their lengths. Another way is simply to count how many lines in each paragraph. The more variety you

have, the more visually compelling your message will be.
Obese paragraphs of uniform length are a turn-off for
readers.

Index #4:   Variety in Your Sentence Structure
We tend to speak in a simple subject-verb-direct
object fashion. And when it comes to writing, we tend to
record our thoughts using the same syntax. If you believe
that variety is the spice of life, you will understand how
variety can also be the life of your parsing. Here are
alternatives to the basic noun-verb-noun format. We'll use
the famous saying, "Don't cross your bridges until you
come to them" as our exemplar. (This sentence begins with a
verb, by the way, so we already have our first alternative to
the noun-verb-noun structure: starting the sentence with a
verb.)

<u>Start with an Expletive</u>
No, we don't mean the four-letter words that got
Richard Nixon into so much taped trouble. Instead, we are
referring to the linguistic sentence-opener that uses phrases
such as "It is...." or "There are...." Periodically, use an
expletive to begin your thoughts. Our oft-quoted aphorism
would then sound like this: "It is critical that we not cross
bridges until we come to them."

Start with a Gerund

Simply for the sake of variety, we can begin our sentences with this verb form that usually ends in "ing." The original saying would sound like this with a gerund: "Crossing your bridges before you come to them can mean wasted time and energy."

Start with an Adverb

The effective writer has numerous tools at her fingertips for bringing a fresh slant to the influence-points being made. One such syntactical tool is the adverb, which tells when and where, how and to what extent. To pique a reader's interest, your original sentence could be re-written this way: "When you get to the bridge, then you can cross it."

Start with a Preposition

These short words introduce a group of words. The whole group, the prepositional phrase, provides more information about the basic noun or verb. You could use a preposition in this way, "In the interest of time, avoid crossing bridges until you come to them."

Start with an Infinitive Phrase

One of the world's most frequently quoted lines begins with an infinitive phrase: "To be or not to be." Applied to the original sentence, the revision might read, "To cross a bridge mentally before you come to it physically is usually a waste of time."

Start with a Dependent Clause

Grammar-meisters know such clauses begin with subordinating conjunctions--words such as when, if, while, although. The new saying, starting with a dependent clause, could be this: "If you cross your bridges before you come to them, you will be sorry."

Index #5: The 1:11 Ratio

Effective writers have a limited number of prepositions in their spoken and written expression. Here's why. Too many prepositions will make your words sound choppy, and your sentences seem immature. This is a sentence with an excessive number of prepositions: "We placed an ad in the month of December in the *Times* for the position of accounting clerk in our office in Encino." Ideally, you will have only one preposition for every 11 words. The example has 23 words; consequently, it should have two, three at the most, prepositions. Instead, it has seven, far exceeding the ratio. How would you rewrite it to eliminate most of those prepositional phrases?

_____

_____

_____

Index #6:   The 1:5 Ratio

Find a communication you recently wrote that you consider clear in its intention. Now circle the first five verbs you come to. Was only one in the passive voice? If so, you are conforming to the ratio employed by the most powerful communicators.

Index #7:   The 1:8 Ratio

Use the same written communication. Place your pencil point on any word on the page and encircle eight words in a row. Do this four times, using any starting point. Among those 32 words, you should have four active-voice verbs.

Index #8:   The 70/100 Fraction

Think about some of the most significant expressions you have encountered in your lifetime. Perhaps the words of Martin Luther King resonate within you: "I have a dream...." Or John F. Kennedy's famous paraphrase, "Ask not what your country can do for you. Ask what you can do for your country." It might be a Native American quotation, such as this from the Nez Perce chief, Hinmaton Yalatkit, "The earth is the mother of all people, and all people should have equal rights upon it." Or this from Eleanor Roosevelt, "You must do the thing you think you cannot do." Other examples can be found in the Bible and numerous additional sources.

No doubt you'll find those sentences with a majority of monosyllabic words have had the greatest impact upon you. One easy way to determine if you are overusing those sesquipedalian words is to count off 70 words in a row. Then go back and count the number of syllables. The lower the syllable-count, the better. One-hundred syllables in a 70-word selection is an excellent range to be in.

Index #9: Format

There are several effective ways you can employ visual impressions to convey a verbal message. We'll present you with an example and then ask you to identify the typographical aids that helped convey that message. The original passage looked like this.

As I have mentioned on numerous occasions, if we fail to plan, we can plan to fail. Not having a workable plan has a serious impact on our sales operation. So, we have to make planning a definite aspect of sales. Those who are involved in planning should continually evaluate our product lines, as well as our competitors'. Quarterly reports should be prepared and shared with the sales staff. The final section of these reports should include projections of possible trends in our industry. In addition, our finance department should be meeting with our salespeople to prepare projected budgets for the next five years. Those budgets should consider the cost of training to make our sales staff informed, well-trained, and familiar with the company's objectives. Therefore, it is obviously imperative that interdepartmental adherence to this directive will enhance our chances for success. I trust each of you will comply with this new program.

A dense paragraph such as this is uninviting, to say the least. By using some simple formatting techniques, we can immensely improve the clarity and thus, the impact-power of this communication.

Planning Recommendations:
Quarterly Reports/Budget Projections

In a further effort to merge our planning and sales team project, the following program will be implemented as of this week.

1)   Quarterly Reports: Planners will prepare quarterly reports, which will conclude with projections of possible industry trends. These reports will be shared in a quarterly meeting with the sales staff.

2)   Budget Projections: By the end of May, the finance department will submit to me a projection of costs for the next five years. That five-year projection will be done with the assistance of the sales department and will include the usual budgeted items as well as training costs. With input from sales, planning, and the finance departments, I believe we can achieve superior results in sales this year.

☑   Can you identify four typographical elements that enhance the clarity of the message? (The first has been supplied for you.)
1.   The use of boldface

2. _____

3. _____

4. _____

Index #10:   Readability Level

Just as your style of dress requires an understanding
of convention and situation, so, too, should your style of
writing reflect an understanding of convention and situation.
You would never wear a tuxedo to the company picnic, nor
would you wear blue jeans to a formal dinner party.
Similarly, you would not use doctoral-dissertation language
in a memo about the company softball team, nor would you
use a casual, chatty tone when writing to request a job
interview.

Understanding what type of reader is likely to be
involved in different situations means altering your writing
style to fit the occasion. Fortunately, it is fairly easy to
determine the readability level of your documents.

Think for a moment about all the measuring
instruments we use or others use in our behalf on a given
day. For atmospheric pressure, there is the barometer. For
earthquake magnitude, the Richter Scale is used. There are
thermometers for fevers, pedometers for distances you walk
or run, speedometers for measuring speed, odometers for
measuring miles driven, and pentameter for determining if a

line of poetry has five feet or not. Not surprisingly, there is a scale to measure the level of difficulty in business writing.

Devised by philologist Robert Gunning, the Fog Index uses simple fractions to measure the effort your reader must expend to understand something you have written. To calculate this index, divide the total number of words in a passage you have written by the total number of sentences in that passage. Then add that number to a second whole number. The second number is obtained by dividing the total number of hard words, multiplied by 100, by the total number of words. Once you have these two whole numbers added together, you multiply that total by .4.

(To determine if a word is "hard" or not, just count the number of syllables it has. Three or more syllables qualifies it for the hard category. There are three exceptions to this hard-word rule, though. If a name has three or more syllables and is fairly common, such as "Mississippi," you would not count it hard. Also considered not hard is a compound word, composed of several short words [like "mother-in-law"]. The third exception is a word whose third syllable ends in "es" or "ed" [words like "entrances" or "repeated"].)

The higher the Fog Index for a given passage, the less readable it is. Because the index equates with the number of years of schooling required to read a passage once and comprehend its meaning, a level of 20 or higher is really inappropriate for the business world. If the average newspaper is written at an eighth-grade level, there is no need to write on a graduate-school level when communicating with co-workers.

Michael Barone, Senior Staff Editor,
Reader's Digest:

"Influence is the capacity to persuade others to do what you want them to do. The reason for influencing must be based on trust. If others do not trust you, they have no reason to be influenced by you. Influence is separated from manipulation by the honesty of intent."

Other Means of Influencing

When all is said and written, what remains in the minds of your listeners or readers? Yes, they should have an over-all grasp of the salient points of your message. But what will cause them to probe and prod, to ponder and pursue your words? Typically, the more memorable your phrases, the more likely your audience is to be bitten by the sound of your message. And, consequently, the greater your influence will be. Think of the last time someone tried to influence you on an issue of some import. Record here what

the other person was hoping you would do as a result of
being influenced

_____

_____

_____

_____

What stands out in your mind about the effectiveness
(or non-effectiveness) of that person's efforts?

_____

_____

_____

_____

Things To Remember If You Want To Be Remembered

#1   The Verbal Twist

A single sentence can capture the mind and
sometimes the heart of those whom you wish to influence.
Amid the hundreds of words you will use in your influence
effort should be one group that the listener or reader can take
away. With the verbal twist, you can create sentences that
continue to influence long after you have used them. This
sort of sentence uses the content in the first half and twists it

118

around to create an equally meaningful thought in the second half. Some examples follow:

Jesse Jackson: "I was born in the slums but the slums were not born in me."

John D. Rockefeller, Sr.: "A friendship founded on business is better than a business founded on friendship."

LeRoy Satchel Paige: "Age is a question of mind over matter. If you don't mind, it don't matter."

Henry S. Commanger: "Change does not necessarily assure progress, but progress implacably requires change."

Anonymous: "If you lead through fear you will have little to respect, but if you lead through respect you will have little to fear."

#2   The Unexpected Outcome

One way to make your listening or reading audience sit up and take notice is to stop before the expected outcome and pronounce an unexpected outcome. Quickly, they will move from complacency to contemplation or some other mental mode. To illustrate, when a period is placed after the word "fancy" to stop the sentence from veering into the familiar, you are forced to contemplate the meaning of the words in a new way: "In spring, a young man's fancy." (Unspoken is the reason for such attention to attire, namely, the hope of attracting young women.) Similarly, the observation that a book in the hand is worth a hundred on the shelf surprises us with its fresh variation on a familiar theme. Here are other examples.

Anthony Burgess: "Laugh and the world laughs with you; snore and you sleep alone."

Mark Twain: "If you have to swallow a frog, don't stare at it too long."

Anonymous: "Every great acorn was once a nut that stood its ground."

#3   The Juxtaposed Opposite

To enter the rarefied stratum of super-influencers, you have to give careful and extensive thought to the way you express your thoughts. If you wish potential influencees to remember your words, to tell you later they'll never forget what you said about one issue or another, you have to choose your expressions carefully. One way to achieve memorability is to place opposites together in the same sentence. Here are examples for you to study.

Arab proverb: "You may forget with whom you laughed, but you will never forget with whom you wept."

John F. Kennedy: "Too often we enjoy the comfort of opinion without the discomfort of thought."

Anonymous: "It's easy to know all the answers if you don't bother to listen to the questions."

Japanese Proverb: "To live long, keep a cool head and warm feet."

Earl Wilson: "Success is simply a matter of luck. Ask any failure.

Tombstone in Celano, Italy: "As you are, I once was. As I am, you will be."

#4   The Repeated Phrase

The ancient Romans may have been the first to know the power of the repeated phrase: "I came, I saw, I conquered." Numerous other influencers over the ages have depended on this device to make their message a memorable one.

Mario Cuomo: "By creating the largest defense budget in history.... By escalating to a frenzy the nuclear arms race. By incendiary rhetoric."

Abraham Lincoln: "Government of the people, by the people, for the people."

Marchant: "To be a success in business be daring, be first, be different."

Judy Columbus: "Leadership means being called aggressive and saying 'thank you.' It means not always being liked. It means being a risk-taker."

Peter Drucker: "In industry, in government and in medicine, research is the search for new utility."

Kitty Carlisle Hart: "The arts soften the city's hard edges, the arts appeal to what is best in our character. The arts, frankly, make us want to live here."

Chinese Proverb: "Great minds discuss ideas; normal minds discuss events; small minds discuss people."

Jesse Jackson: "I have marched with him. I have debated with him. I have argued with him. I have disagreed with him. I have learned from him."

#5   The Definition

Whether on a job interview or in a meeting, whether at a social event or at a seminar, we all want to be heard and to know our opinions matter. Sometimes we speak for the sheer pleasure of exchanging ideas, other times we speak because we wish to influence others to action. Definitions not only provide a vehicle for easy transportation of our thoughts, they also allow us to decide how fast, how appealing, how efficient we want that vehicle to be.

The following examples from real-world interview situations illustrate how the definition can serve to make a point and influence the potential employer to hire the candidate. (If you have conducted interviews, you know that after a while it is hard to keep the candidates straight, just as houses, after six hours of house-hunting, become scrambled in your memory.) Standing out from the crowd can be achieved through our choices of words. One candidate was given the ubiquitous prompt, "Tell me about yourself."

She replied, "If you truly want to know who I am, I should tell you that I'm a non-conforming conformist. By that I mean I will conform to the policies, procedures, expectations that are part of the job. But if I am ever asked to do something I consider unethical, I will *not* conform."

In another scenario, an applicant for a supervisory position was asked what she thought the primary job of supervision was. She thought about the origin of the word and then responded, "The supervisor is the one who, quite literally, has a 'super' vision. She is expected to oversee what is happening in her department, not to micromanage it but to align what others are doing with the organizational vision and mission. She has to know the big picture in order to determine if all the pieces of it are falling into place as they should." Additional examples follow.

A. A. Latimer: "A budget is a mathematical confirmation of your suspicions."

Christopher Quill: "I believe that genius is an infinite capacity for taking life by the scruff of the neck."

Lon Watters: "School is a building that has four walls, with tomorrow inside. "

#6   The Comparison

"A diamond," it's been said, is really "a chunk of coal that made good under pressure." Comparisons like this can serve not only to amuse an audience but to give them food for thought and even for mental regurgitation. Such comments are repeatable and in the re-telling, influence spreads. Organizational leaders use such comparisons all the time.

Peter Silas: "We can no longer wait for the storm to pass. We must learn to work in the rain."

Ben Sweetland: "Success is a journey, not a destination."

Bonnie Pruddin: "You can't turn back the clock, but you can wind it up again."

Aristotle: "Poverty is the parent of revolution and crime."

Frank Capra: "A hunch is creativity trying to tell you something."

☑   Return now to that situation in which someone attempted to influence you concerning an important matter. Using one of the six techniques just described, re-write that person's message to make it more influential than it originally was.

124

———————————————————————

———————————————————————

———————————————————————

———————————————————————

Preview   The next chapter studies the many faces of trust, a salient feature on the influence-map. You'll learn how it is built and how easily it can be destroyed. Additionally, the importance of trusting relationships is emphasized, especially when we empower others to implement our influence projects. The chapter concludes with an interview of a government manager, who believes in taking care of his people so they can take care of business.

INTERVIEW

Joseph Gennaro, President, Kinetic Communications, Los Angeles, California

People in leadership positions regularly use language to influence others. In my practice as a business writer, seminar leader, and communication consultant, for instance, I rely largely on linguistic ability to persuade prospects first to meet me, then to purchase my services. And since I've been doing this for 15 years, I suppose I'm doing it right. Of course, I have lots of backup ammunition I bring to an initial meeting: recommendations, evaluation of my work, a great-looking capabilities brochure, and a rather long, impressive client list. But all of this material wouldn't carry nearly as much weight if I weren't able to use language convincingly both on the phone and in person.

It seems people still want or perhaps need to be persuaded to put their money down, even when it's not their own. By knowing how to assure that Kinetic Communications will either make them happy or ease their pain in some way, I will often land projects others don't...or can't. Once I have a training project--usually seminars to deliver in-house--the hard part is over. After they place their first order, my work, which is also based largely on my effective use of language to get across key points, must speak for itself.

126

After first-time buyers observe me present an initial workshop, they tend to become long-term clients (assuming they have a training budget for such).

Truth be told, not many people in business today can rise even to near-leadership positions --never mind top leadership positions--unless they've used language effectively on their way up. Once, well before I launched Kinetic Communications, I was a corporate employee. I used good writing as a vehicle to more than double my salary virtually overnight, as I moved from one company to another. I still use this story (with a bit more detail) in the business-writing workshops I present, to bring home the importance of using language well. And since every participant would very much like to double his or her salary quickly, I have no difficulty getting them to pay close attention to the importance of using language effectively.

DO:

-- Attempt to turn the question back to the questioner.

-- Try to improve upon past performances.

-- Go out on a limb, as long as you can live with the consequences. If not, go out on a verbal limb instead.

-- Periodically check your writing to see if you have the 1:11 ratio (preposition to words).

-- Use an unexpected conclusion once in a while.

-- Use definitions and comparisons.

-- Observe others if you are serious about improvement.

-- Be careful about making statements that are too emphatic.

-- Double-check the figures you cite.

-- Play with words.

-- Issue appropriate challenges.

-- Use parallel structure as warranted.

-- Compliment your audience if you can do so sincerely.

-- Appeal to positive emotions such as pride.

-- Let honesty of intent guide your influence actions.

DON'T:

-- Go into a question-and-answer period without having anticipated tough questions and rehearsed the answers to them.

-- Minimize the power of stories.

128

-- Let your sentence length exceed an average of 15 words.
-- Start every sentence the same way. Bring variety to your syntax.
-- Overuse the passive voice. (Ideally, you will use it only 20% of the time.)
-- Overuse long words. (A good balance is 100 syllables for every 70 words.)
-- Think your message will stay in people's minds without repetition.
-- Confuse your audience if you hope to lead them.
-- Twist the meaning of words to circumvent truth.
-- Overlook the benefit of having a friend critique your presentations.
-- Try to hide the truth if there are problems. Address them before your opponent does.
-- Hesitate to set up structures such as a dichotomy ("past" and "present") or natural associations ("sunlight" and "warmth").
-- Fail to use figures to back up your points.
-- Rely solely on backup ammunition or linguistic prowess. Use both to create a powerful and lasting impression as you work to influence others.

YOU WILL:

-- Find support among audience members.

-- Seldom go wrong if you use relevant and suitable humor.

-- Lend weight to your argument by citing precedents and/or authorities.

-- Make the look of your written communication more inviting if you vary paragraph length.

-- Be considered an effective writer if you have one action verb in every eight-word passage.

-- Reach virtually any business audience with a readability level of 8 or 9.

-- Run the risk of being laughed at if your language is obscuring your point.

-- Keep your audience's attention by being unpredictable from time to time.

-- Find catchy phrases useful, those based on alliteration or rhyme, for example.

-- Help debates get off to the right start with a statement of positive purpose.

-- Be remembered more easily if you use turnaround or twist-around phrases.

-- Take the sting out of venomous remarks by restating them more positively.

-- Find converting a comment to a question helps you address it more easily.
-- Have to persuade others to put their money, time, or faith in you. Influence doesn't occur without work on your part.
-- Find your career growth stunted if you don't communicate well.

YOU WON'T

-- Always be able to answer questions that are raised: some merit further investigation at a later time.
-- Benefit from regarding objections as attacks (although some might be). Regard them as an expression of interest from people who are typically competent and concerned.
-- Hold reader's interest very long if you always use sentences of the same length.
-- Capture the reader without making use of typographical aids.
-- Be able to weasel your way out of a tight spot very often without appearing untrustworthy.
-- Maintain interest long if you use polysyllabic words.
-- Sound fresh or stimulating if all your sentences are the same length.

-- Have much verbal pizazz if you do not use stylistic devices such as personification once in a while.
-- Succeed as an influencer unless you can excel at both offense and defense.

Chapter 4
Influence & Trust

~~~~~~~~~~~~~~

Overview   When we influence, we do so in the hopes of
making a difference. Something will change in the
environment, in the relationship, in the organization, if we
are successful in our efforts. But it's nearly impossibly to
influence others to make change if we have not earned their
trust. This chapter examines both general and specific ways
of doing that.

It encourages you to know your influencees, to say
what you mean, to mean what you say, to use qualifiers as
needed, to develop a sixth sense, to listen well, to share
information, and to make and keep promises. Building trust
is important. Equally important is demonstrating trust. We
do this by empowering others to follow their instincts while
we step out of the way. In his interview at the end of the
chapter, Stephen Robertson pulls together all these elements

133

as he speaks of his #1 priority: taking care of the needs of his staff so they, in turn, can devote their time and energy to protecting the environment.

Making a Difference

Given the betrayals we have experienced in our lifetimes--betrayals that are a normal part of the maturation process but also betrayals by global, national, and organizational figures--it is little wonder the average person is imbued with a healthy skepticism by the time he enters the workforce. Once there, he is again subjected to trust-erosion as one new alphabet-soup program replaces another, as waves of downsizing wash over the workforce while corporate profits and CEO salaries appear safe, riding the crests of those waves. So distrustful have employees become about the security of their own positions that wry commentaries such as these have evolved: "Optimists bring their lunches to work, pessimists leave the car running in the parking lot."

The cynicism has not gone unnoticed by those responsible for making the very decisions that cause trust to be eroded. Soul-searching is becoming as critical an issue as strategy and profitability in many corporate camps. According to a recent article in *Training*, ("Cue the

Compassionate CEO," January 1997, page 16), "The business leader of tomorrow will be a compassionate soul who cares about the environment and believes that corporations bear a social responsibility for the welfare of their workers and the community."

Caring about the environment and *doing* something about the environment are two different things. Without evidence of the latter, the former may seem like sound without substance. Believing that you have a social responsibility and acting in socially responsible ways are two sides of the same coin. If regarded as two separate coins, a distance can develop between buyer and seller, speaker and listener, manager and employee.

The business leader of today, many would agree, is seldom regarded as a "compassionate soul." Consequently, trust is not the coin of most business realms. Today's employees, it seems, are more wary than ever of placing too much faith in governing bodies or organizational bureaucracies. According to corporate trainer Linda Edison of Oneonta, New York, it's important for leaders--especially those who have chosen or who are chosen to influence others--to let hindsight become foresight for the future, to ensure the mistakes of the past are not repeated in the future. She cites the phrase "going postal" as an extreme example of what can happen when working conditions create more stress than security. Violence, she observes, has become for some the raft to which the shipwrecked mind clings.

If the organization is not offering security, employees may have to establish their own. Experts like author Charles Handy encourage employees to become "portfolio people," moving as hired heads from project to project, company to company, creating their own security in the process. Portfolio people trust themselves to take care of themselves; they no longer depend on womb-to-tomb employment. They gravitate toward placing faith in themselves instead, making a difference in their own professional lives before worrying about the differences to be made in the corporation's life. Self- or company-motivated, though, we need trusting relationships. Without them, influence cannot be exerted and differences cannot be made.

Trusting relationships are predicated on several factors. It was journalist Edward R. Murrow who observed, "To be persuasive, we must be believable; to be believable, we must be credible; to be credible, we must be truthful." In and of themselves, neither persuasion nor credibility nor truth will ensure that trust will be built. But each of these elements is an important part of the ethical formula for influencing others. Failing to apply the formula accurately and patiently means failing to make a difference.

Numerous reasons prompt people to make a difference in the world, or at least in their small corner of it. For some, difference-making is part of their family history. For others, it may be the result of a religious influence. For others still, it may be the awareness that it's time to give something back, to leave the world a slightly better place for their having lived in it. A recent survey, conducted by Pinnacle Worldwide ("Fast Facts," *Sales & Marketing Strategies and News*, Special Project Planning Issue, 1997, page 33) found the ability to make a difference was the top job reward listed by senior executives at Fortune 500 companies.

What difference would you like to make--in your life, in someone else's life, in the organization for which you work, in the circles in which you travel? Asking this question is the starting point for influence-projects that have both impact and integrity.

☑ Think of a new influence-project you would like to explore, one you've not listed in preceding chapters. Begin by noting here some way in which you would like to make a difference--for the organization that employs you, for the community in which you live, for the people who constitute your nuclear and your extended family, for the associations of which you are a member, for those who are less fortunate than you--the possibilities are unlimited.

_____

_____

_____

What is driving this interest? Exactly why have you chosen this difference as the one you are most committed to making?

_____

_____

_____

Whom would you have to influence in order to ensure this project is carried out effectively and successfully?

_____

_____

_____

(We'll regard you as the leader of this project, and those whom you must directly or indirectly influence as your team.)

Whatever the rationale that is prompting you to have an impact on others, whatever your position inside or outside an organizational structure, it will be difficult if not impossible to make a difference without being able to influence; and difficult if not impossible to influence without earning trust.

Earning Trust

Giving either 0% or 100% of trust is an effective way to work cooperatively with others. Contradictory as it may seem, both approaches work well. Some leaders start off by trusting all their team members completely. (The same is true of team members in their relationship to their leaders.) Then, if subsequent incidents show that trust should not have been given so quickly or so freely, they may subtract some percentage of trust they give to certain individuals. (In their own minds, at least, they acknowledge that trust levels could be raised again later.)

Others start off giving virtually no trust at all. Little by little, as they learn the extent to which others can be trusted, they extend more and more. The dichotomous choice between no trust and complete trust is made more difficult by the numerous possibilities that exist within these extremes. Just listen to what others have to say on the subject. "The chief lesson I have learned in a long life is that the only way to make a man trustworthy is to trust him; and the surest way to make him untrustworthy is to distrust him and show your distrust," asserts Henry Stimson. And Frank Crane observes, "You may be deceived if you trust too much, but you will live in torment if you do not trust enough." Adding a touch of realism are the words of Finley Peter Dunne, "Trust everybody, but cut the cards [yourself]."

No matter which approach you take, you will find trust-building does not occur overnight. It is an incremental process, which can be enhanced by practicing the recommendations the trust experts preach.

Know Your Influencees

At the beginning of a seminar at an army base, the instructor approached one of the participants and asked, "Do you trust me?" The participant immediately answered in the negative. When the instructor asked why, the participant logically replied, "Because I don't know you." Those who are serious about earning and extending trust can not do so in an interpersonal vacuum. They have to reveal things about themselves so prospective influencees can know who they are and what they stand for. The opposite is true as well: the more we know about others, the more readily we can determine if they can be entrusted with the goal of making a difference.

To the fullest yet most professional extent possible, get to know the people with whom you will be working. Even in a one-time-only situation, such as a presentation to an audience you may never see again, you can make simple overtures that bespeak your willingness to trust and your wish to be trusted. Before the program starts, you can, for example, stand at the door instead of behind the podium. Greet people, ask them questions, allude to the presentation they are about to hear.

At the beginning of a meeting you may be chairing, learn people's names, invite their thoughts (and record them), establish some common ground. If attendees do not know each other, you can take a few moments for an introductory or ice-breaking activity, such as this: each person tells two things about himself, one of which is a lie. The others then try to determine which revelation was the lie.

(Even if participants do know each other, you can periodically engage in a self-disclosing probe such as this, "When you think about your work environment, what lights your fire?" After everyone has replied, you can then ask, "When you think about your work environment, what burns you up?")

Knowing your influencees means doing your homework. Knowing what their pet peeves and pet passions are can only enhance the appropriateness of the various presentations you make to them. When you are making a pitch to colleagues or those above you in the hierarchy, you need to give thought not only to the content of your remarks but also to the context in which they will be delivered. It will take time to learn interests and idiosyncracies, for despite the many hours we spend together in the workplace, we seldom know what lies beneath the surface of our co-workers.

To verify this assertion, try the following experiment. Ask ten people at random, "What is the last time your supervisor or manager asked you what is the greatest contribution you can make to the organization?" Chances are, the majority will either say, "I've never been asked that question" or "Not for a very long time." Most of us, supervisors or colleagues, are so busy doing what we are paid to do that we feel we cannot take time to know our co-workers better than we do. And yet, without some show of personalized interest, trusting relationships take longer to build.

To illustrate, by demonstrating personalized interest, we can prevent the following problem. In their rush to be known as team players, team members often accept assignments that do not match their special talents. If the team leader, for example, asks, "Ahren, would you take on the task of analyzing these data by our next meeting?" Ahren might agree--just to let others know he is not a shirker, that he as willing as the next person to pitch in and see the work gets done. And yet, analysis may not be his strong suit. Ahren may in fact be much better suited to tasks of a creative nature. Without knowing his talents, though, the team leader will understandably mis-assign the work to be done.

Learn what people do in their life outside work. The skills applied to social, athletic, and community causes could easily be transferred to the work site. The person who coaches a Little League team, for example, has learned quite a bit about motivating, organizing, coaching, and dealing with conflict. That knowledge has value in the work site as well.

Ivan Seidenberg, chairman and CEO of NYNEX, asks his employees periodically to tell him what is happening in the workplace ("My First Job," compiled by Daniel Levine, *Reader's Digest*, January 1997, page 90). Invariably, he admits, they inform him of things he did not know about. He relies on this information source because when he was a mere 18 and working as a janitor, he engaged in a conversation with the building superintendent who informed him that some firms pay for their employees' schooling. He mentioned telephone and electric companies in particular. Young Seidenberg obtained an application for the telephone company and has worked at no other company since.

An observation from Wal-Mart's Sam Walton echoes the wisdom of knowing how others think--regardless of their station in corporate life: "The key to success is to get out into the store and listen to what the associates have to say. It's terribly important for everyone to get involved. Our best ideas comes from clerks and stockboys." As reflected in the words of Sam Walton, what separates mediocre management from exceptional management is the degree to which managers truly listen to their employees.

Say What You Mean (without Getting Fired)

Honesty has to be woven into the fabric of trust. Without trust, as we know, influence seldom occurs. However, there is value in moderation. Honesty that is not couched in compassion may actually weaken our influence. It may even cut away the fragile threads of trust we have worked hard to establish. As an influencer, you have to find the appropriate way of saying what has to be said and saying it in a way that does not offend.

Consider the understandable (and probably justifiable) strength of a new secretary's assertion, "This filing system has got to go." She is saying exactly what she means. However, the honesty of her observation may prove to be insulting to the person who originated the existing filing system. Toning down the strength of our assertions, as appropriate, still allows us to speak sincerely but not abrasively. An alternative: "This filing system certainly is an easy one to learn and to maintain. However, I've thought of a few ways we could improve upon it, based on what we did in my other company. I'd like to explore improving upon what we have."

A fine example of speaking your mind without alienating your listener comes from *New York Times* sports writer John Kieran. Dissatisfied with the salary he was earning and determined to quit if he didn't get a raise, Kieran marched into his boss' office and spoke a mere 14 words: "Mr. Ochs, working for the *Times* is a luxury I can no longer afford." Fourteen words, but enough to get him the raise he wanted.

Despite trust-busting experiences we may have had in the past, most of us remain willing to give others the benefit of the doubt and to trust again. But we are a bit more cautious the second or third time around. We expect to take people at their word. And where their word proves unreliable, we quickly withdraw the trust we had been willing to extend. The message for influencers is clear: if you can't follow through, don't make the promise. Better to promise less and deliver more than to promise more and deliver less.

☑   You can gain practice here with saying what you mean but saying it so that listeners want to follow your lead. Lee Iacocca, for example, has commented that the language of leadership consists of "strong, simple words that tell people things they don't want to hear. It's a leader's job," he asserts, "to get people to believe things they don't want to believe, and then to go out and do things they don't want to do."

While such reluctance is not part of every influence situation, it is part of a great many. The words you choose to convey your leadership message will either invite involvement in the change you are effecting or will distance your followers from it. In the following exercises, think of what you wish you could say, then reflect on what you want to happen and what you don't want to happen. Finally, fashion a message, using strong and simple words, that touches upon what you influencees may not want to hear or believe. The message should be persuasive enough to get them to do things they probably don't want to do.

1)   Here's what you want to say: "This coffee room is a mess. How can you people eat in such a pigsty?"

- Here's what you want to happen: Employees will assume some responsibility for keeping the room clean.
- Here's what you *don't* want to happen: You don't want one person to get stuck with the job. You don't want others to be so resentful they make it *dirtier* than it is.
- Here's how you could say it so others will do what has to be done:

  _____

  _____

  _____

2) Here's what you want to say: "Why can't you get along? You act like spoiled kindergartners, thinking the whole world revolves around your petty concerns."
- Here's what you want to happen: Two quarreling employees will learn to get along so more time can be spent on work and less on feuding.
- Here's what you *don't* want to happen: You don't want to make matters worse. You don't want to lose the friendship of either or both. You don't want to be viewed as a meddler. You don't want the situation to divide the work unit further by having others take sides.

- Here's how you could say it so others will do what has to be done:

  _____

  _____

  _____

3) Here's what you want to say: "Only a numbskull would refuse to attend training programs. Don't you realize that what you earn depends on what you learn?"

- Here's what you want to happen: Employees will attend training with a positive attitude and will use what they've learned when they return to work.

- Here's what you _don't_ want to happen: You don't want to appear holier-than-thou or smarter-than-thou. You don't want the employees to feel you are forcing them to attend the class.

- Here's how you could say it so others will do what has to be done:

  _____

  _____

  _____

Before returning to the responses you wrote above, think about the communications that corporate bodies have to deliver. Ideally, such communications are characterized by

148

integrity. To illustrate, film giant Eastman Kodak has built a culture based on five key principles: integrity, respect for the individual, trust, credibility, and continuous improvement. Each bespeaks concern--concern for corporate values, for corporate (human) resources, and for corporate profits as well.

☑ Which of these five elements--integrity, respect for the individual, trust, credibility, and continuous improvement--are apparent in the responses you prepared for the three preceding situations?

1) _____

_____

2) _____

_____

3) _____

_____

Delivering Bad News

The Sandwich Technique

A number of people endorse the "sandwich" technique. It works like this. If you have negative information to impart, let's say to a subordinate, you begin the appraisal interview by pointing out the good things the person is doing. Then, you address the areas that need improvement. You conclude by pointing out additional positive actions the individual displays. Many managers swear by this technique.

We suggest a more direct approach for this reason: today's employees are better informed than ever. They are familiar with this technique and so, when their supervisor begins listing the admirable aspects of the individual's performance, they are not even listening--waiting instead for the other shoe to drop. Their trust is held in abeyance during the recitation of positives.

What's the alternative? To take full advantage of this influence-opportunity, and to avoid the impression that you may be mouthing soft insincerities before the hard truth, we recommend you isolate the most serious problem with the individual's performance. Discuss it at length, learn why the individual may be having difficulty with it, offer suggestions for improvement.

Once a plan of action has been established, you can conclude with a summarizing statement such as this. "Hector, now that we have a handle on that one aspect of your performance, I want to mention the many other aspects that you are handling quite competently. If your job could be divided into eight primary aspects, you are doing just fine with the other seven. Please, continue exactly as you have been doing with...." You could then list the other job requirements with which the person has demonstrated considerable competence.

The Good News/Bad News Technique

Certain verbal "crutches" have permeated the business world to such an extent that they are actually crippling creativity. For example, the pervasive "Have a nice day," has reached such mind-numbing proportions that many people cringe when they hear it. In fact, in some police departments, officers are forbidden to use the phrase after issuing a ticket to motorists. Their superiors have deemed the phrase insulting and have compared it to rubbing salt in a festering wound. To wish someone well after issuing a ticket smacks of perversity. And perversity is a guaranteed trust-buster.

Another crutch is the "I've-got-good-news-and-bad-news. Which-do-you-want-first?" method. Psychologically, many seem to believe, the recipient will be so euphoric after hearing the good news that the bad news won't seem so bad. (Or, after hearing the bad news, the good news will go a long way toward lessening the depression created after the first news release.) You can find more straightforward ways to present information that may not be well-received. For example, "There are two things I'd like to discuss with you today. First, an aspect of your performance that I feel needs improvement. Second, the opportunities that may arise if that improvement is achieved."

What are other straightforward ways of delivering the combination of good news and bad news? Reflect on your own experiences and determine what worked and what did not.

☑ What are some bad-news messages that have recently been delivered to you? List them here and tell if they were delivered in a way that earned your trust or that influenced you toward positive action.

Message #1:_____

Did the message-deliverer earn your trust? _____

Why or why not? _____

Message #2:_____

Did the message-deliverer earn your trust? _____

Why or why not? _____

Message #3:_____

Did the message-deliverer earn your trust? _____

Why or why not? _____

Through analysis such as this, we can glean insight into the methods that constitute effectiveness in influencing others. Preparing ourselves by developing a one-construct-fits-many-situations repertoire, we can cover a multitude of spins.

☑ Several bad-news-to-be-delivered examples follow. The less effective response is presented for you. Your task is to supply a more effective, influential message, one that inspires trust.

Situation #1: You have failed to meet a commitment.

Ineffective: "I won't be able to ship the materials to you next week as I had promised."

More effective:_____

_____

Situation #2:   You, as team leader, have learned the team's proposal has been rejected.

Ineffective: 'Well, guys, just as we expected, our brilliant leaders have failed to see the merit of our proposal. Poof! All that hard work down the old toilet."

More effective: _____

_____

Situation #3:   Senior management, in a cost-cutting mode, has decided that neither the annual Christmas bonus nor the annual Christmas party will be given this year.

Ineffective: "You can call me Scrooge if you like, but there'll be no ho-ho-ho's around here this year. We can't afford the Christmas bonus nor the usual Christmas party."

More effective: _____

_____

In the Appendix you'll find additional sample messages. Compare them to what you've listed.

Turning a Phrase

Carpenters, seamstresses, and others whose professional lives are dependent on metrics know the importance of measuring twice and cutting once. Outstanding influencers, in their own right, know the importance of thinking twice and speaking once. Often, just one word is sufficient to move a person from a receptive to a hostile frame of mind. For example, if an error were pointed out to you this way, "Jan, you've made a mistake in the projections column," you would probably regard that statement as having a neutral valence. In other words, it would neither anger you nor make you feel especially good.

Now, let's see what happens when just one word is added: "Jan, you've made a mistake in the projections column, again." This time the valence of the sentence has definitely gone in the negative direction. Further, you will probably be less receptive to learning what you have done wrong.

As tempting as it frequently is to rely on sarcasm to emphasize a point, leaders and other effective influencers resist the temptation. One way to force yourself to remain professional is to think, "What outcome do I wish to achieve here?" The outcome will probably never be "to hurt someone's feelings." Rather, you are probably hoping greater accuracy or more cooperative work relationships will result. In either case, sarcasm will not advance the cause.

Another example that shows how a single word can vitiate influence is the word "today" in this sentence: "Today the ABC Company has given quality a prominent place in its mission." Although the writer probably did not intend it, the implication is that in the past, quality was given a less prominent position or perhaps no position at all.

Which of these two statements do you find more comforting? This: "The contamination is not believed to pose an environmental or public health threat." Or this? "The contamination does not pose an environmental or public health threat."

The first almost suggests the company is hiding behind the words, "is not believed to." You can just imagine them saying at some point in the future, when the contamination is learned to have been a real threat, "Well, we didn't think it was serious, but unfortunately, we were wrong." By comparison, by the strength of its assertion, the second sentence is much more reassuring (assuming one is willing to trust the company making it).

Finally, imagine high-ranking officers being asked at a press conference about police action that resulted in the death of several citizens. A reporter asks, "How could this have happened?" The police chief begins to explain. Which of these two statements helps us understand the actual chain of events and the responsibility for them: "A decision was made to drop the flare bomb." Or, "I decided we had to drop a flare bomb."

Mean What You Say

World-recognized communications expert Dr. Albert Mehrabian of UCLA asserts that without repeated reinforcements, people forget within a month 90% of what they have learned. To influence means to effect lasting change, not just feel-good moments of motivation immediately following the delivery of your message. The trust you have worked so hard to build needs to be periodically reinforced. Then, it can serve you over a prolonged period as your plans are being realized.

Short-term effectiveness is good, but long-term effectiveness is decidedly better. How committed are you to achieving long-term influence? Take this self-assessment to find out.

☑ The words Always, Usually, Sometimes, Seldom, Never are written below the continuum line. Respond to each statement by placing an X on the line to show the frequency with which the statement applies to your patterns of acting and thinking.

1. I |_____| I
   Always   Usually   Sometimes   Seldom   Never
   I firmly believe that once is not enough when relaying
   important information.

2. I |_____| I
   Always   Usually   Sometimes   Seldom   Never
   I know where to draw the line between making the
   message familiar and making the message seem like
   overkill.

3. I |_____| I
   Always   Usually   Sometimes   Seldom   Never
   When I work on teams, others compliment me on
   keeping the mission constantly before us.

4. I |_____| I
   Always   Usually   Sometimes   Seldom   Never
   I am creative enough to know how to deliver the same
   message in different ways.

5. I |_____| I
   Always   Usually   Sometimes   Seldom   Never
   My influence strategy includes a schedule for re-
   delivering the message.

Did you have three or more answers in the "Always-Usually-Sometimes" area of the continuum? If so, you have all the makings of an effective influencer. If not, within the statements are suggestions for developing your follow-through skills. For example, #5 states, "My influence strategy includes a schedule for re-delivering the message." If you have not incorporated such a strategy into your influence plan, consider how you could.

Use Qualifiers

Metacognition is the ability to analyze what you are saying or doing while you are in the midst of saying or doing it. In a sense, you step outside yourself and mentally evaluate the process in which you are involved. The following scenario illustrates what we mean by "metacognition." Julio and Bill have been friends for a long time. Although their careers have gone in different directions--Julio is an assistant movie producer and Bill a securities analyst--they still get together several times a year for dinner and a movie. We find them now leaving the theatre and discussing one action-packed scene in particular. Bill says, "Wasn't it incredible the way he rode the motor cycle through that marina?"

Julio replies, "The stunt man who did that must have a lot of spunk. Did you notice the camera angle, by the way, when he was flying over the top of the boat?"

Bill didn't notice it and there's no special reason why he should have. He's not in the least bit attuned to visual effects. But as a film producer, Julio was able to enjoy the movie on one level, and to enjoy the special effects on another level at the same time. With his metacognitive mind, he is able to watch the movie not only in terms of the plot line, as the average person does, but also in terms of the cinematic process.

Able influencers, in a way, are so aware of words and their impact that they choose their words very carefully, even as they speak them. This duality of consciousness cautions them to use qualifying statements at the appropriate times; it prevents them from making promises they can't keep; it develops trust by demonstrating concern for others.

√ This sixth sense, the metacognitive mentality, allows you to think ahead to possible pitfalls in the words you have just uttered and to make verbal provisions for offsetting the negative potential. (By the way, if you are sensitive to body language, you will often be able to tell when something you have said may have offended someone. If you pick up on it, you can do some quick verbal backtracking to prevent an angry or disgruntled response.) In the three situations that follow, record a qualifying statement that may help keep the speaker's feet on the ground (and out of his mouth).

Situation #1:   "Many of you are involved in activities outside work that have taught you any number of valuable skills. For example, some of you probably spend every weekend coaching your son's soccer games or hockey games. In doing so, you are actually learning some valuable management skills."
   What qualifying statement would you add? _____

_____

Situation #2:   "There have been a number of rumors flying around here. I'd like to address them now. The one I hear most often is that the store is going to close. Believe me when I tell you the store is *not* going to close."
   What qualifying statement would you add? _____

_____

Situation #3:   "Several research reports have shown the average female employee would rather work for a man than a woman. My own experience bears that out. The worst boss I ever had was a woman. All other things being equal, I'd rather work for a man than a woman any day."

What qualifying statement would you add? _____

_____

The danger in Situation #1 is the assumption that only boys play sports. As soon as you realize that girls are playing on weekends too (in fact some of the coaches are probably their mothers), you can amend your potential faux pas this way: "Just as your daughters are learning about teamwork by being part of a baseball team, you, as coach, are learning how to optimize chances for collaboration."

The manager in Situation #2, telling employees quite emphatically that the store is not going to close is clearly speaking with conviction and, we must assume, absolute honesty. The problem here is that the manager cannot control the future. Even as he speaks, decisions are perhaps being made above him to file for bankruptcy! It is wiser to add a qualifier such as this, "I have been assured of this. Of course, things can change. We may learn tomorrow that a closing is impending. But let's operate on the basis of what we know now and not speculate about what we don't know."

This situation is based on a real-life scenario. The manager spoke from the heart. Unfortunately, his assurances were belied by senior management's decision a month later to close the store and lay off all its employees. The manager appeared to have been lying, or at best to have been withholding information.

Again based on an actual situation, the third speaker was absolutely accurate in the research she cited. Further, she is absolutely entitled to express her opinion. In so doing, however, she alienated at least one person who was thoroughly satisfied working for a woman and at least one person who felt she was demeaning women managers in general. A simple qualifier such as this could alleviate the potential for alienating the audience: "Of course, my experience is not the same as everyone's. Many of you have probably had excellent women supervisors."

Listen Well

Influence requires using a wide array of inner-directed tools--tools such as introspection, analysis, and imagination. These tools help us choose the right words when we attempt to sell our ideas or our products. Power selling is the wise use of those tools in outer-directed ways. It means, for example, listening so well that we validate the worth of other people, thus increasing the likelihood that *they* will listen even more attentively to the ideas we are proposing. This special ability is perhaps best captured in the distinction made by an Englishwoman whose name history failed to record. She moved in London's upper circle, though, and so had the good fortune to dine on two separate occasions with Gladstone and then with his political arch rival Disraeli.

Asked to compare the two, she replied, "When I left the dining room after sitting next to Mr. Gladstone, I thought he was the cleverest man in England. But after sitting next to Mr. Disraeli, I thought *I* was the cleverest *woman* in England."

When others trust us, they feel good about us and our intentions. They also feel good about themselves. Good listening skills, because they evince an ideally sincere interest in others, are integral to building trusting relationships.

√ For the following self-assessment, you will be asked not only to rate yourself on a scale of 1-5 regarding your work-related listening behaviors, but also to supply the name of one person who would probably agree with your assessment. Try to get a different name each time (internal customer, external customer, supervisor, team member, co-worker). As you may have expected, you will then be asked to contact that person to learn what number he or she really would give you in reference to the statement. Discuss any discrepancies.

Use this scale to describe how well each statement applies to you.

1	2	3	4	5
not at all	occasionally	often	usually	always

1. __ I listen to customers (internal or external) well enough to know what they want from me, from the outputs they receive from me, from my department.

    Name of person who might verify this numerical rating: _____

2. __ I take notes as others speak so I don't have to interrupt and yet I don't have to worry about forgetting what I wanted to say.

    Name of person who might verify this numerical rating: _____

3. __ I try to make the environment conducive to good listening.

    Name of person who might verify this numerical rating: _____

4. __ I try to spend about 50% of the conversation listening and the other 50% speaking.

    Name of person who might verify this numerical rating: _____

5. __ I give feedback on the most salient parts of the conversation.

    Name of person who might verify this numerical rating: _____

6. __ I listen to what is said as well as to what is not said.

    Name of person who might verify this numerical rating: _____

Share Information

There are those who believe that knowledge is power and that by keeping all the knowledge to themselves, they will have more power than others. Such behavior has been described by management experts as "silo-ism"--keeping knowledge in, keeping people out. The strategy is a manipulative one. It smacks of self-aggrandizement and dishonesty. In time, silo-ism will destroy whatever trust once existed between influencer and influencee. Without a doubt, this underhanded strategy, used by "destructive achievers," runs counter to the proven benefits of an open-book management style.

The open-book style gives employees--any and all employees--a chance to look at the books, to learn about revenues, stock values, assets, liabilities, profits, and costs. When they can't look, when they lack data about operations, employees simply cannot understand how their jobs impact the bottom line. Supplying them with financial knowledge lets them see the big financial picture and their part in it. Consequently, they are more inclined to act in responsible ways. Further, they are more likely to trust what they are told because they have learned the reasoning behind the decisions.

The results of a study by Watson Wyatt Worldwide ("Is Management Blocking Employee Touchdowns?" *Workforce*, November 1997, page 14) found the majority of 9,144 American employees had not been given the skills they need to do their job (57%), nor the information they need to achieve goals (62%).

When training is provided in a comprehensive manner, when management demonstrates its commitment over the long haul, when confidential financial data are shared, loyalty and credibility invariably grow. And trust is strengthened. Of course, a little knowledge can be a dangerous thing. If the company is undergoing hard times, profit and loss statements might generate rumors and lead to fears of job loss. But even in worst-case scenarios, most people appreciate knowing the truth. Most people appreciate knowing their trust has not been misplaced.

Make and Keep Promises

When 150 executives from some of America's largest companies were asked what it meant to be a team player, they said it was the ability to meet deadlines. ("Pleasant comes 3rd," Rochester *Democrat & Chronicle*, June 9, 1997, Business, page 5.) You may have had a different answer altogether but for many, being able to trust others to do what they said they would do by the date they promised to have it done, is a vital component in the productivity equation. By contrast, when promises are broken, when deadlines are ignored, when accountability is not emphasized, trust is hard to give (for influencees) and hard to get (for influencers).

For the most able influencers, their word is their bond. Are you yourself bound to bonds? Think about the last month of your personal or professional life. What promises have you made? List the most important of them here.

1. _____ _____
2. _____ _____
3. _____ _____
4. _____ _____
5. _____ _____

On the line to the right, tell whether or not those promises have been kept.

Whom will you soon have to influence? _____
For what reason? _____
_____
What assurances can you offer that individual? _____
_____
_____
What is the likelihood that your promises will be kept (and that trust consequently will be engendered)? Is the likelihood high or low?_____

Naturally, there are times when a postponement is the only way out of the deep hole we have dug for ourselves. In such cases, advise those who are depending on you as soon as you can of the delay. Work with them to establish alternate plans.

Signs of Trusting

Assume you are the leader of a team you rely on to execute your vision. To what extent do you have faith in their ability to do the right thing? How can you, as a leader, demonstrate your trust in their competence? Perhaps the best bit of advice we can share comes from General George S. Patton, who advised other leaders to "give direction, not directions." You may think there is not much difference between these two styles of leadership--after all the little letter "s" is all that separates them.

It may be a singular letter, but it makes a singular difference. The leader who trusts, gives direction. That is, he explains the mission and then trusts that his subordinates will execute it to the best of their ability. He believes their experience and their commitment will guide them to make the correct choices. The micromanager (derogatorily referred to by subordinates as "manajerks") will spell out, step by step, exactly what is to be done. Ironically, what the micromanager dictates as the best way of doing something is often less effective than the way someone close to the process would have performed the task. Micromanagers, in effect, are saying they cannot trust others to do what should be done.

√ Regardless of the position you hold, when you attempt to influence others, you are assuming a leadership position, if only for a short while. Think of the last time you played such a role, and then answer these questions concerning that situation.

	Yes	No
1. Do you create a question-receptive environment?	___	___
2. Do you present both the upside and the downside of the project?	___	___
3. Do you admit you make mistakes?	___	___
4. Do you invite others to share their ideas?	___	___
5. Do you acknowledge ideas that may be better than your own?	___	___
6. Do you share credit willingly?	___	___
7. Do you routinely thank others for their contributions?	___	___
8. Do you think you have all the answers?	___	___
9. Are you reluctant to ask for help?	___	___
10.Do you feel you have to be in control of everything?	___	___
11. Do you tend to keep others waiting?	___	___
12. Do you generally feel it's easier to do things yourself than to depend on others?	___	___
13. Do you secretly feel superior to most people?	___	___

If you had four or more "yes" answers in the first seven and three or more "no" answers in the second set of six, you are more trusting than untrusting.

Signs of Being Trusted

There are many ways trust is made manifest. Verbal exchanges are only one way. (Ironically, for some people, just hearing the phrase "Trust me" is enough to make them run in the opposite direction.) If you have learned to read body language, you will be able to pick up the signs that your influencee trusts you and is being influenced by what you are telling him. When the receiver of your verbal messages, though, glances at his watch, yawns, folds his arms in front of his chest, taps his foot, glances at papers on his desk, and/or has a blank look on his face, it will soon be apparent that you are not getting through to him.

Further, the other person will not be actively engaged in your presentation, using silence as a protective shield or, worse yet, as a retaliation. Not only will you have no verbal involvement from him, you will not have physical involvement either: there will be no nods, no note-taking, no smiles of encouragement. Or, if there are questions/comments, they may be accusatory or derogatory in nature.

-- You have a number of choices for altering the negative tone of such a conversation or presentation.

-- You can stop and try to find out if what you are sensing is accurate, "Is this a bad time, Jim?" or "Has something I've said disturbed you?" Be prepared, of course, for an honest reply and deal with it accordingly.

-- You can diplomatically end the meeting and try to re-schedule it.

-- You can invite the person to give you feedback on what has been said so far.

-- You can turn to another communication medium. "Jim, I sense that you have something else on your mind today. Why don't I summarize the points I was making and send them to you in a memo?"

-- You can confront the issue. "Jim, we've both been burned before. I realize it's hard for either one of us to operate now with total trust in one another. We may not ever have total trust, but I really believe we can operate with more trust than we are now showing to one another. What can I do to increase the degree of trust you have in me?"

Empowering through Trust

Organizational leaders throughout the nation, throughout the world even, have found that empowered employees work more productively, more happily, more healthfully. While the concept of delegation has been around for thousands of years, the concept of empowerment is a more recent outgrowth of the quality movement.

There are some parallels between delegation and empowerment. The latter, however, requires a greater amount of trust. Delegation is more limited in scope and duration than empowerment. When a manager delegates, he is essentially asking an employee to take charge of a task and see it through to completion. The employee may not ever do that particular task again. Responsibility is limited for both the delegator and the delegatee.

By contrast, an employee who is empowered is in a permanent state of heightened responsibility and authority. He has demonstrated competence and so has earned the ongoing trust of his manager. At this elevated level, the employee may be given the authority to manage a certain project. Or, he may feel sufficiently empowered to request a certain project be assigned to him. Thus, empowerment is more like a two-way street than is delegation.

☑ There are two simple ways to determine the degree of empowerment you and co-workers have (or believe you have). First, imagine your immediate supervisor has suddenly learned he cannot return to work for the next three months. You have just received an e-mail explaining his absence and telling you how to carry on in his absence. What are his instructions likely to say?

1. _____

_____

_____

Ask the same question of at least five others in your department, i.e., what would the boss probably say in terms of what has to be done and how it should be done while he is not there? After this informal poll, analyze the answers. Within them typically lies a fairly accurate assessment of the culture of empowerment.

2. On a scale of 1 (absolutely unempowered) to 5 (fully empowered), how empowered do you feel you are? _____
Now, ask the same question of as many other people in your department as you can. While reality and perceptions often diverge, you will probably find most people giving the same answer. If the numbers fall primarily in the 1 and 2 range, determine what factors are leading people to feel unempowered. Similarly, if the numbers are primarily 4's and 5's, ascertain what conditions are enabling people to feel so empowered. In either case, work to eliminate the negative forces and to increase the positive ones.

175

With an average of 3 or lower, you can and should make some overtures to increase the trust levels so the empowerment levels can also rise. These are but a few of the possibilities. Check off three you would be willing to try.

☐ Meet with the department manager to discuss the results of the ratings.

☐ Encourage co-workers to participate in an empowerment project.

☐ Read and circulate an article about trust in the workplace.

☐ Learn more about financial operations.

☐ Offer to assist your boss with a project you know he does not enjoy doing.

☐ Benchmark with another department or organization in which trust runs high.

☐ Raise the trust issue at the next department meeting.

☐ Form a team to investigate ways to raise the trust levels.

☐ Distribute an e-mail quote a day (concerning trust and/or empowerment).

Unfortunately, the process of letting go of power is a frightening one to some middle managers. They fear that empowerment may strip them of their power and perhaps ultimately of their jobs. Further, some fear empowerment may reveal certain employees know more than the supervisor does or may have an expertise greater than his own.

On the other hand, there are employees who are afraid to be empowered. With empowerment comes risk--the risk of taking on more responsibility and of being blamed if the project fails. But the other side of the empowerment coin is the self-confidence that grows as we demonstrate our capability. With demonstrated capability comes the opportunity to work with less supervision. When we are trusted, as a rule, we rise to the demands of the occasion.

Above all, though, supervisors and their direct reports must work as partners, with information flowing freely between them. Supervisors cannot simply turn over the reins of authority and then walk away, expecting all will be done as it should be done. And employees cannot assume full authority and think they can operate with no managerial input. Rather, there is an ongoing exchange of ideas and information, with assistance sought as needed and assistance given as requested.

Preview   Chapter 5 examines the difficult choices influencers must sometimes make between exactness of content and appropriateness of context. With numerous examples of those who made the wrong choice, the chapter maintains that honesty is still the best policy. It concludes with remarks from an executive concerned with the impact of anxiety on communication attempts.

INTERVIEW

Stephen Robertson,
Regional Contaminants and Spill Coordinator,
U.S. Fish and Wildlife Service,
Department of the Interior,
Albuquerque, New Mexico

A number of spills, mostly oil spills, occur each week, typically caused by transportation accidents or pipeline breaks or navigation incidents. Most of them are small. Fortunately, spills of the magnitude of the Exxon Valdez occur very seldom. Our field offices, of course, understand the urgency of the situation, and so contacting them is really a matter of following a pre-established routine. In addition, depending on the severity of the situation, we reach those managers in the closest field office. Whenever there is a sensitive natural habitat that needs protecting, we take immediate action.

The media of course, is always very interested in potential threats to the environment. In particular, they are concerned with the impact of spills on wildlife. They home in on the after-effects because they know it grabs the public attention. In the wake of the Valdez disaster, legislation was passed and we now have the Oil Pollution Act of 1990. We work closely with other agencies and effectively operate in an emergency management mode via the Incident Command

System. Within this system, there is a designated person or group in charge of media contacts. We feed them the factual information we have and they in turn piece it together into press releases and press conferences.

In terms of the need to influence on a more direct level, I have been blessed with excellent assistants. I've not had to break unpleasant news regarding their jobs or job performance. Nonetheless, I've worked to develop trust with them. I make certain not to ask others to do things I would not do myself.

In every job, there are things we like doing less than other things. But those things have to be done, by me and by my staff. Support is one of the ways I influence others to do what they might not be inclined to do otherwise. For example, I make sure personnel actions that need to be taken are taken (awards, promotion, reinstatement). Those become my highest priority until they are completed. I cannot do this job on my own, and my people need to be confident that they don't have to worry about their job status and advancement. My priority is to take care of their needs. In turn, they can devote their time and energy to protecting the environment.

DO:

-- Be willing to trust.

-- Realize trust-building is a gradual process.

-- Promise less and deliver more rather than the other way around.

-- Think carefully about the words you are choosing when you have bad news to deliver.

-- Attempt to learn more about the organization's bottom line and how the work you do, and the work your department does, impact that line.

-- Look for signs that indicate trust is occurring in the communication exchange.

-- Ensure the communication flow is ongoing. No matter how trusted/trusting you are, no matter how empowered or empowering, periodic progress reports have to be shared between employees and supervisors.

DON'T:

-- Forget those things that are integral to making a difference: truth, credibility, persuasiveness.

-- Overlook the importance of knowing others.

-- Fail to include at least one of these principles--integrity, respect, trust, credibility, continuous improvement--in your messages of influence.

-- Ignore the statistics regarding how much of what we have learned is forgotten in a very short time unless it is repeated and used.
-- Wait until the last minute to inform others if you have to break a promise or if you can not meet a deadline.
-- Hover, hold on, or treat people like children if you wish to be an effective delegator.
-- Fail to have a predetermined action plan so crises can be managed effectively.

YOU WILL:

-- Have to begin your influence undertaking with decisions concerning what difference you want to make and why.

-- Find unexpected talents residing in all kinds of people, in all kinds of jobs.

-- Have to decide when and if to use the sandwich technique or an alternative.

-- Be able to develop metacognition so you can quickly engage in damage control before the damage becomes irreparable.

-- Have to demonstrate you trust others by giving more information regarding what has to be done and less information regarding how it should be done.

-- Reap numerous benefits, as will the organization, from working in an empowered manner.

-- Find the media (even if it's only intramural or local) can help promote a cause you want to influence others to adopt.

-- Probably get some good ideas if you ask others, "What can I do to earn your trust?"

YOU WON'T

-- Be able to earn trust easily without knowing what style of trust you subscribe to (and sharing that with others).

Do you start with 100% and subtract accordingly or start with 0% and add as warranted?

-- Always be able to say exactly what is on your mind. Some words do need to be driven home with a hammer. Others need to be encased in a velvet glove.

-- Need verbal crutches when you learn to rely on your own creativity.

-- Listen if you are talking. Aim for exchanges that have 50% of each behavior.

-- Learn how competent your co-workers are if you are not sharing both responsibility and authority with them.

-- Succeed in empowering yourself or others unless fears are addressed and dealt with.

-- Be able to do this in every situation, but take care of the needs of others when you can.

Chapter 5
Influence & Appropriateness

~~~~~~~~~~~~~~~

Overview   The influencer bent on reaching others
through ethical means often finds herself balancing on the
beam labeled truth. That truth can be expressed in ways that
are abrasive or tactful, unkind or compassionate, offensive
or diplomatic. Truth must be told through the mouthpiece of
integrity. Yet, political correctness must be considered as
well. This chapter will help you balance the need for
unvarnished facts with the need for listener-receptivity.

It will also help you avoid remarks that are impolitic,
in part by showing how a single word can have a damaging
effect on individual and corporate personas. The damages
attendant to lies are also explored as are the sins of omission.
You can speak up for what is right without alienating others,
without having to resort to unethical means. Self-deprecating
humor is but one of the ways to accomplish this. Even when

(perhaps especially when) using electronic media, you can be efficient and ethical.

Bruce Cryer of the HeartMath Institute explores the need to step back from situations that can be misinterpreted and to consider them from a wider perspective. He speaks of managing our emotions so that ethics and not ego rules our communication.

Political Correctness

An interesting dichotomy overhangs the communications we use to influence others. On the one hand, we have been trained since childhood to tell the truth. As we mature, though, we learn how devastating truth can be, especially truth expressed in the baldest, boldest terms. And so we learn to temper our words, ideally, to maintain the integrity of the idea we wish to impart without sacrificing the feelings of those for whom the idea is intended.

We find further evidence of this dichotomy in the very definition of the adjective "politic": it can mean both "having practical wisdom, prudent, shrewd, diplomatic" but also "crafty or unscrupulous." Throughout *Principled Persuasion*, we have worked to define the line that separates the two definitions. The intent behind your influence efforts bears additional repetition: when an overture is made to influence others for self-benefiting purposes only, the overture lacks integrity. By contrast, when the action is taken to benefit both oneself *and* a larger community without causing harm to others, then the action can be described as an ethical one.

Think about the most powerful people in your organization. How political are they? Is their behavior practical, shrewd, and/or diplomatic? Or, does it reveal a lack of scruples? Are they getting ahead at others' expense or expending their own energies to move others/other causes ahead? We believe it possible to be both political and politically correct as you influence others. Integrity is the *sine qua non* or absolute requirement for doing so.

Be an Office Politician

There's an up side to office politics as well as the much-discussed down side. By attending to the following guidelines, you can make office politics work for you and others as you seek to improve existing conditions. Being a political animal may actually be good for your professional health.

-- Cite the big picture or overarching mission that connects you. The Reverend Jesse Jackson did this in a masterful way when a number of his supporters were complaining about their hotel accommodations in Libreville, Gabon. He literally scolded them for forgetting what their mission was: not to be pampered by the amenities they were accustomed to having but rather to build a partnership with the African delegations. He reminded them of the spirit of the conference and downplayed the fact that cabs were hard to find and rooms were less luxurious than they are in New York.

-- Recognize but don't side with the various factions that may be vying for power. Neutrality is a difficult state to maintain but if you wish to influence others via your trustworthiness, then you must find ways to recognize the differences without encouraging division.

-- Develop your politicking skills and use them for the organizational good. You'll need to strategize, to optimize resources, to articulate a vision, to use power wisely, to deepen your understanding of human nature, and to put these attributes forward to advance a common cause.

-- Emphasize outcomes. If any one power source is trying to emerge, explore with them exactly who or what they are triumphing over. Point out that if time and energy are wasted in negative politicking, everyone loses. Destructive achievers seldom last long.

-- Carve out your own turf rather than go to war over turf that has already been staked out by others. The development of a special expertise on which others depend will allow you access to the stratum in which power players operate.

-- Watch what you say. Until you have learned the lay of the land, keep your observations to yourself. For example, a newly hired analyst was asked by her boss to perform a certain task. The boss spoke quickly and then disappeared into a meeting. The secretary overhead the conversation, smiled sympathetically at the analyst, and then remarked, "That Todd. He's always in a hurry. He never quite explains what he wants, does he?"

The analyst considered this an invitation to exchange confidences and shared a few mild complaints. It wasn't until two weeks later that she learned the secretary and the boss were actually an item and that the secretary's scolding remarks about him had actually been spoken in an adoring manner.

-- Separate nonsense gossip from no-nonsense business possibilities. Don't invite gossip, but if it is shared with you, avoid commenting on it and refuse to pass it along. Business information is a different story altogether. If you hear of things that warrant further investigation, you

189

can make discreet inquiries without revealing where you heard them.

-- Curry favor with the poor and unknown as sincerely as you do with the rich and famous. In other words, be respectful of everyone so no one can accuse you to playing up to a particular level of importance. Courtesy, diplomacy, and perhaps even charm should be extended to everyone you meet, not just to those whose positions outrank your own.

-- Acknowledge the fact that you may have enemies. Work on cultivating their friendship before the enmity turns to bitterness.

-- Recognize that your future bears little relevance to your present circumstances. Before investing too much time or effort on office politics, even the most beneficial of such politics, take stock of what the future has in store. You've no doubt long since realized that the days of womb-to-tomb employment are a thing of the past. Further, you've probably heard the predictions that we will have seven job/career switches by the time we retire. And, by the year 2005, approximately 50% of the work-force will be temporary or contingent workers. The time that could be spent on office politicking may in fact be better spent on preparing yourself for the shifting job market.

☑   The following are real-life occurrences in which political incorrectness had some messy ramifications for those who spoke unwisely. Had you been the individual involved, what could you have said afterwards to atone for your verbal sins?

1.   A well-known speaker addressed a group at a breakfast meeting sponsored by the American Society of Association Executives (ASAE). In his remarks, he shared his suggestion that an athletic team paint the visiting-team locker room pink. That and subsequent physical actions that reinforced certain stereotypes evoked criticism by the Association's Executive Human Rights Caucus. As reported in *Successful Meetings* ("ASAE Apologizes for Speech," December 1994, page 31), the speaker, a well-known sports psychologist, failed to see the problem. He maintained he had not intended to offend anyone and that, in his opinion, he had not done so.

    Nonetheless, the ASAE issued an apology. If you had been asked to write that apology, what would you have said?

_____

_____

_____

2. You are the corporate Counsel for a famous manufacturer of athletic shoes. You have just received a request from a schoolteacher who wishes to use your well-known, three-word advertising slogan in a speech she will deliver to other teachers. The cause is a worthy one and the resulting publicity can only enhance the company image. Nonetheless, the phrase is copyrighted. What words would you use to deny permission?

_____

_____

_____

3. You are president of a Fortune 100 company that has been cited for willfully violating Occupational Safety and Health Administration (OSHA) standards. Because the rumors are flying among employees, you have decided to release a special bulletin to allay fears and quell speculation regarding the $1.5 million in civil penalties. What specific points would you make?

_____

_____

_____

Compare your answers to the politically correct and thus influential statements that were actually made. Turn to the Appendix to learn if your thoughts match the actual thoughts of these influencers.

Off-the-Cuff Remarks that Can Collar You

It's fairly easy to *prepare* remarks that are politically correct. But the more often we appear in the public eye, the more common is the reporter's or audience question that requires on-the-spot thinking. For example, during the 1988 political campaign, President Bush was asked by a high school student if he would pardon Oliver North for his involvement in the Iran-Contra incident. True, the President did some politically smart side-stepping, but his rationale for doing so was sound.

"The question is for me--pardon imputes guilt. And therefore I have refused to speculate on this because I want to see this man have a fair trial." ("Bush hopes North found innocent of charges," Rochester *Democrat and Chronicle*, September 16, 1988, page 5A)

When you've had the luxury of time, though, and you still reveal insensitivity, then your remarks will come under deserved fire. On the third floor of a well-known American firm are photographs of the organization's leaders over the years. They cover the entire wall except for the large caption at the top, which reads, "The men who have made our company what it is today." On second glance, you realize the photos are indeed all (white) males, a fact that had escaped you when you first walked by.

While it is no doubt historically accurate that the leaders of this particular company have all been men, emphasizing that fact in the caption only intensifies the impression that women and minorities have little opportunity for upward mobility in this particular firm. Worse, the caption suggests that only white males have contributed to "making the company what it is today."

It would have taken very little to convert this diversity-insensitive statement to one less offensive. What alternative can you suggest? _____

_____

As your career expands and your feet move higher on the corporate or entrepreneurial ladder, you gain visibility. Accordingly, you must carefully weigh your words. In all likelihood, most of us will not attain an international status, like that of England's Prince Philip, head of the World Wide Fund for Nature. And so, we will probably not be asked to comment on whale rescues, as he was. The Prince likened the rescue to a circus act and thus set off vehement protests from animal rights activists.

In response to his interest in hunting, he exacerbated an already controversial situation by observing that killing animals for money is no more moral than killing them for sport. Perhaps in an effort to extricate himself, he then extended the convoluted analogy to prostitutes and wives.

The prince said a prostitute is no more moral than a wife, even though they are both doing the same thing.

While the prince's position will remain secure, no matter how degrading his remarks, *your* position may in fact disappear if your remarks are culturally insensitive. The costly Texaco scandal should make us all sit up and take notice. Less recent but equally damaging on the personal level were Jimmy The Greek Snyder's comments about why blacks were better athletes than whites. Despite his self-described "heartfelt apology," he lost his job with CBS.

Remember Neil Bush's reference to supporters of Pat Robertson? He described them as "cockroaches" spilling out of the "baseboards of the Bible Belt." Even his subsequent claim that he never intended to offend anyone did not lessen the sting of his words. Nor did his embellishment that he was alluding to their work ethic and their ability to organize quietly.

More amusing but no less powerful in its impact was the remark made by a county health department official in Fresno, California. In a local television interview, the official was discussing a rat infestation problem in the county. He made the unfortunate comparison between their droppings and unwrinkled raisins. Raisin industry officials immediately demanded the employee be fired. A letter-writing campaign was even launched in protest. Raisin industry leaders unrelentingly refused to accept an apology for the "stupid remark." ("They're Raisin' the Roof Over Remark in Fresno," *Los Angeles Times*, January 20, 1988, page 21)

☑   These are among the least sensitive/most damaging remarks ever made by those used to the political limelight. Can you match the speaker to the verbal powder keg he ignited?

a)   Dan Quayle
b)   INS Commissioner Ezell
c)   Japanese politician Yoshio Sakurauchi
d)   Interior Secretary Bruce Babbitt
e)   Secretary of State Al Haig
f)   Gary Hart
g)   Correspondent Bob McNamara
h)   Fred Drasner, CEO, *U.S. News & World Report*
i)   Pat Buchanan

1) "I am in control here!"
2) "I thought they might start putting your picture on milk cartons."
3) "Women are less equipped psychologically to handle business problems."
4) "If anybody wants to put a tail on me, go ahead. They'd be very bored."
5) "Eat your heart out."
6) "There are some bad buys out there who ought to be punished. There are probably some bad women out there, and they out to be punished in a different way."
7) "What a waste it is to lose one's mind or not to have a mind."
8) "Denver is a town that's never been No. 1 in anything but carbon monoxide levels."
9) "U.S. workers are lazy, illiterate, inferior, and overpaid."

The press loves to report those careless comments that can easily transform an exchange of words into a war of words. Even in the best of companies, such comments are made from time to time. Internal policing may make spokespersons more cautious, but even measures such as the ones taken at Intel Corporation will never solve the problem completely. Intel management awards a dog muzzle to any employee who makes an inappropriate remark to the press.

The first muzzle award was presented to the company's attorney for having remarked, "Negotiating with the Japanese is like negotiating with the devil." Even the company's president, chief executive, and senior vice president have been "muzzled" ("Speak no evil," *Incentive*, November 1997, page 14).

A recent book (*Inside Intel* by Tim Jackson) reveals that Intel leaders have particular demands about language. They insist that managers use the word "leads" and not "dominates" in reference to Intel's position in the market. They also conduct raids from time to time: raiders come into executives' offices unannounced, cart away files, and hunt through them for careless phrases that could be damaging in a court of law.

On a related note, Eastman Kodak was severely and front-pagedly criticized for choosing the word "de-selected," KodakSpeak for "fired" ("Kodak job cuts 'unfolding,' William Patalon III and J. Leslie Sopko, Rochester *Democrat and Chronicle*, December 2, 1997, page 1). Business analyst Michael W. Ellmann observed the word probably made matters worse by creating a dehumanized impression of the downsizing. He alluded to an Orwellian essay describing the government's use of euphemisms to camouflage their ugly actions. The action seems especially uncaring in light of Kodak's long-standing emphasis on certain core values such as trust and respect.

Political Corrections

There is not a person alive who has never made a mistake. More critical than the mistake, though, may be the way we apologize for it. We can smoothly or awkwardly deal with the "culpa" that has "mea" written all over it. We can learn or not from people like General Norman Schwarzkopf, who has had to eat humble pie publicly on occasion. In a television interview, he recommended the march against Iraqi forces be continued, implying that he had disagreed with then-president Bush about bringing an end to the war between the two nations.

Schwarzkopf's subsequent apology was simple, straightforward, and professional: "I am extremely sorry that a poor choice of words on my part in any way would result in dishonor cast upon you." (Note he didn't retract his opinion.)

His remarks are reminiscent of those made by businessman Lee Iacocca, who was asked how he felt when he learned of the death of his hated former boss, Henry Ford II. Simple, sincere, and smart enough to avoid reference to how he probably really felt, Iacocca replied, "My sympathies go out to his family."

Before his death of a brain tumor, Republican organizer Lee Atwater realized the harm he had caused by his zealous words on behalf of his party. He offered apologies for their cruelty and seeming racism--qualities he denied having. The objects of his remarks, Michael Dukakis and a state senator named Tom Turnipseed, accepted the apologies and believed the sincerity of them.

Developing the habit of looking ahead to the possible harm our words may cause others and ultimately ourselves, means making a good investment in the future. To illustrate, David Brinkley will perhaps be remembered more for his remarks on his final show than for the 15 years he hosted it. He apologized to President Clinton on that show for having made disparaging comments on election night about the President, who, claimed Brinkley, "has not a creative bone in his body. Therefore he is a bore and always will be a bore."

Brinkley began his apology by reading something he had written years before: "It may be impossible to be objective, but we must always be fair." He then went on to explain that Election Day had been a long day and that he was quite tired by the end of it. He alluded to his remarks as having been both "impolite and unfair" and then expressed his regrets concerning them.

As with most things in life, there is a wrong way and a right way to do the right thing. Your attempts to atone for your first mistake may be even more grievous than the original sin. Such was the case with former White House Chief of Staff John Sununu, who was taken to task for using taxpayer monies for his personal travel.

The only influence he exerted in his apology was a negative one: "Clearly no one regrets more than I do the appearance of impropriety produced as a result of the events surrounding my recent travel. Obviously, some mistakes were made. Certainly, I regret that my own mistakes contributed to this controversy."

[√] If you had been responsible for preparing these remarks for the Chief of Staff, what would you have said differently? _____

_____

_____

The choice of the word "regret" left eyebrows raised on the faces of political and armchair analysts. Some felt it did not suggest he was sorry for his actions at all. Instead, they felt, he was sorry he was caught engaging in them. A second point of much debate was the phrase "appearance of impropriety." The implication here is that he feels the travel wasn't improper at all but he realizes it may have seemed that way to the public. A third problem is the passively described phrase, "mistakes were made."

The implication is that many people made mistakes and he was just one of the many who made them. Finally, the word "contributed" seems designed to lessen the severity of the problem. Sununu's actions, in truth, didn't *contribute* to the controversy. In essence, they *were* the controversy.

Truth and Consequences
Lying, Lying Everywhere

According to Reid Psychological Systems, ("They Lied," *OfficeSystems 97*, August, 1997, page 9), more than 95% of college graduates in a recent survey admitted they would give at least one false statement in order to get a job. Psychologists tell us children are already lying by age 2. And only one-third of executives surveyed by Robert Half International rated honesty and integrity as the most important attributes a job candidate should have ("Honesty is asset," Rochester *Democrat and Chronicle*, April 14, 1997, page 3). As a nation, we've become jaded by unending exposure to sex, lies, and videotapes that capture both.

(You may recall the startling statement issued by Pat Robertson about the kind of people who are qualified to govern. When *Time* magazine questioned him about the assertion, he denied ever having made it. "I never said that in my life," he declared. Compounding the foolishness of the assertion was the foolishness of the denial--it had been made during his *taped* television show, after all. Provided with the evidence, he weaseled his way around it by asserting he had made the remark as a minister and not as a politician.)

Three lessons emerge for would-be influencers: Make your assertions as carefully as possible, for words can blow up with a force akin to TNT. Secondly, if your assertions have come back to burn you, face them honestly. Three, recognize the possibility that others may not be telling the truth and must be dealt with in a fair but firm manner.

☑ How would you have handled this situation? You are a manager in a well-respected firm. Not only does the company have an ethics policy, but they ask each employee to read it once a year. Part of the policy states that anyone who knowingly lies on an employment application will be discharged. (Job applicants are informed of this when they interview with the company.)

Now it has come to your attention via the rumor mill that one of your most skilled employees lied on her resume when she was first hired. You ask to meet with her and confront her with the allegation, which she promptly and regretfully acknowledges. What do you do now?

_____

_____

_____

     Although you will not always have the luxury of time in problem-solving, when you can explore options, alone or with others, you will often come up with ideas that simply would not have occurred to you when forced to think on your feet. In this situation, the manager could have told the employee she had to think further about the appropriate course of action. Then, she might have used a problem-solving technique called Janusian thinking.

     This method of analysis is derived from the ancient Roman god, Janus, whose double-sided profile was printed on coins with one face looking back over the year that had just ended and the other face looking forward to the year about to begin. (January is named after him.) Essentially, Janusian thinking requires us to think in opposite terms. The opposite of firing someone would be hiring someone. As strange as it may sound, a very workable solution emerges here.

If the employee is *not* fired, then it make the ethics statement a very weak one indeed. If the policy is basically a toothless paper tiger, one that will not be enforced, why have it in the first place? Why make employees read it each year? In a larger sense, it is dishonest to promise certain actions will occur in reaction to certain other actions and then to break that promise.

On the other hand, the employee has since proven to be not only skilled and upright, but is in fact the most productive employee in the whole department. The manager is truly reluctant to let her go. But a Janusian compromise is possible here: Fire the employee for having violated the terms of the policy by lying on her application. Then, because her job is now open, allow her to apply along with other applicants for that job. She may decline to do so. Certainly, that is her choice. On the other hand, she may opt to re-apply for her job and if she truly is the most qualified candidate, she should be re-hired.

With sufficient time to explore several courses of action, you can almost invariably influence with integrity. You can make decisions that are equitable for all involved, even if the situation prompting the decision was rooted in unethical behavior.

Honesty May Be the *Only* Policy

In a similar vein, successful salespeople (whether they do this for a living or as an everyday aspect of a job such as your own) introduce objections themselves, rather than hope the objections never arise. This approach has multiple benefits:

1. You can prepare yourself with facts and figures that will offset the strength of the objection.
2. You can strive for win/win consequences by moving closer toward the perfect fit between your offering and the influencee's needs.
3. You will develop trust and respect for the honest manner in which you deal with others.

Attorneys often introduce potentially damaging facts about a witness *before* the other side can do so in an effort to convince the jury they have nothing to hide. Doing so diminishes the explosive effect the evidence might have had if introduced by opposing counsel.

We live in a time where cynicism runs rampant, when patients deliberately call doctors by their first names to assert equality, when exposure to countless hours of television has made us attuned to discrepancies between what is said, what is meant, and what is done. We have become scanners of nuances, readers of subtext, decoders of duality in thought and action. We can read bottom lines, tops of the lines, drawn lines, fine lines, and what's between the lines. We are social sophisticates who know, for example, that good old country boys may be only one of the four terms they choose to describe themselves.

Today's falsehood detectors are finely calibrated because information abounds for those concerned with such detection. Dr. Paul Ekman's article, for example, "How to Tell When Someone Is Lying" (*Bottom Line Personal*, October 15, 1993, page 9) actually tells how to spot a liar by the words, vocal characteristics, and body gestures she employs. (A liar, asserts Ekman, is more likely to make incomplete gestures--such as shrugging only one shoulder instead of two to indicate she doesn't know the answer to a question when she may really know it.)

Sometimes in this world of inflated claims and hyperbolic hype, less may really be more. Witness the real-estate agent who used all the inflated descriptions that have become standard in house-for-sale ads. Unfortunately, months went by without a single offer, for the reality of this quite ordinary home, juxtaposed with the puffery of the descriptions, left prospects quite disappointed when they actually saw it.

Then the realtor had an idea: he would tell it like it was. The truth read, "Small cabin. Rickety roof. Slanted floors. Rusty water. Five little rooms. But a creek flows by, the birds sing in the woods, and a couple could be happy here. Although the place has electricity and phones, you might not want to use them." The place sold in two weeks ("I Sell, Therefore I Exaggerate," Robert Nylen, *Selling*, October 1994, page 74, Reprinted with permission).

Sins of Omission

There's the law. Then there's the letter of the law. Only your conscience can steer you clear of the ramifications that result from breaking either or both. You may be legally pure but morally tainted by your decision to circumvent propriety. Presidential advisors know this, which is why they withhold information, thus affording deniability to the one in charge.

You may remember how soundly President Bush was criticized for his one-word omission from a speech he delivered in Massachusetts. He told his audience that the state had lost jobs under Michael Dukakis' governorship. This was true--the state had lost *manufacturing* jobs--but overall employment had risen over a four-year period by more than 200,000 jobs. An inadvertent or deliberately misleading omission? No one will ever know. But we do know many came forward to set the record straight.

The paintbrush of professional tarnish can be applied to us no matter how innocent, no matter how unintentional, no matter how unthinking our words or actions are. Consider the corporate trainer who was approached at the end of a training program and was accused of being prejudiced. The accuser had no way of knowing how untrue the charge was. All she knew was what she had seen and heard--and she had seen and heard allusions to white males only the entire training day. The omissions led her to believe the trainer was prejudiced.

☑️   You may be sending out negative messages to those you wish to influence, without even being aware that you are doing so. No matter how high your personal integrity actually is, if you are *perceived* to lack it, the perception will override the truth. Set aside a few moments now to examine how your spoken and unspoken messages may be conveying truths, half-truths, or even non-truths to others.

1.   How does my office look? _____

_____

What message might this "look" be conveying to others? _____

_____

2. What is my behavior typically like at meetings? ____

_____

What message might this behavior be conveying to
others? _____

_____

3. What elements constitute my communication style? _

_____

What message might this style be conveying to others?

_____

4. With whom do I associate at work? _____

_____

What message might these associations be conveying
to others? _____

_____

5. What is the quality of my work? _____

_____

What message might this be conveying to others?

_____

Sixteen hundred years ago, St. Augustine wrote,
"When regard for trust has been broken down or even
slightly weakened, all things will remain doubtful." However unintentional the weakening may be, when integrity is
compromised, little is left. If you are sending messages that-
-deliberately or inadvertently-- are eroding trust, your efforts

210

may become suspect and your best intentions may be doubted. This is a truth attorneys and administrators alike understand. So, too, do those with powerful selling skills.

By Your Words You Shall Be Known

Psycholinguistic experts know that one's choice of words can be as revealing as the results of lie detector tests. One horrific example is the plea Susan Smith made to the public at large after her two sons were reported missing. With her husband at her side, the seemingly distraught mother begged for their safe return. The problem, according to legal and psychiatric analysts, is that she used the past tense in reference to them, while her husband spoke in present-tense verbs. Investigators correctly surmised she already knew they were dead because she had drowned them.

Forensic analysis of the Unabomber's manifesto offers further testimony to the ability of a skilled linguistic investigator to ferret out identity. Another case captured the public's attention for a while. It was less serious, for no crime had been committed, but intriguing nonetheless. Despite several denials, protestations, and downright lies, journalist Joe Klein was finally unmasked as the author of *Primary Colors*, which offered no protective coloration at all. Here's why. Donald Foster, a professor of English at

Vassar College, discovered with the aid of a computer what he called "lexical overlap" in the writing of Klein and the Anonymous author of the book.

Both had a tendency to employ adjectives that ended in "y," such as "talky" or "slushy." ("Not Very Neatly, 'Anonymous' Comes Clean," *U.S. News & World Report*, July 29, 1996, page 13). And both used a word, "unironic," that you will not find in your dictionary.

☑ Keep a tape recorder on in your office for an entire day. (Advise others who are conversing with you that you are doing so). At the end of the day, play it back and analyze your speech. Use these questions to deepen your understanding of your own words.

1. Do you find yourself using favorite words over and over? _____ If so, what are they? _____

    _____

    If not, are you pleased with the extent of your vocabulary? _____

2. Did you sound abrasive, rushed, stressed? _____
    If so, what can you do about it? _____

    _____

3. If someone who did not know you listened to this tape, would she think you were executive material? Why or why not? _____

Assuming you wish to be considered executive material, what will have to change? _____

_____

_____

4.   If a tape were made of the person you consider the best possible example of influencing with integrity, what similarities would there be between that tape and your own?

_____

_____

What differences? _____

_____

Speaking Your Mind

In the course of daily living and working--no matter where you work or what kind of work you do or even if you work at all--you are bound to encounter people whose behavior is "anti-social," as authors Robert Giacalone and Jerald Greenberg describe it (in *AntiSocial Behavior in Organizations*). You can remain silent when you encounter such things as lying, theft, harassment, rumor-mongering, defamatory language, racial, ethnic or religious slurs. But in doing so, you are in a sense silently endorsing such behavior.

Understandably, fear may be governing your actions, or, more appropriately, your non-action. There is a

213

possibility that retaliatory actions would be taken against you. Or that speaking up could make you an outcast. And yet, it is possible to simultaneously influence others to cease anti-social behavior. Let integrity and tact govern your words.

√ The following dialog actually took place. Although Donna was reluctant to create a scene, she also felt a need to advise the speaker that she found a particular word, when used as a verb, distasteful.

Donna: I'm so glad we could all get together for lunch today.

Alice: Me too. It's been so long since we've seen each other. Oh, I really like that handbag. Is it new?

Donna: This thing? It's old, girl, old. I got it when I was in Morocco eight years ago.

Alice: Honestly? Did you get it in the casbah?

Donna: As a matter of fact, I did.

Alice: Did you have to jew down the merchant?
(Frozen silence)

Donna: Alice, I'm surprised to hear you use that word in that way. Even if I weren't Jewish, I would find it objectionable.

Alice: I am so sorry. I did it unthinkingly. I promise, I'll
           be very, very careful in the future.

Donna: (raising her water glass), I'll drink to that.

The moment was an unpleasant one but--given its brief
duration--it had a lasting impact on the group. Here are
additional situations in which (deliberate or unknowingly)
anti-social or dysfunctional behaviors may be impeding
harmonious relations. Select one and then write a dialog like
the one above illustrating how a person could speak up for
what is right without permanently alienating the other
person.

1. The boss (correctly) suspects she is being told only
    what others believe she wants to hear. She has asked
    you to be honest with her and to tell her why this is
    happening. She also wants to know what has been
    kept from her.

2. You are troubled because favored employees get the
    most interesting assignments where you work. You
    have decided to speak to your supervisor about it.

3. Your manager has made it clear he will not socialize
    with any woman after work for fear romantic rumors
    will start. So, he goes to sports bars or out to dinner
    with various men on the staff. You are not really

interested in socializing, but you know some important information is shared in these after-hours get-togethers. You have vowed to infiltrate the old-boys network. What will you say to your manager?

4.   You have created a monster of sorts. After a particularly valuable training program several months ago, you typed up your extensive notes and distributed them to department members. It took quite a while but you were willing to do it because the course was so informative. The problem now is that you've signed up for additional training. Your supervisor has already stated her expectation that you will do the same thing again. You need to advise her you don't have that kind of time without appearing as if you are unwilling to share knowledge with others.

_____

_____

_____

_____

Content and Context

Impeached Arizona Governor Evan Meacham once contritely observed, "If I had to do it over, I would have realized earlier that style is sometimes as important as substance." Often the content of what needs to be said undergoes revision according to the context in which the communication will be delivered. Being able to play the political game means knowing the rules, virtually all of them unwritten, and then being in the right place at the right time with the right people, saying and doing the right things. Your technical expertise, it's been observed, represents 90% of any job. The other half is politics.

There are ways to get the credit you deserve--legitimate, ethical, professional ways. For example, if you long to point out to your boss that the feather she wears so proudly in her cap, came out of your tail (as you worked it off), you are not alone. Credit-stealing occurs at a great many levels, in businesses small and large, in public and private organizations.

We know of one woman whose boss invariably took the credit for the achievements of others. She happened to meet her boss' boss in the elevator one day. She seized the opportunity to let him know the major report he had just received had been written by her, even though her boss' name was on it.

When the executive casually asked, "How are you?" she replied, "Much better now that the Jones report is done. I've been working on that so long I'm dreaming about it at night! I don't know if you've had a chance to see it yet, but if not, I think you'll find it interesting reading."

Three sentences--and just enough time to ride three floors with the executive. In a way that did not demean her boss but did reveal her own input, the woman managed to "influence with integrity." Granted, it would seem she was the primary beneficiary of the action, but there are times when it is necessary to set the ethical record straight. Also, in the long run, the organization itself may benefit from such action, for the people who are truly contributing, rather than stealing credit for contributions, can be identified and called upon again.

√   Presented below are the contents of five messages that, if delivered appropriately, will influence others to take positive action. Your job is to give considerable thought to the context in which these messages should be delivered. Consider the *where* and *when* as well as the *what* (What words should be used? What words should not be used? What topics should be avoided?) and the *how*. (What body language and vocal characteristics should accompany the words? What should precede the message? What should follow the message? How should silence be used? How and when will feedback be elicited?)

1. Content: You are troubled by a co-worker's inappropriate attire.

   Context: _____

   _____

   _____

2. Content: You feel team members should refrain from using profanity.

   Context: _____

   _____

   _____

3. Content: A co-worker's frequent tardiness is impacting your own efficiency.

   Context: _____

   _____

   _____

4. Content: Your supervisor has a bad habit of criticizing employees in public.

   Context: _____

   _____

   _____

5. Content: You believe office collections for charity put too much public pressure on people who may not want to give the specified amount or give to a particular charity.

   Context: _____

   _____

The more people with whom you can discuss the various possibilities for direct-but-delicate communicating, the more quickly you will sensitize yourself to the subtleties of stylistic choices. Make a pledge to yourself: before the week is over, you will have discussed both content and context alternatives with at least three people whose opinion matters to you.

Actor Dick Van Patten,

"I try not to influence on impulse but to deliberate about the person I am influencing and why I want to influence him or her. As a child actor with a stage mother who influenced me quite a bit, I'm grateful for the influencing that has enriched my life."

Self-deprecating Humor

Sometimes an honest admission or even a laugh-at-yourself statement wins an audience over more than an impressive listing of our accomplishments. (A well-known presenter, Dr. William Work, once sat through a long iteration of his accomplishments. When he finally took the podium, he commented, "Thank you for that impressive introduction. My father would have loved it. My mother would have believed it!")

Of course, if you are verbally gifted, as Orson
Welles was, you might be able to combine the two elements:
self-deprecation plus accomplishments. He was once asked
to lecture in a very small town to an audience so small it was
virtually non-existent. He began with a synopsis of his
career.

"I'm a director of plays," he is reported to have
announced, "a producer of plays. I'm an actor of the stage
and motion pictures. I'm a writer and producer of motion
pictures. I write, direct, and act on the radio. I'm a magician
and a painter. I've published books. I play the violin and the
piano."

He paused then in the recitation of his successes,
surveyed his audience, and ruefully asked, "Isn't it a pity
there's so many of me and so few of you?"

☑ Quickly note here some way in which you hope to
influence others in the near future. Select a situation you've
not used before. _____

_____

_____

Now check off one of the following self-deprecating
remarks and then tell how it could be woven into the body of
your persuasive message.

☐ "Boy, the things I do for England." --Prince Charles, after trying snake meat for the first time

☐ "Is sloppiness in speech caused by ignorance or apathy? I don't know and I don't care." --William Safire

☐ "There are more pleasant things to do than beat up people." Muhammad Ali

☐ "I would never join any country club that would have me as a member." --Groucho Marx

☐ "When ideas fail, words come in very handy." --Goethe

☐ "When I was kidnapped, my parents snapped into action. They rented out my room." --Woody Allen

☐ "I'm going to speak my mind because I have nothing to lose." --S. I. Hayakawa

☐ Other: _____

How could you use the selected self-deprecating line to make your message more interesting at least and more influential at best?_____

_____

_____

E-Mail Ethics

The information highway has transformed the nature of work. Once regarded as someplace we went to get done

222

what we were being paid to do, work, for many of us, now resides in cyberspace. To get to this virtual workplace, we need only turn on our computers and we're there. This new work environment has a culture and language all its own-- and expanded promise and pitfalls for would-be influencees. Accordingly, because this "terra" is still relatively "incognita" rather than "firma," the chances for mistakes to be made and rules to be broken are high.

If you've not yet heard the horror stories revolving around the unethical or improper use of e-mail, you soon will. If you are an employer who has failed to develop an e-mail policy, the threat of extensive legal costs may soon be facing you. When Siemens Solar Industries, for example, discovered a particular e-mail message in the computer system of a subsidiary they had just purchased, they sued, claiming the subsidiary had known the new technology was not going to work prior to the sale.

Another critical offshoot of the new technology is the avalanche of e-mail messages that tie workers to the computer for hours each day. In many places, the medium is used for messages of a personal or gossipy nature, thus wasting valuable hours that should be spent on other pursuits.

The policy governing use of e-mail should stipulate that mail sent out during company time, using the organization's name, must be business-related. An offensive e-mail message, with its capacity to reach hundreds of people in a short amount of time, could easily make your organization liable for damages in the six- or seven-figure bracket. (Even if your firm is found innocent, the legal costs to fight the charges can overwhelm.) The policy should be monitored and violations should be immediately enforced.

Recommendations for the proper care and handling of the e-mail medium include:

-- Responding to e-mail with the same promptness given to faxes, mail or voice-mail messages.

-- Don't shout (i.e., use all capital letters) when writing e-mail messages. Avoid wordiness, but do give as much attention to grammar, punctuation, and spelling as you would in a regular letter or memo.

-- Do fill in the subject line. It saves the reader's time.

-- Given the tracking that can be done and the fact that messages that can go far beyond the intended recipient, employees must communicate according to clearly established guidelines. A simple test is to ask, "Would I be willing to put this message on a post card for all to see?" If not, the message doesn't belong in e-mail either.

-- The daily bombardment of e-mail messages can swamp an already-sinking workforce.

-- Information overload is a reality; therefore, use this medium sparingly. Minimize opinion-giving and eliminate trivial messages.
-- Know that privacy and e-mailing are mutually exclusive. What you write on company time belongs to the company.
-- Think twice about the medium you've selected for the message. Not everything you have to say should be said electronically.

Voice Mail Values

Voice mail is inescapable, with 75% of Fortune 2000 companies using, misusing, and/or abusing it. Can you employ this ubiquitous bit of electronic gadgetry to make your communications more influential? The answer is a resounding "yes." Given the stress factor and the pressed-for-time feeling most employees have, though, you have to keep those recorded communications simple and straightforward.

Here are recommendations for achieving excellence via your telephone emissary.
-- Begin with your name, your organization (if appropriate), and your purpose for calling.

225

-- If there is a connection, state it in the first few seconds. (For example, "We met at the trade show in Las Vegas last week." Or, "My former boss, Nancy Forrest, suggested I contact you.")

-- If you've not met nor yet established a working relationship, use the person's last name at least once. If you've achieved recognition-status, use the first name at least once.

-- For messages of considerable import, reduce your main point to a ten-second "pitch." Begin by writing out a whole page, specifying your purpose and your expectation/ hope for the ultimate outcome. Then, reduce that page to a single paragraph, again delineating the result you hope will be achieved if the person is influenced to do what you want her to do. Finally, condense the paragraph to a single sentence.

-- Make it worth the person's while to call back. Mention something you will explain in greater detail when she returns the call.

-- If you're asking for something (a donation, service on a committee, an interview, information), pull out your metaphorical biggest guns. You might tell who benefits from the charitable donation, who else is serving on the committee, where the interview will be published, et cetera.

-- If it's not worth the person's while to call back, say so. ("There's no need to call back. I just wanted to let you know I received the conference outline.")
-- Specify a time when you'll be there to take the call and thus avoid telephone tag.
-- Advance the action. Tell the other person what you wish her to do or what she should have ready when she calls back.
-- Give your phone or fax number clearly and slowly.
-- Practice before making the actual call to ensure you can deliver your point in 30-60 seconds.

Preview   Just as flexibility is required for taking full advantage of the various influence situations, in-person or otherwise, you find yourself in, so too is flexibility in your basic style an integral aspect of effective influencing. Chapter 6 discusses the need for "speed, simplicity, and self-confidence" (to use the words of CEO Jack Welch) in your influence endeavors. Whether you work alone to collect your influence-thoughts or work with others in a spirit of fellowship, the ultimate receivers of those influence-thoughts will benefit from your willingness to consider alternatives.

INTERVIEW

Bruce Cryer, Vice President, HeartMath LLC, Boulder Creek, California

In an era when business is moving at such high speed and inputs are increasing exponentially, there is a tendency is engage in knee-jerk communications. We respond without thinking because we have so little time in which to think. It's critical for those of us in positions of influence to stop and think before we speak. We have to consider seriously the audience to whom we are speaking, to anticipate what might be the range of responses to the message we have to impart.

It's easy to skip that one fundamental consideration, whether we are speaking live or in writing or even by video. Projecting ahead to imagine how people might respond forces us to address those possible responses. And so, we can save tremendous strain and stress and avoid unintended consequences.

Stopping that internal juggernaut long enough to have a wider perspective is not easy. It may mean we have to obtain feedback from constituents, both in advance of the communications interaction and after it has occurred. But the failure to do this can result in misunderstanding, hurt feelings, and alienation. The potential for negative consequences is tremendous.

These days, everyone feels rushed--not only the decision-makers but also those who feed information so the decisions can be made, as well as those who will feel the impact of the decision. Too, a great many people have pretty high levels of skepticism. People are on the lookout, no matter what message they receive, for the cover-up, the covert rationalization. Culturally, I see we are engaging in cynicism at increasingly higher levels and increasingly lower ages.

As a nation, we have primed ourselves to look for the worst and to fear the worst. And so, those interested in influence have a special obligation to think how their words might be misinterpreted. My personal bias on this issue is that a lot of the communication errors that are made, a lot of the gaffes that occur, can be traced back to a lack of emotional management. In many people and even in many business entities, there is an identification with winning at all costs. There is an ego vanity that dictates what will be said and how it will be said. When ego rules content, then we wind up with insincerity and manipulation.

Here at the HeartMath LLC, we know that most people are subject to tremendous pressure, to non-stop stress. In fact, I've just returned from a trip to Asia and there it is even worse. The fall of several of the Asian economies is causing massive fear, reactive responses, poor communication, and emotional impulsiveness. Many people are not operating from an objective or deliberative standpoint. Anxiety is taking its toll.

I suspect the issue of fear-driven communicating is becoming a societal issue, rather than solely a personal problem. The entire focus of our organization is giving people the tools to deal with these issues. It's possible to get emotions working on your side, to view yourself as victor and not victim, to stop the reactive process, and to neutralize the negative emotional impacts. These techniques are not designed to repress or suppress emotions, but to have them serve as fuel for the highest good, rather than fuel for the fires that can leave us scorched.

We are entering a new frontier for organizational and personal concerns with quality. As Daniel Goleman and others have shown us, developing emotional intelligence may be the smartest thing we can do for ourselves. That is an inside job.

DO:

-- Recognize the dual nature of circumstances surrounding truth-telling and politics.
-- Develop your politicking skills. Use them for the common good.
-- Treat everyone respectfully.
-- Realize that from time to time you are bound to say something you will regret afterwards. How you handle the apology can erase or exacerbate the situation in the minds of others, especially when the public is privy to the exchange.
-- Know that the sins of omission can be as damning as the sins of commission.
-- Pay equal attention to the content of your words and the context in which they are delivered.
-- Avoid the tendency to use knee-jerk responses.
-- Continue to develop your emotional intelligence.

DON'T:

-- Hesitate to be an office politician, guided by integrity. Because no office is free of politics, we endorse using the system to make a positive difference, rather than letting the system use you indifferently.

-- Let destructive achievers override you. To offset their forcefulness, talk about the tremendous waste associated with game-playing or, worse yet, with negative politics.
-- Overlook reality. If you suspect others are harboring bad feelings about you, learn why and try to resolve the situation before it gets out of hand.
-- Compound the original sin by trying to weasel your way around or out of an awkward situation.
-- Forget that the perception of truth can be more powerful than truth itself.
-- Hesitate to get the credit you deserve but do so only in ways that do not jeopardize your career.
-- Regard communication as a process of hitting the bull's eye target. Rather, anticipate the range of responses that could be created with your message and adjust as necessary.
-- Think of the process as a one-way street.
-- Let ego rule the content of your influence efforts.

YOU WILL:

-- Be able to garner support by reminding others of the overarching mission.

-- Have to develop some wariness if you intend to become a political animal.

-- Be moving on at some point in your career, in all likelihood. Don't invest too much time, energy, or emotion in the present circumstances.

-- Find Janusian thinking beneficial in a variety of situations calling for effective influence.

-- Discover that honesty, properly presented, truly is the best policy.

-- Find others analyzing your words as well as your actions to learn more about you.

-- Be able to use self-deprecating humor from time to time in order to quickly establish bonds with those you wish to influence.

-- Need to abide by the organizational e-mail policy. (If none exists, assume a leadership role in preparing such a policy.)

-- Influence more powerfully if you obtain and use feedback, before, during, and after a communication exchange.

YOU WON'T:

-- Be regarded as trustworthy if you don't maintain neutrality.

-- Manage time very well if you can't separate personal gossip from talk about business happenings.

-- Be able to escape the additional scrutiny that comes with career advancement. Learn to think carefully before you speak.

-- Equate exaggeration with persuasion if you are influencing with integrity.

-- Be able to halt antisocial behavior unless you take a stand against it.

-- Have to regard voice-mail as a business bane if you follow a few simple suggestions.

-- Be able to overcome all the skepticism that exists, but you can guide others more skillfully to the correct interpretation of your words.

-- Manage influence well without managing your emotions well.

Chapter 6
Influence & Style

~~~~~~~~~~~~~~~~

Overview   Considerable attention is given in this chapter to the adaptive style, and to the speed, simplicity, and self-confidence General Electric's CEO so prizes. Influencers, like military strategists, have to be able to move in unplanned directions, in response to challenges presented while they try to execute careful plans. Businesspeople, too, may find the logical flow of their presentations interrupted, and so a new tack has to be taken.

Jack Welch, the speed czar, puts his staff through workouts. We recommend you build your influence muscles by doing a modified workout of your own. In this chapter, you will also be reminded of the remarkable power a single person can exert, especially if he is willing to engage in self-scrutiny.

The substance of influence (directness, compassion, diplomacy) is also explored. But, the emphasis is not entirely inward. You will learn more about *koinonia*, the atmosphere of harmony, as opposed to hostility, in which ideas should be explored. Finally, Dr. Albert Mamary reinforces the need for such harmony as he discusses building partnerships predicated on trust.

The Styles of Influence
The Adaptive Style

Entry into a new decade, a new century, a new millennium, and perhaps even a new age inevitably produces contemplation, albeit a contemplation conducted in bite-size chunks as we digest our fast-food for thought. As we think about the meaning of life and the purpose of work, we cannot avoid the entanglements caused by relinquishing the old and embracing the new. As we strive to hold on to the best of the past while creating the best for the future, we often find ourselves on a psychological tightrope. The only safety net is the one spelled f-l-e-x-i-b-i-l-i-t-y.

As bumper stickers remind us, we have to "adapt or die." The very urgency of the words lends a frantic pace to days already characterized by a pace of change that leaves us breathless. And yet, without clinging to a stable constancy, a core consistency, we may soon find ourselves being swept up and left adrift as the winds of change howl around us.

The nanosecond nineties have paved the way for a new era, hallmarked by "speed, simplicity, and self-confidence," according to General Electric's CEO Jack Welch. If you are not displaying these elements in your influencing, you are probably not leading very effectively. Before we take a look at the extent to which your influence efforts reflect speed, simplicity, and self-confidence, let's consider this paradox--flexibility based on constancy--in terms of both businesspeople and trial attorneys.

The businessperson making a formal presentation or briefing is permitted to do just that--without interruption, without having to change course. Such situations require more constancy than flexibility, for the script is adhered to. Yes, during the question-and-answer period, you may have to think quickly on your feet but you will seldom have to deviate from the prepared import of your presentation. Less formal influence situations require the same kind of careful preparation, but they require greater flexibility, for you may not have a chance to execute your game plan, you may not be fortunate enough to proceed in a constant fashion through the influence points you intended to make.

Like coaches, lawyers and able influencers need to adapt to changing thrusts, often in the form of challenges

237

that interrupt your intended sequence. Here is where speed, simplicity, and self-confidence are critical.

The Speedy Style

People who appreciate orderliness, who thrive in settings that have a place for everything and everything in place, who like to gather extensive information before making decisions, often have trouble operating in a culture of chaos. Unfortunately, the chaos is here to stay, so futurists tell us. Within a decade, information pressure will be 32 times greater than it is today. (In no time at all, predictions of 500 television channels will be realized.) We're already swimming in a sea of intellectual inputs. Soon, we'll we drowning--unless we learn some powerful strokes, learn when to tread water, learn when to get out of the water. (The assessment of choices is explored further in the "Create Your Own Workout" section on page 252.)

Of necessity, today's influencer has to process rapidly information that may be entirely new or unanticipated. Unless he is able to respond quickly, the influencer may lose control of the discussion he in fact was hoping to lead. Consider Melinda Gates, wife of Microsoft's leader. Her incisive style, as described in Julie Bick's *All I Really Need to Know in Business I Learned at Microsoft*, was fascinating to watch, but no doubt intimidating if you were the object of it. During business presentations, Gates will often ask a question that ignores the carefully prepared slides, the painstakingly crafted proposal. For her truly penetrating questions, she wants bottom-line answers. This is the sort of situation for which you, working to influence others to accept your ideas, will have to be ready.

Is it possible to develop this skill of quickly receiving, analyzing, and responding to unexpected data, questions, information, or challenges? The answer is yes, but, not surprisingly, a qualified yes: skill development takes time. The exercises that follow will get you started.

Two bits of advice first, though: 1) Remember that all you need are words and you have been using words since you were one year old. Even if you don't have the ideas to be expressed in words, you can still use words intelligently either to admit you don't have specific knowledge, or to provide related knowledge, or to ask for more time. 2) The words you need constitute a universe. You simply have to reach for the right stars in that universe and unite them to express your ideas. The faster you can find the stellar combination, the more impressive your response will be. These exercises (and others like them that you can devise yourself) force you to move quickly to select specific, related elements in that verbal universe.

☑ Imagine you are applying for a job, determined to influence the prospective employer to hire you. The interview, however, takes an unexpected twist. The interviewer, after fully describing what the job entails, suddenly hands you a piece of paper, a pencil, and says, "I'm going to leave the room now, but I'll be back in a half hour. During that time, tell me what you'd do if you were hired." (This is a technique recommended by the likes of author/consultant Ken Blanchard.)

Now assume you are applying for the job of your dreams and you've just been asked to do the very same thing. What would you write that would positively influence the outcome?

Use a separate sheet of paper. Give yourself a half hour. Then show your response to someone who does a lot of hiring. Ask him to honestly assess your response, to tell you if it was good enough to land you the job.

☑ You'll need to set a timer for this exercise. Read through the directions first and once you understand what you have to do, then set the timer for one minute. This is the task. Using some letter other than "s," think of three things (all nouns) that apply to the process of influencing with integrity. For example, your words might be *trust, tact,* and *truth.* If you're ready, set the timer now and begin.

240

1. _____

2. _____

3. _____

There are all kinds of assessments to gauge your ability to think well and fast under pressure. The following is a simple test--one that you'll probably enjoy taking. Follow the same procedure: read the instructions over until they are clear to you and then set the timer--for two minutes this time.

List twenty titles (of books, songs, plays, operas, poems, television programs, movies, et cetera) that contain a reference to either a color (such as the movie *Blue Velvet)* or to a geographic location (such as *April in Paris).*

1. _____ 11. _____

2. _____ 12. _____

3. _____ 13. _____

4. _____ 14. _____

5. _____ 15. _____

6. _____ 16. _____

7. _____ 17. _____

8. _____ 18. _____

9. _____ 19. _____

10. _____ 20. _____

You can easily prepare all kinds of other tests for yourself--
20 titles that contain a woman's name or a reference to time
or date. You could even play with 20 names of animals,
birds, or insects spelled with just three letters. Or, 20 names
of body parts spelled with five letters, like e-l-b-o-w. The
possibilities are endless and endlessly valuable in sharpening
your wits. Your self-confidence will grow in leaps and
bounds, too, as you develop your concentration abilities;
they let you choose the right galaxy of terms from a whole
universe of possibilities.

As we've mentioned, whenever you attempt to
influence others, you are playing the role of leader. And
your communication skills are inseparable from your
effectiveness in this regard. If you are not articulate, you are
not inspiring confidence in you as leader or in the worth of
your leadership project.

☑ 1) Through practice (and a commitment to be
disciplined) you can easily develop the ability to think well
on your feet (or even in your seat). One of the simplest
techniques is to start each morning at work by opening a
dictionary to any page at all, letting your finger fall on a
word, and then tape recording your thoughts about that
word. Do this for a whole month and at the end of each

week, analyze your off-the-cuff remarks and prepare a written critique of yourself.

2) Another technique is to take any combination of five letters: s-r-e-t-l, for example, and create as many sentences as you can in a five minute period. The first word in each sentence would begin with the first letter in the combination, "s," in this case. The second word must begin with the second letter ("r") and so on. Once a given word has been used, it cannot be used again. "Silly realtors evade technical leases" is one possible sentence for the combination of letters here.

Work your way up to the apex: 20 sentences in a five-minute period is considered proof of exceptional, truly outstanding verbal facility.

3) A final suggestion requires the assistance of a colleague. Each morning for a full month, when he sees you or calls you on the phone, he will ask you a truly challenging question and permit you only one minute to respond. For instance, the question could be related to current events in the organization, in the nation, in the world. Or, it could be related to your views on a given issue. It might even pose a philosophical question or perhaps even an absurd question designed to catch you off guard.

The Simple Style

We've noted repeatedly that influence will be limited if you lack simplicity in your style. How do you *get* that simplicity, you may be wondering. It's probably easier than you think. If you can follow a five-step process, one that you first learned in junior high school, you will be able to liberate your ideas. You'll replace fluff with forcefulness and pomposity with hard-hitting points. Remember, your written words serve as a permanent record and so deserve special attention. As Lee Iacocca was fond of saying, "If you want to be the best, you have to separate yourself from all the talk about quality. And put it in writing."

1) To begin, find all forms of the "to be" verb and encircle them. When conjugated, this verb uses "am," "are," "is" in the present tense; "was" and "were" in the past tense; and "will be" in the future tense. Also of concern is any form of the word "be," such as "has been," "had been," "might have been," "should have been," et cetera. (Note: when coupled with an active-voice verb, such as "is walking," you do not have a form of "to be." It is only when the conjugated forms stand alone ("She is grateful") or when it stands next to the past tense of a verb ("This report was prepared by me") that you have to worry.

2)   Next, locate all the prepositions and encircle them. Many of them can be eliminated.

3)   In the third step, you have to dig out the action in the sentence--it may be very deeply buried beneath the fat. Practice with this, an actual government statement:

The purpose of this standard is to assist in the achievement of increased discipline in contractors' work measurement programs with the objective of improved productivity and efficiency in contractor industrial operations, since it is evident that excess manpower and lost time can be identified, reduced, and continued method improvements made regularly where work measurement programs have been implemented and conscientiously pursued in the government.

When faced with a monster sentence of this ilk, it helps to ask: What do they want to do? The answer will help you understand what they are trying to say: "They want to increase discipline in work measurement programs." A second question, applicable to this sentence is, Why? The answer: "To improve productivity in operations." A corollary is another Why?, the response to which would be: "When the government implements method improvements, it can identify and then reduce wasted manpower and time."

The actual action was camouflaged in the word "increased," which was used in the original as an adjective instead of a verb. Its power was stripped away because of this.

4)   The fourth step entails converting the action to an action verb. We saw it in the preceding example when "increased discipline" was changed to "to increase discipline." A slight difference, you may be thinking, but a difference that packs a lot of power, particularly when applied to a lengthy document. Uncovering the verbs, asking simple questions such as "Who did what?" will invariably lessen the complexity of the sentence, thus making it much easier to understand.

5)   Far too often, we waste time at the beginning of sentences and the beginning of memos by saying things that don't need to be said. Get to the point immediately if you wish to achieve simplicity in your influence messages. To illustrate: "It is the purpose of this memo to advise you that offices will be closed from December 24 to December 29, in honor of the Christmas holiday" wastes 11 words at the very start.

Of course the memo has a purpose. Otherwise, you wouldn't be writing it. Again, we know it is intended to advise the reader of something, so why point out the obvious? Thoreau's advice to "simplify, simplify, simplify" applies with equal logic to possession and expressions alike.

After all, there's a very good reason why the K.I.S.S. Principle ("Keep it simple, silly!") is still around.

☑   It's your turn now. Take this 30-word sentence and reduce it if you can to a mere 5 words. Yes, it is possible. All you have to do is follow the five steps just outlined for you.

There is a great deal of suspicion on the part of the secretaries in our office in Middlebrook toward the secretaries in our office in Meadowbrook at the present time.
Your revision _____

_____

(Check in the Appendix later to see how you fared and to find other practices.)

Perhaps the best (and most humorous) rationale we can provide for the importance of simplicity when influencing comes from a government office. A plumber wrote to them one day, saying that he had been using hydrochloric acid for unclogging pipes and asking if it would do harm to the plumbing. The office wrote back in typical bureaucratese: "The efficacy of hydrochloric acid is indisputable as a means of removing accumulated substances in the lining of pipes although the ionic residues are incompatible with metallic permanence."

The plumber was actually flattered to be addressed in such a scientific way and decided to drop them another note to thank them for endorsing his discovery of hydrochloric acid as an efficient pipe cleaner. When the agency received the note and realized they had completely misled him, they immediately fired off a much simpler communication: "Don't use hydrochloric acid! It eats the h _ _ _ out of pipes!"

This message the plumber understood.

The Self-confident Style

If you have made excellence in the influence process one of your top priorities, then you probably already have a fair amount of confidence. But life has a way of shaking us all up once in a while. If Marilyn Monroe, regarded by many in her day as the world's most beautiful woman, could show up late over and over because she felt she didn't look good enough for the camera, then it's easy to understand how fragile the human psyche really is. Daily, life presents reasons to lower our self-esteem. However, there are a number of things you can do keep on building your faith in yourself. A few are listed here.

<u>Review Your Raves</u>

From time to time, particularly if your self-confidence is waning, you should take five minutes and a sheet of paper to list all the things you have accomplished in your life since elementary school days. List all those achievements that have made you proud--it might be awards or honors you have been given, promotions, selection to a particular committee or team, the way your children have turned out, or the relationships you have with friends/ family. It might even be specific moments, for example the time your supervisor complimented you on an idea you proposed.

This short self-esteem injection does wonders for the soul. It helps restore self-confidence that may be fraying because of some incident that you probably won't even remember a year from now. An alternative to reviewing your raves is to have "shelf-esteem." Purchase a small, inexpensive shelf and install it in your home or office. On the shelf, you would place tangible evidence of your accomplishments.

Such activities help repair the small rips that occur in the fabric of confidence and competence, a fabric we have been weaving since children. Making mistakes is not the problem. The problem is being so crushed that we cannot learn from those mistakes, cannot put them behind us and move along.

Mind What You Say

Appoint someone you are close to to listen for certain expressions in your everyday speech. There is no need to put yourself down with statements like these: "This is really a stupid question, but could you explain why....", "I know I should know this but could you tell me just once more how to....", "I must be dense or something because I still don't get...." And yet, people do it every day of the week.

Let your assertions bespeak your confidence in your idea. "This is really going to make a difference" is much more confident that "It is my opinion that the results that will ensue will have an impact on the objective we are trying to attain." The second sentence is limp. It has no personality. It is hard to feel excited about it. (It is also unnecessarily long.)

☑ Listen to someone like Tom Peters on television and you'll have a good sense of the persuasive power self-confidence exerts. (Although his style may be a bit more dynamic or slang-filled than you would choose, it is undeniably effective.) As you translate these sentences for ones that sound more self-confident, aim for a style somewhere between the highly formal or conservative and the highly hyperbolic or in-your-face style Peters uses.

1) Perhaps if we could just give it a try, at least once, then we could decide if it is worth pursuing. Your confident alternative: _____

   _____

2) I know you're all very busy and you probably won't have time to serve on this committee with me, but I figured nothing ventured, nothing gained. Your confident alternative: _____

   _____

3) My idea probably isn't as good as Joe's, but if it's okay with you, I'd like to put it on the table now, if you don't mind. Your confident alternative: _____

   _____

4) I've been doing a lot of thinking, and I know you've been doing a lot of thinking too, about the safety issues that have been worrying us for quite a while now. I mean, one of these days, there just might be a fire and we are going to have a very hard time getting out of this building with all of those boxes blocking the door. Of course, I don't mean to sound as if I am criticizing the clerical staff, because I know they are doing the best they can. And I know all of you are doing the best you can, and I am certainly doing the best I can, but I

really think something has to be done or this situation could turn into a very serious problem. Your confident alternative: _____

_____

Create Your Own Workout

No, we don't mean getting physical (although many experts endorse doing something physically exerting in order to get pumped up on more levels than one). By workout, we mean doing something akin to what Jack Welch does with his direct reports.

The sessions are more mental *workout* than physical, and require employees to analyze situations with the speed, simplicity, and self-confidence Welch insists upon. Participants use these sessions in part to take unnecessary *work out* of their jobs. And, they can *work out* problems together. The term, then, has three beneficial outputs.

A group of 40-100 people from all ranks and functions convenes and is briefly addressed by their manager, who provides an agenda of topics or issues that deserve attention. He then leaves the room. The group breaks into teams and each tackles one part of the agenda-- listing complaints, proposing solutions, preparing presentations for the third day when the manager returns to work with the group.

He of course has no idea of what has been discussed. All he knows as he sits in the front of the room is that senior executives are there to watch and that he will be given proposals for which he must make a decision then and there. Each team makes its proposal. The manager is limited to three choices only: agree to the proposal, say "no," or ask for more information by a certain date. That's it.

The sessions have proven to be highly effective--on many levels, not the least of which is the hundreds of thousands of dollars saved by the ideas presented. Think of how you can use this system with family, friends, co-workers, or any other group of which you are part. You may not have the luxury of a week-long retreat, but you should be able to present the situation and ask others to think of possible solutions and resolutions.

☑   1)   What group do you wish to influence in some way? _____

2)   List here the issues in your relationship with them (and their relationship with each other) that need resolution. Then present the list to them.

a) _____

b) _____

c) _____

d) _____

3)   Explain how the workout works. Then give them your list and ask them to come up with solutions or things they would like to try in order to improve the situation. Give them one week to think about the improvements and to prepare a proposal. Set up a time and place for re-convening.

4)   Ask a trusted friend or co-worker to be present when the solutions are presented to you by the group.

5)   Meet with the group at the appointed time. Have them present their ideas one at a time. You can ask questions, but at the end of five minutes, you must agree to the proposal, say no to it (and tell why), or ask for more information by a particular date.

6)   Afterwards, have your observer provide you feedback regarding your ability to speak with speed, simplicity, and self-confidence.

Just as people who manage stress know how to spend their stress-dollars wisely (they wouldn't spend a dollar's worth of hypertension on a five-cent problem), so do influencers know how to align time with importance. H. L. Mencken's observation, "For every complex problem, there is one solution that is simple, neat.....and wrong," underscores the need to move slowly with complex problems and their resolution. By contrast, you must develop speed for those decisions that have minimal impact upon mission.

And, you must develop the wisdom to know when to postpone and when to act quickly, as illustrated by the workout strategy used in corporate or familial settings. If the long-term consequences of the decision are negligible, make the decision quickly. If a quick decision could cause irreparable harm, ask for more time or confer with others. (In an emergency, as opposed to a business-decision situation, of course, you may have to act immediately.)

As daunting as these time pressures may be for the influencer, there are always opportunities in them. Lying embedded in virtually every problem to be solved, every decision to be made, is a result waiting to be realized. The more you work out with situations with reluctant buyers of the ideas or products you have to sell, the more skilled you'll become in responding speedily, simply, and self-confidently.

Remain Flexible

Professor Fred Fiedler of the University of Illinois
espouses a contingency theory of management. Your
response to a given demand, he asserts, should depend on
three things: the nature of the problem, the nature of the
people involved, and the nature of the situation. Having the
same managerial style for all people, for all situations, and
for all circumstances will yield tentative, tepid results.
Better, he maintains, to have a style so flexible it can fit
varying demands.

Your style of influence, similarly, should contain
generally effective elements. These might include, for
example, your willingness to listen as much as you talk.
(Are you self-confident enough, flexible enough to increase
that willingness on the basis of this observation by Albert

Einstein: "Everyone has had an idea that could change the world"?)

☑   In terms of general verbal skills, take the following quiz to learn more about your own perceptions of influence. Check the appropriate box to indicate whether you agree or disagree with the statement (or whether it is true for you or not).

	I Agree (True)	I Disagree (False)
1) Author Raymond DiZazzo asserts the primary cause of failure in both personal and professional lives is poor communication.	☐	☐
2) You should sound different at home than you do at work.	☐	☐
3) Whenever I see or hear an effective communication technique, I try to incorporate it into my own style.	☐	☐
4) I'm fairly astute at knowing when to back off and when to press on.	☐	☐
5) I can read people fairly well.	☐	☐
6) I believe you're never too old to learn.	☐	☐
7) A good command of verbal skills will make you more self-confident.	☐	☐

8) I set and met a goal to improve one aspect of my communications style within the past year.

☐   ☐

9) Words can either defuse or escalate a conflict.

☐   ☐

10) Master influencers adapt themselves to the needs of the situation, people, and job to be done.

☐   ☐

A majority of answers in the left-hand column suggests you are indeed willing to change, to consider new possibilities and new prospects. Even if you had a majority on the right-hand side, the quiz statements should point you in the direction of improvement possibilities.

Let's put your proclivities to the test, another test, that is. This one asks you to think of some project that you would have to influence others to adopt. But this time, we'd like you to think on a grander scale. Are you already beginning to quake at the prospect? If so, remember that at this point, the project is a paper-project only. Deciding to transfer it from paper into the reality-realm will depend on your leadership and your passion about the importance of this possibility.

Remember something else if you are doubting the power of one person to effect change in the world: think about people like Rosa Parks, Nelson Mandela, Lech Walesa, Mother Teresa. Think too about Jody Williams, awarded the 1997 Nobel Peace Prize. With a staff of one (herself), she worked from her home in Vermont for a year and a half, relying primarily on the Internet to organize a global ban on land mines.

While we are not endorsing a project of this magnitude, we do believe you can get involved with something large or small that will make a definite difference in your small corner of the world. Your influence can be exerted on an individual or collective basis. To aid in shaping a successful outcome, we'll apply the items in the preceding assessment to this project of your choosing.

☑   Describe here your idea for making a positive change or having an ameliorative impact on some segment of society (the elderly, children, battered spouses, college students, the unemployed, the homeless, those with serious medical problems, et cetera). Or, delineate an idea for improving the workplace in some way (developing basic skills, improving customer service, holding a consortium, celebrating a special day or month like Quality Month in October, et cetera).

What key decision-makers would you have to influence in order to launch this project? _____

How could poor communications cause this undertaking to fail? _____

For this particular group of decision-makers, what should you sound like? What words will help you achieve that sound? _____

Consider all the people you know or know of: whom do you most admire for his or her ability to influence others with integrity? _____

How would this person influence the key decision-makers you have identified? _____

(Would he, for example, shake up their thinking as Tom Peters does? Would she appeal to a common core of decency, as Princess Diana did? Would he employ humor, as Bill Cosby does?) _____

As you think ahead to the first meeting or first approach you would make, what points might you have to back off from and what points will you probably have to move forward with? _____

_____

Keeping these potential influencees in mind and knowing them as you do, what body language should you speak? What body language of theirs should you be attuned to? _____

_____

What new knowledge will you probably have to acquire in order to accomplish your goals? _____

_____

In what specific ways could you project your confidence in the merit of this idea? _____

_____

If you could achieve one goal in relation to your first meeting with these people you need to influence, what would that goal be? _____

_____

What conflict or disagreements might arise in this meeting? What words will minimize the negative impact?

_____

_____

What adaptations to your basic style might you have to make in light of this particular group, this particular project, this particular situation you think needs improvement? _____

_____

By the way, one excellent method of developing the flexibility integral to the influence process takes little time and virtually no effort beyond the mental gymnastics. In a relaxed setting, begin a conversation with a friend as you normally would. Then ask your friend to throw out a business-related word, such as "profits." Your job is to segue smoothly into a discussion of profits and stay on the topic for about two minutes, after which your friend throws out another topic, "morale," for example. You will continue the process until you have covered five words. Ask your friend for his critique before you leave each other, including suggestions to improve your verbal flexibility.

The Substance of Influence

Your style and your substance form two prongs of the instrument successful influencers use. Your style, as we noted, should be an adaptive one. It should reveal the speed, simplicity, and self-confidence we invariably find in the influence styles of rich and famous business leaders. But we find something else in those styles--a sense of concern for others. In *Augustine's Travels*, for example, Norman Augustine roots his success-observations in the soil of integrity. The chairman of Lockheed Martin Corporation speaks at great length about the ethical considerations that must lie at the core of our personal and professional actions.

That substance of concern is also reflected in a recent study by the Johnson School of Management at Cornell University (Pam Mayer, "Profitability and the Common Good," *Leadership in Action*, published by the Center for Creative Leadership and Jossey-Bass Publishers, Volume 17, Number 3, 1997, page 13). In the study, executives from leading companies were asked, "What characteristics will business leaders need for success a decade from now?"

Not surprisingly, the need for teamwork was the one cited most often by executives. Running a close second was the need for compassion. The next section includes suggestions for establishing the kind of teamwork evident in idea-explorations that welcome all viewpoints. First, though, let's examine some world-of-work situations calling for responses reflecting the substantial elements of influence: directness, compassion, and diplomacy.

Mistakes, disasters, and tragedies occur in the world of work as frequently as they do in other areas. As influencers, our responses can reflect these three characteristics--directness, compassion, and diplomacy--or they can be so circuitous that our influence does not extend beyond our own noses. According to James Lukaszewski (Buffy Vouglas, "The Power of Positive PR," *Contingency Planning & Management*, January 1998, Vol. III, No. 1, page 19), a good answer for a bad situation contains an objective for the response you are giving (directness), information about people (compassion), and a limited number of negative words (diplomacy).

This triad of effective influence will work in the most critical of situations--a suicide at work, violence in the workplace, industrial accidents, natural disasters that affect employees, lawsuits that can ruin a company's image, et cetera--but we'll apply them here to less serious situations. The scenarios that follow are more likely to be encountered by those of us who influence in ordinary circumstances (succession planning, possible danger, theft). There are people responsible for influencing the press and public in truly extraordinary circumstances, but their numbers are fewer.

√ Read each case, and then outline your response, to be presented in a memo or actual meeting with the person(s) involved. Strive to include an objective (directness), information about people (compassion), and a limited number of negative words (diplomacy) in your answers.

1. You are the son of, and vice president for, a successful businessman who heads a family-owned business. Your father is approaching his 75th year of life and still has a very firm grip on the reins of power. Your concern is that no succession planning has been done for the company and no will, medical directives, or estate planning has been done for the family. Your father is reluctant to discuss these issues, but you feel the time has come. Draft your approach here by stating your communications objective and then weaving it into the other two substances that comprise effective influence in such cases: compassion and diplomacy.

   What is your objective? State it directly. _____

   _____

   _____

   What information could you supply about your father and about other people, if you were facing similar circumstances? State that information compassionately.

   _____

   _____

What words with negative connotations do you have to use? Express them as diplomatically as possible.

_____

_____

2. The bank for which you run the security office has just been held up for the third time in two years. Although thankfully no one has been seriously hurt so far, employees are expressing fear about their safety. You've even heard rumors that some employees have brought handguns to work.

What is your objective? State it directly. _____

_____

_____

What information could you supply about your employees and/or other people, if you were facing similar circumstances? State it compassionately. _____

_____

_____

_____

What words with negative connotations do you have to use? Express them as diplomatically as possible.

_____

_____

_____

3. The theft of a hard disk drive (containing names, addresses and social security numbers of current and former employees plus bank account numbers on retired employees) from a San Francisco manufacturer has left employees in your nearby company very nervous ("Levi Strauss Disk Theft Spurs Massive Communication Effort," *Contingency Planning & Management*, July/August, 1997, Vol. II, No. 7, page 4). As personnel manager, you want to offer reassurances in a company-wide communication.

What is your objective? State it directly. _____

_____

_____

What information could you supply about your employees and/or about other people, if you were facing similar circumstances? State it compassionately. _____

_____

_____

_____

What words with negative connotations do you have to use? Express them as diplomatically as possible. _____

_____

_____

_____

Substance: Abuse or Appropriate Use?

Our panel's comments reflect all three elements of substantial influence--directness, compassion, and diplomacy. Did your own drafted messages have at least some of these recommendations? If your intentions were integrity-driven, chances are your treatment of substance was appropriate. If you decide, however, after reviewing these comments, that your response could have been more influential, let the points guide you in the future, as you combine the substance of influence with your own unique style.

Situation #1:

-- The strong health of the company must be maintained, no matter who is in charge.

-- Succession planning will mean the company can move into the future as the original founder would wish.

-- If the founder's wishes are not made known in advance, family members may not be allowed to make decisions about medical treatment.

-- A living will and an actual will can guarantee the founder's intentions, for his own health and for the health of the family. Consequently, the future operation of the business will be conducted according to his desires.

-- An estate planner and an attorney can handle the paperwork so the founder need invest little time or effort in making these arrangements.

-- The employees of the firm as well as its customers deserve to have continuity of excellence. That can be assured only if formal measures are taken to specify what will happen once the founder retires.

-- The founder deserves to have some time off, if only semi-retirement, and these plans should be in place before he reaches that stage.

-- If he has friends in similar circumstances who have made the necessary provisions, mention should be made of their preparations.

-- A legacy and legend have already been built around the founder. Both should be allowed to continue in the most favorable of circumstances, those he himself has fashioned.

Situation #2:
-- Employees cannot bring guns to work. (Statistics show there is a greater likelihood of harm from accidental discharges than from robbery attempts.)

-- Ideally, additional security measures have been put in place. Advise employees of what they are.

-- The local police department should have been contacted to advise employees what to do if another robbery attempt is made. Safe and appropriate actions should be specified and periodically reviewed.

-- A communications channel should be established to deal with employee concerns, proposals, and rumors.

-- Senior management should emphasize repeatedly its concern for the safety of employees.

-- Senior management should also network/benchmark with other banks that have the same worry. Together, they can best decide what can be done to protect employees and assets. The plans should be made known to employees as they are being undertaken.

Situation #3:

-- Explain the situation and the precautions that were taken to prevent further theft. In the actual situation, the precautions included these steps.

- All present and past employees were notified of the theft, and retired employees were urged to change their bank accounts.

- All area banks were notified of the theft and the likelihood of customers closing and re-opening accounts in order to protect their deposits.

-- Offer assurances.

- The information on the existing employees is the same information that appears in the phone book and any number of other places.
- Employees were given information about how to obtain credit reports.
- The company had back-up disks, thus allowing it to reach all former employees.
- There was a possibility that the theft was simply an act of sabotage and not an attempt to use the information illegally.
- The thieves had not yet misused any of the stolen information.
- New security measures have been implemented.
- The police are still investigating the crime.

-- Invite input.

- Ask for suggestions from employees about ways to prevent a similar theft or to deal with it if it should occur.
- Ask for volunteers to learn more about the situation and to benchmark with other companies or with experts who handle such crises.

Establish *Koinonia*

Questions of style and substance are often individual matters. But as ideas are explored and plans being formulated, we usually find we need to interact with others. Those interactions can be optimized when certain conditions prevail, among them *koinonia*, the spirit of fellowship. When this understanding pervades meeting rooms, flexibility of thought occurs more readily, for people are not focusing energy on contentious issues. When you and others are examining thoughts on a high level of cognition, when you can isolate the ideas and not be concerned with covert agendas or overt hostilities, the best outcomes can occur much more readily. With brainstorming, a mental kinship evolves. With *koinonia*, a mental and emotional kinship prevails.

By contrast, when dishonesty, narrow- or closed-mindedness pervades the setting, the worth of ideas is pushed aside and the worth of individuals seems to come to the forefront of the discussions. How can you reach the state at which freedom of thought is valued and bitterness is avoided? A few suggestions follow.

-- Emphasize that in idea-exploration, there are no right or wrong ideas. There are ideas and there are opinions, and when the majority of opinions agree on the seemingly best ideas, the best outcomes are more assured.

-- Have some ground rules that permit ideas to be nurtured until they are either overruled or accepted. Otherwise, verbal toxins can kill good ideas before they have a chance to be born.

-- Push pettiness aside by making frequent mention of purpose.

-- Welcome differences of thought. Groupthink can spell danger for all involved.

-- Have a "conversion cop" who will ring a bell or wave a red flag in the air whenever someone is trying to forcibly convert others to a particular viewpoint instead of merely listing its merits.

-- Allow time on every agenda for the unadulterated pursuit of creative possibilities.

-- Set aside a time when people can say exactly what is on their minds without being embarrassed, ridiculed, or attacked.

-- Treat each person as if he had a million-dollar idea in his head. Otherwise, you may filter his idea through the sieve of your own opinion about him, and judge the idea as you judge the man.

Preview   In Chapter 7, the emphasis shifts from rapidity of response to appropriateness of response. You'll acquire greater diplomacy as you follow the suggestions and work on the exercises. And, you'll learn when sugar-coating is acceptable and when it should be avoided at all costs. The interview at the end of the chapter explores creative responses and how to make them less threatening to those who in the long run can profit from them.

INTERVIEW

**Dr. Albert Mamary, Executive Director,
Renewal for Better Schools and
the Partners for Quality Learning Alliance,
Binghamton, New York**

A long time ago, I vowed to take the word "no" out
of my vocabulary. Instead, whenever I received a request
that would set precedent or change the terms and conditions
of the existing contract, I would say, "Help me find a way."
In my head, "no" is an ugly word. It implies that I have the
power and you do not. Interestingly, the more you give of
yourself and the more power you give away, within certain
parameters, the more it comes back to you. By asking for
meaningful involvement, we can say "yes" to possibilities
that we've never thought about. We can share the power.

If we could only understand that "all of us" is better
than any one of us. My greatest fear as a leader was that
people were overextending themselves. I knew the extent of
their dedication and that concerned me. I used to tell the staff
they were trying to give too much back to the organization
and to the system but their response would be, "It's good for
kids."

When people know they are valued and trusted, they
are eager to demonstrate commitment. At least that's been

my experience. When we, as organizational leaders, act out what we say, when we actually live by the words we speak, people know our sincerity. When that trust is reciprocated, the organization can go faster and farther than we ever thought possible.

We do not always know, though, who can make a contribution. We think we know because of what we have seen and heard in the past. But we simply do not know how much people can contribute. Previously untapped talent and recognized talent should both be used to drive organizations toward excellence. My philosophy has always been, "Everyone has a wonderful brain. If you don't think they do, just pretend they do."

Even when employees' viewpoints do not match management's viewpoint, we have to trust them and show we care about them. They have to see, hear, feel, and taste the organization's respect for what they have to say. The very fact that they are saying it indicates concern.

Once the trust has been built, a systems approach comes next. The quick-fix approaches may give us the illusion of a fast solution, but not a long-lasting one. While a hot solution is rarely bad, it alone will not change the organization or company over the long haul.

Sometimes I ask people, "What is the first thing you do when you are putting a puzzle together?" Some people say they concentrate on the corners; others say they find the unusual shapes that fit into other unusual shapes; but the best answer, of course, is to look at the big picture first. The same is true on the organizational level: we cannot fit the pieces together if we do not have a sense of the big picture.

You may remember the man who juggled so many plates all at once on the old Ed Sullivan Show. This is a good analogy for any organization today. Even if the performer's back was to the audience, he would respond to the gasps of the audience when a plate was ready to topple, always managing to save it just in time. The systems approach is the only way we can identify and keep all those plates going at the same time--not the fix-of-the-day or the flavor-of-the-month.

For any organization to maintain progress and develop continually, it must view its employees as the most valuable resource. When employees feel valued, they will view change as necessary and the results will be long-lasting. When conditions permit them to be meaningfully involved, they will assume responsibility for their own behavior, productivity, and renewal. Most people want to be responsible and do a quality job, but without the conditions of trust, caring, and respect, organizational and personal renewal and improvement are almost impossible to achieve.

Renewal and self-assessment are the thrusts toward sustaining momentum. We cannot keep asking people vague questions like, "What can we do to get better?" or "How can I improve?" Most will work hard when they know what the answers look like. We need leaders and those they lead working together to determine the attributes and performance indicators that spell excellence. Once this is done, each person can continually self-assess against the agreed-upon performance indicators and continually adjust for improvement. Renewal through self- and co-assessment is the only way to excellence.

DO:

-- Develop flexibility.
-- Remind yourself periodically that the best-laid plans may be upset just as you are presenting them. Develop the ability to respond with speed, simplicity, and self-confidence.
-- Ask who is doing what to determine what action is occurring in a sentence.
-- Plan a workout session of your own.
-- Realize that poor communication can cause failure in both your personal and your professional life.
-- Keep yourself open to change.
-- Act as if everyone has a "wonderful brain."
-- Consider using the system approach to problems rather than a piecemeal approach.

DON'T:

-- Overlook the importance of speed as a competitive advantage.
-- Forget to engage in exercises that will develop your ability to think well and fast.
-- Forget to review your raves from time to time.
-- Minimize the importance of networking.
-- Ever think that one person alone cannot change the world.

-- Think a hot solution will last very long.
-- Let too long a period go by without engaging in some self-renewal.
-- Let egos replace *koinonia*, the spirit of fellowship.

YOU WILL:

-- Find it useful to ask some questions about decisions you have to make.

-- Inspire greater confidence as your communication skills improve.

-- Find it difficult to motivate others if your sentences do not pulsate with energy.

-- Discover that the contingency theory of management can be applied to your style of influence.

-- Achieve permanence when you put salient information in writing.

-- Be forced to think more creatively if you take the word "no" out of your vocabulary.

-- Find commitment growing as employees feel more trusted and more valued.

YOU WON'T

-- Manage time very well if you cannot screen decisions to determine how much of your time they deserve.

-- Keep writing dense sentences if you get rid of passive voice and excessive prepositions.

-- Be able to hear yourself uttering self-defeating statements unless you train yourself to listen.

-- Be able to use the same communication style in every scenario. Your job-speak should not sound exactly like your home-speak.
-- Have to solve every problem alone. Involve others.
-- Be able to place some pieces in the puzzle without a sense of the big picture.

Chapter 7
Influence & Impact

~~~~~~~~~~~~~~~~

Overview   Having specific lines in your hip pocket
enables you to extricate yourself easily from situations that
can be awkward, embarrassing and even possibly offensive.
By using these pre-determined lines, you can sugar-coat
your refusal to answer, thus maintaining positive working
relationships with those who may have pushed you for
answers.

     The D-I-R-E-C-T Approach is also presented in this
chapter. With its emphasis on Dialog, Inquire, Response,
Environ, Contact, and Tie up, the method encourages
connections between influencer and influencees.

     Sugar-coating, as examined in this chapter, refers to
the process of making the hard-to-swallow easier-to-digest.
It does not refer to being sinful in the process: hiding

negative information, having predetermined outcomes, or using silence unethically.

The hard-to-swallow ideas are often generated by creative thinkers. The six elements that stimulate creative thinking and creative environments are explored in the interview with Floyd Hurt.

Top-of-the-Line Responses to Bottom-Line Situations

Into each of our lives come people who knowingly or inadvertently back us into a corner. Sometimes they simply want information, other times they want favors. Worst of all are the times when they use deception or trickery to superimpose their wills upon ours. The very best advice we can offer is to have a pocketful of punch lines. Pull them out as needed and save yourself from being verbally mangled or venally manipulated. Here's how.

Has this ever happened to you? You are having an ordinary discussion with someone, perhaps talking about your new house. Suddenly, you hear the ominous words, "I know it's none of my business...." You know the next word is going to be "but." And sure enough, the person continues, "but how much did you pay for it?" Or, "How much did you get when you sold your old house?" Or, "How can you afford to live in a neighborhood like that?"

Because you've been raised to be honest, your first inclination will be to give the person the information she is seeking, even though you may be thinking, "You're right. It really is none of your business." But a comment like that could strain a relationship when you'd prefer to maintain a cordial relationship. How do you prevent the strain and still not reveal information you consider private or personal?

Reach into your figurative hip pocket, the one stuffed with good responses, and pull out something like this, with a smile on your face, "My mother always taught me to circumvent questions about money. And so, I'm going to follow her advice. But let me tell you, it's worth every penny we paid for it. The deck alone is perfect for...."

Another ploy is to repeat your refusal in a novel way. Let us say someone asked you how old you are and you don't like to talk about your age, for whatever reason. Again, with a smile, you could reply, "Why, thank you very much." The person may try to correct a non-existent misunderstanding. "Perhaps I didn't make myself clear. I was asking how old you are."

In return, you would repeat, "Thank you so much." (The bigger the twinkle in your eye, the better. Very soon, the person will get the message that you are not going to

285

divulge this information. If you continue saying it, you will be able to influence the other person (you want her to stop asking such personal questions) without violating your integrity (you have a personal policy of not revealing certain types of information).

☑ Take this real-life situation. Your neighbor has approached your spouse on the golf course with this request, "Could you give this to your spouse when you get home? I don't have a sewing machine (or electric drill) myself so I thought Gerry could just take a minute to do this for me." Your spouse dutifully complies.

A week later you meet the neighbor at a social function. You do not wish to create hard feelings. On the other hand, you have enough of your own woodworking (or sewing) to do. How can you make your point without being too pointed?

_____

_____

_____

The person caught up in this dilemma had the advantage of time to prepare her response. But you can use this kind of response even when you are put on the spot. She said to the neighbor, "Jon gave me the mending. I had to put it at the bottom of the my to-do list but I'll get to it, I promise." Although it only took her five minutes to do the repairs, the time factor was secondary to the point she wanted to make: she had enough of her own work to do and didn't want the neighbor developing a pattern of dependency. She waited a whole month before giving her husband the mending to be returned. And she was never asked again for sartorial assistance.

What if the situation involves someone presenting an idea that you honestly feel is not very valuable? An able administrator we know responds with a two-word imperative statement: "Persuade me." The burden of proof (explaining why it won't work) is shifted to the shoulders of the proposer, who has to prove why it will.

Often, in the process of exploring the idea's worth, the idea-proposer comes to her own realization that the idea is not a very good one. On the other hand, sometimes the idea, as it is being dissected, has more allure than the administrator first thought. In such cases, she ends up approving it.

To be sure, there is no way you can be prepared for every situation requiring diplomacy or calling for a direct message of influence. Nonetheless, by having a wide array of responses available, you'll be better prepared for the awkward moments that bedevil us all.

For practice, we're providing ten situations here, as well as the bottom-line point to be made. For each, you will make that point strongly enough so that you'll not be trapped in such awkward circumstances in the future. (Lines are deliberately left blank so you can fill them in according to the specifics of your own situation.)

1. You have made a presentation at staff meeting and are awaiting a critique from your colleagues. The first evaluation is given, but the speaker, your manager, is evaluating your appearance and not your proposal. The remark is devastating: "I hope you don't intend to present this to our client dressed the way you are."

<u>Bottom line</u>: You don't want the group's focus to shift to an unpleasant exchange. You decide the snide remark can be dealt with later, in private. The bottom line is that you want feedback on your proposal.

Here's the hip-pocket parlance that will work in numerous comparable situations when someone uses a professional setting to make an unprofessional remark:

"Don't worry about _____. Let me have your input about _____ instead. That's more important to me right now."

2. You are caught in the middle of an interoffice squabble. One individual is badmouthing another. You like both of them and wish they could learn to get along.

Bottom line: You don't have time for petty quarrels like this, and you don't want to be dragged into them in the future.

This line, a speaking-from-the-hip (pocket) line, usually works admirably: "I'm surprised to hear you say that. _____ speaks quite highly of you." The badmouther, perhaps because she is surprised, perhaps because she feels guilt, usually backtracks.

Now, if the second person in fact is making disparaging remarks about this speaker, then you cannot use the line. Instead, you might say something like, "I'm sorry to hear that. But we have a bigger problem to contend with. Have you heard that _____?" Move right along to issues more deserving of your and their time.

3.   The veiled barb is no less damaging than its uncovered cousin. In fact, sometimes the intimated insult is even worse, because it leaves us wondering if the person was really directing her comments toward us and if so, how many other people feel as she does. Imagine you had a family emergency and were an hour late to work. Your boss was most sympathetic, but at lunchtime you overhear a remark that sounds as if you were meant to overhear it: "Some people think they can waltz in here any time they want. They don't even think about how hard it is for the rest of us when they're late."

<u>Bottom line:</u>　At least when the disparaging remark is out in the open, we can deal with it at face value. We advise speaking with the other person so the issue or perhaps an underlying issue can be identified and discussed. If you were imagining the slight, you can make light of it. If not, your insulter has a chance to deal directly and to tell you honestly what is troubling her and why.

You might say, "I sense you have a problem with my _____. Let's talk about that now so it won't stand between us." If the other person denies the implication you thought you heard, you need not apologize. Instead, speak in positive, affirming tones. "Good. I'm glad I asked and that I was wrong. It's best if our communication can be open, don't you think? I've found that submerging real feelings usually leads to problems later on."

4. 　If you have the unpleasant task of reprimanding someone (this advice applies equally well to employees and children), you will often find them sidetracking your charges by involving others. For example, you are a team leader and one of the team members has repeatedly failed to complete assigned tasks on time. When you speak with her about it, she may try to sidetrack: "Cecelia is late with her assignments more often than I am and yet you never speak to her about it."

Bottom line:　　You want to meet the objective of dealing with the problem face-to-face with this person. Whether or not there is truth to the charge being leveled against *you*, you are meeting for another purpose altogether.

Sidestep the sidetracker. If you wish, you can point out that Cecelia's actions will be dealt with at another time, in another place. Try something like this, "We're here today to talk about *your* assignments, _____, and the difficulties it creates for the team as a whole when you don't follow through."

5.　　You are a secretary who does work for several people. As a rule, they are respectful of your multiple priorities and time commitments; they have empowered you to juggle the workload as you see fit. There is one manager, however, who seems to feel her needs take precedence over everyone else's.

Bottom line:　　You want to be fair to all concerned. Work is work, you believe. In one sense, it doesn't matter whose work you are doing. But you are professional enough to give priority to real priorities, not to status. You want to make sure that described urgencies truly are such.

Try this: "_____, I can easily stop what I'm doing and take care of your report right now. But, I'll need you to explain to _____ why I'm not finishing her report as I said I would. If you can clear it with her, I'll be happy to work on yours."

(This is a technique known as requests-and-promises. It works no matter who is making the request. More complex situations, though, should have the details of the exchange recorded.)

[✓]   In the remaining five scenarios, you will have a chance to hone your influence abilities. You task will be to get your message across without resorting to either abrasiveness or apology.

6.   You find co-workers, supervisors, and subordinates alike who are prone to taking the monkey off their own back and planting it firmly on someone else's. In fact, when you are aware of the monkey-transfer taking place, you'll probably be surprised at the ingenuity behind the attempts. Some people will resort to guilt; others to flattery, sympathy, or guile; still others will appeal to your basically nice nature. Simply put, they want you to do their work for them. Bottom line: You want to ensure productivity levels remain high but you do not wish to be solely responsible for them. Being too efficient or too concerned can actually add stress to your life and subtract accountability from the lives of others.

What could you say? _____

7. You don't mind hearing opposition to your ideas. However, you have one colleague who makes outright, damning declarations. She can condemn a proposal that took three months to prepare with a one-second comment: "Ridiculous." On occasion, her pronouncements run the length of an entire sentence, but they are always spoken with a definitiveness that brooks no further discussion, or so it seems.

Bottom line: You don't want to appear contentious, but you do want the ideas you are proposing to be debated at least before their fate is sealed forever.

What could you say? _____

8. Although you can never quite be certain, you believe a colleague is making borderline sexist comments. You can't be certain because they can be interpreted in more than one way. Plus, your colleague is careful enough to say things with a smile that appears quite sincere.

Bottom line: You feel you have to take a stand, for yourself and others. You hesitate to make accusations, but you do want your tolerance limits to be known.

What could you say? _____

9. An individual in a position slightly higher than your own has a way of dismissing you. You don't know if she is aware of her actions or how they make you feel, but it is not uncommon for her to greet someone else and start talking to that person even though you and she had been in the middle of a conversation. Or, she fails to introduce you to others who come along. Sometimes, in the middle of a report you are giving, she starts doing something else, as if you weren't even there!

Bottom line: Your self-worth is on the line here, or at least some of it. You can't afford to antagonize this person, but you don't like feeling as if you are invisible either.

What could you say? _____

_____

10. Even though you respect a particular colleague's abilities, you find her non-stop whining tiresome. She is making a significant contribution, no doubt about it, but she complains incessantly about any and all aspects of the organization. You feel she is indirectly undermining morale in the office.

Bottom line: You don't want to dampen her enthusiasm for her work, but you do want to dampen the gripe-embers she continues to flame.

What could you say? _____

_____

The D-I-R-E-C-T Approach

How often have you lamented, or heard someone else lament, "It wasn't what she said as much as the way she said it"? With so much of the communication message dependent on factors other than words, the power seller and the power influencer know how to work a room or situation in order to maximize both input and output. One approach that will help you do just that is the D-I-R-E-C-T Approach. Each of the letters represents the first letter in another word related to tools you can use to persuade others of the worth of your idea.

D = Dialog   In the most time-honored sense of the word, to dialog is to talk together, to establish harmony through an open exchange of ideas. Neither party attempts to dominate the conversation or the thinking of the other person. There is a parity to be seen and heard, not a monologue. If the other party cannot understand your viewpoint, she will never be persuaded to it. And if you do not comprehend the rationale behind her failure to embrace it, you cannot hope to persuade fully.

If your dialogs are equal and even, you will be listening at least fifty percent of the time.

I = Inquire   Not only does asking questions enlighten you and the question-answerer, but the process demonstrates your interest in the things she is

295

expressing. Inquiry qualifies as much as imitation in being a high form of flattery.

R   =   Respond   In both physical and verbal ways, you can show the sincerity of your interest in what others are saying. Physically, you can smile, maintain eye contact, jot things down, or show by your posture that you're attentive rather than bored. Verbal gestures include saying "uh huh" while nodding, or "I see" or "Hmmm" to indicate the point is one that makes sense to you.

E   =   Environ   This verb means to surround or to encircle. It probably makes you think of its noun cognate, "environment." When you are being direct in your influence efforts, you attend to the surroundings and their impact on the recipient of your influence message. By paralleling or synchronizing your message and its medium, you stand a much better chance of getting your concept across and having it remembered. One way to environ substantially is to match the import of the message to the surroundings. If it is a serious message, for example, you may want to meet in a quiet conference room. If the message contains good tidings, a noisier, people-filled setting may be more suitable.

C   =   Contact   Make some physical contact at least once during the course of your presentation. If you are addressing an individual or small group, you could shake their hands upon completion of your report. In a one-on-one setting, you could briefly and lightly touch someone's arm, as if to say, "That's right!" or "We could do this, too!" As the other person is leaving your office, you might give a pat on the back to signal, "Great. I'm glad this is settled." Contact also means keeping in contact, as appropriate, once your initial influence overture has been made.

Solicitors know, for example, that if people have displayed a willingness to give to a charity once, they can usually be counted on to continue making a contribution, often in annually increasing increments. But the subsequent contact is an integral part of this influence-equation. Sales people also know that it can take as many as ten interactions to close a sale.

T   =   Tie up   Bring closure to each exchange in which you have attempted to influence someone else. This closure could mean thanking her for her time, repeating the agreements that have been reached, telling what the next steps will be, et cetera. The end of the conversation/speech/pitch/presentation is your last opportunity to assert the authenticity of your request, your final opportunity (at least for that day) to point your listener or reader toward the realm in which possibilities are emerging.

The following anecdotes, one for each word in the D-I-R-E-C-T Approach, are provided to reinforce the importance of direct dealing when it comes to influencing with integrity.

Dialog   In a humorous effort to move below the layers of artifice that often characterized conversation at White House affairs, President Franklin Roosevelt sometimes said outrageous things, just to prove his point that meaningful dialog was virtually impossible in such social gatherings. In standing lines, for example, when people made the inevitable query, "How are you today, sir?" he would sometimes reply, "Fine, thank you, I just murdered my grandmother this morning." No one ever even heard him, or if they did, they no doubt thought they had *mis*heard him and failed to ask for clarification.

One guest, however, whose listening skills were superior to most others', stopped and asked, "What did she do to deserve that, sir?"

Inquire   A request for further information can influence others by revealing our own point of view on a subject. When Winston Churchill was approached by a loud American woman at a reception, she demanded to know, "What are you going to do about those Indians?"

Churchill sought clarification: "To which Indians do you refer? Do you refer to the second greatest nation on

298

earth, which under benign and munificent British rule has multipled and prospered exceedingly? Or to the unfortunate North American Indians, which under your present administration are almost extinct?"

Respond   Your responses can have great significance, sometimes even when they are misinterpreted. In this historical example, we learn how one man's response was turned around and used to influence him. Frederick II, King of Prussia from 1740 to 1786, was a man of firm convictions. One of those was that General von Winterfeldt was not worth his time or attention. The two men happened to meet in Potsdam and the general saluted the monarch, indicating his respect and his willingness to let bygones by bygones. But Frederick used a physical response that clearly showed how little he thought of the general: he turned his back on him.

Von Winterfeldt quickly ran after the king and said with enthusiasm, "I am happy to see that Your Majesty is no longer angry with me." Frederick could not resist inquiring what led the general to that conclusion. "Your Majesty has never in his life turned his back on an enemy," was the clever observation, the basis for a reconciliation between the two.

Environ   Samuel Goldwyn was a tough
negotiator. Once, in the middle of a heated dispute at his
home, one of his colleagues tired of the debate and walked
over to look out the window. After spotting a simple
happening in the animal kingdom, he called the others to join
him. "Here we are fighting," he commented, "and this
marvelous, peaceful event is taking place under our noses."
He then chided his colleagues for being unable to work
together. Goldwyn walked over to see the sight: a mother
quail and five tiny offspring. The magic didn't last long for
Goldwyn, though. "They don't belong here," he snapped
and returned to the battleground.

Contact   In this case, two famous men
contacted one another following a misunderstanding. The
cleverness of their exchange was probably sufficient for
restoring their friendship to its former status. Composer
Giacomo Puccini sent his friends cakes at Christmas every
year. Just before one particular holiday, however, he fought
with the famed conductor Arturo Toscanini. To his dismay,
he learned he was too late to cancel his order: the cake had
already been delivered to Toscanini. Determined to make
certain the gift was not regarded as an attempt at reconciliation, he sent a telegram to Toscanini: "Cake sent by
mistake."

Toscanini was a man of equally few words. His return telegram read: "Cake eaten by mistake."

Tie Up The intention was the right one, to tie up the altercation, but it failed in this case because Ernst Lubitsch spoke English as a second language. The acclaimed film director was in the middle of a heated argument with playwright Edward Knoblock. Lubitsch was so angry he walked off the set, but then returned, hoping no doubt to have the last word and a devastating one at that. Unfortunately for him, the most withering closure he could muster was: "How do you do?"

Sugar-Coating: Sins and Scintillas

There are fine lines to be drawn whenever we engage in the process of influence. When you are in a heightened, metacognitive state, you are constantly evaluating your speech and your actions to ensure you are not crossing any ethical lines. As we've noted, if a given decision or solution effects positive change for you *and* others, the action is worthy of pursuit. When you are the only one, however, who can be listed as the primary beneficiary of derivative gains, the influence you are exerting quite possibly is being done in your behalf alone.

Apart from the broad, brush-stroke questions of gain, finer brush-stroke questions emerge. One concerns the best way to make information palpable so your influencees won't "choke" on it. Are such considerations ethical? Of course they are--assuming they are truly done with the best interests of others at heart. What if the actions are taken for selfish reasons only? Then the sugarcoating will cause others to feel they have been set up or buried in a snow job. Restoring trust after such feelings have emerged will be virtually impossible.

As difficult as medicine sometimes is to take, we ingest it, knowing the ultimate outcome will be improvement. If the pill has been coated with sugar, it does not mean the medicine has been diluted or tainted--the end result is the same, but the sweetened glaze makes it easier to swallow. Verbal sugar-coating functions in much the same way: it softens the hard facts--not to disguise them, mind you, but to place them in a context that does not overwhelm the influencee. Using the metaphorical pill example, sugar-coating makes the hard-to-swallow easy--to-digest.

Sins To Avoid Committing with Hard-to-Swallow Messages
#1 Hiding Negative Information

Again, there is a fine line here. Strategic placement of negative information is acceptable. Not citing it, burying it so deeply it is overlooked, or having the print so fine it is impossible to see, smacks of unethical influence. (You may remember the car advertisements that were recalled, because while the manufacturers complied with the legal requirements to put financial data at the bottom of the television ads, the figures came and went so quickly it was virtually impossible to read them. Such tactics represent "sins.")

☑ Read these three memos and look for information that is either strategically placed, sinfully placed, or ineffectively placed. Look, too, for other elements that will influence in either a positive or negative way. Note your thoughts on the lines following each entry.

Memo A

Dear Ms. Jones:

I would like to attend a stress reduction seminar the first week in March. The cost is fairly high but it should be worth it. I know that early March is a hectic time when we play catch-up with all the work that didn't get done while we were working on budgets, but this seminar is held only once a year and I don't want to miss it. I am confident my secretary will be able to handle my work while I attend.

Your impressions: _____

_____

_____

_____

_____

Memo B

Dear Ms. Jones:

As you know, I am concerned about the effect stress is having on office morale. Therefore, I would like to attend a seminar sponsored by ABC University in early March. The cost, compared to the cost of time lost due to stress-related illness, is negligible. I've learned another member of the Executive Committee, Francis Seneca, attended last year and found it quite informative. The approval form is attached. Please return it to me by the end of the week.

Your impressions: _____

_____

_____

_____

_____

Memo C

Dear Ms. Jones:

When we met recently for my performance review, you suggested I learn more about stress reduction techniques. I assured you I would, and was pleased to learn that ABC University is offering a seminar on this topic the first week in March. Because our budgets will have been completed by then, it's an ideal time, I think, to attend.

Because of the school's proximity, we need not worry about the usual lodging costs. So, the only fee is for the tuition itself: $1500. Upon my return from the seminar, I'd be happy to share what I've learned with the department, thus reducing the per capita cost, in effect, to $150 per person. The enrollment is limited, though, so I'll need your approval by Friday if I am to attend.

Your impressions: _____

_____

_____

_____

_____

Now compare your impressions with those noted by our panel of experts.

Critique of Memo A

There are several problems with this communication, the combination of which stamp it as a failure in terms of its influence potential. There is an incomplete reference to the cost of the seminar ("fairly high"). The omission of the exact amount will leave the supervisor wondering and will necessitate an inquiry on her part to determine just how high "high" is. (Once she learns how high it is, she may even feel the writer tried to "pull a fast one" on her.)

The benefits to the organization are not cited. (This is shown in part by the word "I" that appears in three of the four sentences.) The phrase "should be worth it" is tentative. It suggests the speaker is not really certain of the value of the seminar. Compounding the general ineffectiveness of the memo is the emphasis placed on "all the work that didn't get done." It's an unfortunate choice of words, one that is certain to worry the supervisor. The closing, which intimates the secretary is capable of handling her supervisor's work, leaves the reader wondering if the secretary should be placed in charge on a permanent basis.

Critique of Memo B

Our panel felt this was the most manipulative and therefore the least effective of the three memos. The opening line imparts a feeling of guilt: the writer may not be trying to blame her supervisor for the stress or low morale problems, but the finger seems to be pointed in the boss' direction. The line citing cost actually seems like a veiled threat--one designed, you could infer, to make the supervisor approve the request quickly. Otherwise, the memo suggests, the employee might have to take sick leave.

While it is generally a good idea to gain an endorsement (someone else attended and found it valuable), in this case the writer gives the impression that she should be on the Executive Committee. (A second possibility is that the writer's boss is on the committee but is not as learning-oriented as Mr. Seneca.) The last line sounds as if the writer is trading places with her supervisor: she is telling her boss what to do. The very imperiousness of the tone comes across as underhanded, as if the writer is trying to get the supervisor to sign off without really investigating or discussing how the seminar could benefit the department.

307

Critique of Memo C

The panel felt this was the most influential memo, even though it was a bit longer than the others. The overall tone is quite professional, starting with the reminder that the supervisor wanted the employee to learn more about stress reduction. There is a sense of collaboration here, of two people working together toward a common goal. The alignment of the course date with completion date of the budget was also worth noting. Further, the writer points out the savings because the seminar is held locally. Especially influential, the panel felt, was the directness with which the cost was mentioned and its placement: the advantages are noted before the cost is mentioned. Otherwise, if the cost were listed first, the supervisor might see the amount, declare "No way," and refuse to read on. Perfectly acceptable sugar-coating appears in the form of a cost breakdown: the employee offers to take the knowledge back to the workplace. Finally, because the approval needs to be given quickly, the writer emphasizes the deadline without appearing to be demanding.

#2 Having Pre-determined Outcomes

Nimble influencers must walk psychological tightropes. If they can't see the other end of the rope, where safety and success lie, they may find themselves plummeting earthward. Not knowing in advance the outcome you wish to attain, you cannot really lead others toward it. Your vision must be clear, the results carefully researched, the outputs exactly detailed. Otherwise, why should others allow themselves to be influenced by you? To follow a leader into an unspecified future is dangerous, perhaps even suicidal in terms of career or life itself.

The problem for many influencers arises when we are so determined that our course is the only course that we do not permit opposing points of view to shape our thinking. It's good to be definite about the project you are expending your influence energies on. It's fine to determine why and how you are doing so. But if you can brook no additional input, you may be sacrificing excellence to predetermination.

In the following dialog, you will see the Influencer using some sugar-coating. (Underline the one sentence you feel best illustrates her deliberate effort to offset ideas that may not be well-received.) But you also will see her allowing alternative perspectives to reshape expected outcomes. She does not insist others see everything her way. Instead, her self-confidence permits the possibility that her way may not be the best way, and accordingly that it is definitely not the only way.

Influencer: Thank you for allowing me a few minutes at staff meeting this week to run an idea by you. I'll keep it simple this time, and for those of you who are interested, I can give more details at our next meeting. Essentially, I'd like us to volunteer some time to sponsor a Senior Prom for residents at the Silver Pond Nursing Home.

Influencee #1: Hey, wait a minute here. You have a vested interest in volunteering--isn't your great-aunt living there? The rest of us don't have anyone living there.

Influencer: But when you drop money in the Salvation Army kettle at Christmas, you have no idea who it's going to. Since when is charity dependent on knowing the recipient?

Influencee #2: It sounds like a good idea, but right now I'm swamped between this job and my obligations at home.

Influencer: Tell you what. I've spent a lot of time researching this proposal and condensing it to just five minutes for today's meeting. Let me give you the highlights---without interruptions--and then we can discuss it further. First of all, what I'm proposing won't cost you a cent. Second, it will take only one Saturday afternoon--and you can bring along your spouse or friends or your kids and make it a family affair. Third, service to others, as we know from the Muscular Dystrophy Marathon, is the best thing we can do for ourselves...."

Analysis of Dialog

A number of effective influence techniques are evident, even in this short excerpt. Above all, though, we hope you noticed how the influencer took in perspectives different from her own and used them to quickly reshape her proposal. The first alternative perspective expressed drew her into a debate that probably was not the direction in which she had planned to go. When accused of having a vested interest, she no doubt felt compelled to explain herself. And while she was not defensive in countering the objection, the give-and-take exchange really should have been dealt with at a later time, especially because she had only five minutes to lay out her plan.

By mentioning how hard she had worked on the proposal the influencer does two things: validates the importance she is attaching to it, and indirectly asks for their time as she presents it without interruptions.

Virtually any line in the last paragraph could have been underlined as an example of a sugar-coated overture. Having picked up on the time factor as a possible reason for not being involved, and knowing that most people feel they are not earning enough, she squelched both those objections right away. She also reminded the group of their earlier charitable work. In addition, for those who like to devote their weekends to their families, she wisely observed this was an activity the whole family could participate in. Finally, she emphasized the value of service--all of these WIFMs just in the prelude to her presentation!

#3 Using Silence Unethically

Expert influencers utilize verbal tools like those in the preceding example to influence others. A non-verbal tool can be powerful as well. Silence, the very antithesis of what we usually regard as communication skills, is actually one of the most effective. We use it to honor our dead, to express our disapproval, to show our feelings have been hurt, to share our grief. When we are at a loss for words, our very silence expresses our doubt, confusion, love, grief, shame, or wonder.

When power selling, you can use silence effectively. You will know when the other person needs to pursue a line of thought, and you will allow her to do that without interrupting. Manipulative sellers do just the opposite: astute enough to sense an objection being formed, they will rush the conversation along in an effort to sidestep or skirt a possible problem. They don't allow time for deliberation for fear the potential buyer may find reasons for rejection.

Silence itself can be used unethically. Just as nature abhors a vacuum, most communicators are uncomfortable with verbal voids--they want to fill them. The influencer not prompted by integrity knows this and will deliberately remain silent in certain situations, knowing the other person is likely to be so uncomfortable that she will begin speaking. This often leads to revealing more than she should, perhaps giving implausible reasons for rejection because the real reasons are difficult to explain.

Silence can be intimidating at worst, uncomfortable at least, but encouraging at best. Truly, it is a golden commodity, but if you use it as Midas did--for your gain only--you are not developing the kind of influencing skills emphasized throughout this book. Power sellers use silence honorably. They know that sugar-coating needs time to settle, and so will pause to let the import of their words sink in. The use of time in this way aids the mental digestion that should be taking place. Use silence as a palate-clearer and not as a motive-obscurer.

You may never have thought about how you use silence. But by reading books, taking courses, and self-developing, you can evaluate your current communication practices and decide if they need improvement. Are you using silence effectively? In determining wise use of this and any of the other elements that constitute influence, you may find it helpful to assess them via Einstein's definition: "The life of a person has meaning if it enriches the lives of other people materially, intellectually, or morally." Are you using your influence-power to enrich the lives of others?

Scintillas of Sugar-Coating

While we may never reach the level at which sugar-coating is equated with scintillation, we can at least opt for aspiration through inspiration. These historical anecdotes will show how some of the best delivered bitter news with sweetened tact, humor, or quick-wittedness.

Bear Bryant is associated with winning streaks in college football. He once assembled his team and offered some fatherly advice. "This is a class operation," he told them. He then elaborated on his expectations for the young men--including their physical appearance and their attendance in class. He concluded by assuring them, "I don't want any dumbbells on this team." He solemnly said that if there was such a person in the room, he should stand up immediately. When Joe Namath jumped up, Bear could hardly believe his eyes. He asked why the quarterback had stood. "You're not dumb!" he told the young man.

Namath agreed and then revealed his motive: "I just hate for you to be standing up there by yourself, coach."

Financial stature is the focus of the second incident. Nathan Rothschild, the famous London financier, stepped out of his cab one evening and tipped the driver an amount he felt was more than adequate. The driver disagreed and told Rothschild, "Your lordship's son always gives me a good deal more than this." An explanation was quickly forthcoming. Rothschild said he did not doubt the man's word and told him why, "My son has a rich father. I do not."

Sometimes, the sugar-coating tempers an outright refusal when a possible alternative is substituted. Such was the case with Eero Saarinen, the famed architect from Finland. Saarinen was an extremely deliberate speaker, choosing his words with the utmost care and pronouncing each syllable of each word in an elongated manner. Once, during a television interview, the interviewer realized how quickly time was running out and how slowly words were coming out. He asked Saarinen if he could speed it up a bit. The architect lighted his pipe as he decided how to respond. He declined the request but made another offer in place of it, "I could say less," he suggested.

In summary, remember that truth-telling need not be painful, not if you keep the other person's feelings in mind. Think in advance of both the substance of your remarks and the style with which you will deliver them.

Attorney Gerry Spence, for example, uses a familiar technique. Whenever he has painful truth to deliver to strangers, he expresses regret that they are not friends. He talks about what they might have shared if their lives had intersected. He then offers hope that by the time he has finished his presentation, they will know one another better. In the process of sharing the experience they are about to have, he suggests, they just might wind up friends.

Such "framing" softens the edge that sharp words can carry. It sets an overarching tone of cooperation if not conciliation.

Words have an indisputable magic. And if you are determined to be a verbal magician, you will need to find the best framework of words for making bad situations better, and good situations memorable experiences.

Preview Apart from sugar-coating, other ways of using words masterfully and not manipulatively will be explored in the next chapter, which also emphasizes the need to regard words and ideas from a neutral point of view. Integrity gauges, such as the Win3 Test, are presented to help you do that. The interview with Sherri Malouf further reinforces the need for neutrality and also the need to make good use of nestled networks.

INTERVIEW

**Floyd Hurt, Author, *Rousing Creativity*;
President and Founder, Probe, Inc.
Charlottesville, Virginia**

Our work consists of developing the creative bent in people. To create a context in which creativity occurs, we need to develop a culture that regards creativity as the result of deliberate, integrated efforts. Leaders can stimulate the creative process by incorporating six specific elements into their basic style of interacting with others.

1.   *Motivation*   For a mixed group to coalesce into a creative team, there must be a clearly stated goal and an understanding that the creative activity and its results will help achieve that goal. These two aspects of motivation are as applicable to a creative effort as they are to any motivational situation. Any manager who can clearly state what he/she wants to achieve will rally creative people more quickly than the leader with vague or inconsistent objectives.

2.   *Basic Knowledge*   You don't have to be an expert, but you must have at least enough information to discuss the topic and to stimulate thinking about it.

3.   *Tools*   If you want to encourage others to be more creative, you need to have facilitation skills, a knowledge of creative techniques, and a physical

environment in which creativity can be practiced. The space can be any area that is recognized as a place where ideas can be presented without fear of ridicule. Further, leaders who are serious about fostering creativity in the workplace should have a library of books and tapes exploring these and other aspects of creativity. They also should provide consistent training.

4. *Ramrods* Such individuals often come up with ideas that are hard to swallow. They break through the normal order of things and push for new ideas. Few things of any merit are accomplished without that one pain-in-the-neck person who keeps the heat up on a new idea. If your organization doesn't have a ramrod, it may be time to take a close look at why he or she is missing.

If the leader herself is not a ramrod, then her role is to take the hard-to-swallow ideas and make them more palatable. In championing the ramrod, the leader aims not to dilute the strength of the ramrod's ideas but rather to make them more digestible--perhaps by presenting them in more familiar terms, showing how they substantiate existing goals, or by expanding upon them. The more radical the idea, the more work is required to lead the non-radicals past fear so they can understand and ultimately support the idea.

Ramrods don't mind asking tough questions, and tough questions usually expose problems. They also present new opportunities. Realize that ramrods have a hard time with boundaries. They are used to going where their ideas take them. And their ideas often take them outside the boundaries of safe, stereotypic thought. A few toes may get stepped on as ramrods do their thing, but often these are the very toes keeping the doors of innovation shut.

5.   *Systems*   Environments in which ideas flourish usually have systems for recognizing proposals that don't fit the norm. Any really new idea must transcend the normal order of things. Because of this, it is often hard to actually see a new idea in a current context. Leaders may have to step back and re-focus through another lens, listen with a third ear, ask new questions. In short, they have to be able to suspend judgment long enough to step into this unexplored terrain where the new idea is sinking its roots.

6.   *Feedback*   If you want to establish environments in which certain kinds of thinking flourish, you can't stop after initial overtures have been made. Creativity or any of the other abstract nouns associated with high performance need ongoing attention. Leaders need to obtain and provide feedback. Nothing demoralizes creative people faster than realizing their idea has a wooden spike in its heart and not knowing why.

These six components of the creative environment will help foster the kind of leading-edge thinking most companies need in order to survive. Survival issues do create discomfort. However, with leaders willing to explore them, unabashed by radical thinking, and undeterred by the need to make such thinking commonly accepted, organizations can emerge among the fittest that survive.

DO:

-- Have a pocketful of comments ready for those times when you are on the spot.

-- Confront slights (real or imagined) so you can keep the air clear for ideas that deserve to soar.

-- Try to establish a system of requests and promises.

-- Engage in dialog if you are attempting to influence others.

-- Make and keep contact with your would-be influencees.

-- Ensure there is benefit, for yourself and others, to be derived from your influence efforts.

-- Create a context in which creativity can flourish.

-- As leader, make radical ideas more palatable by toning them down as necessary.

DON'T:

-- Let those who influence with intimidation back you up against a wall.

-- Get sidetracked by diversions designed to take the spotlight off the person or the issue.

-- Be deterred by those who dismiss your ideas before you have had a chance to fully present them.

-- Forget to make inquiries.

-- Commit the sin of hiding negative information.

-- Expect people to be motivated if goals are not clearly
   stated.
-- Overlook the importance of having a system for
   recognizing ideas that don't fit the norm.

YOU WILL:

-- Give the idea-proposer a chance to critique her own ideas by saying, "Persuade me."

-- Sometimes find you can achieve a balance among priorities by asking others for their input.

-- Have to take a stand on occasion to let others know what your tolerance levels are.

-- Find others responding better to your influence when you give them affirmations.

-- Want to place information that may be objectionable in a strategic location.

-- Be able to use silence as an ally if your intentions are honorable.

-- Influence indirectly if you have a library of books related to the issue being explored.

-- Need to give and get feedback to keep interest in your project alive.

YOU WON'T:

-- Be able to present your ideas if you are caught up in an unpleasant exchange. Table small issues so you can focus group attention on the large issue.

-- Help others grow if you allow them to place their monkeys on your back.

-- Be able to be totally influential without considering the environment.

-- Have a sense of what comes next unless you tie up your influence efforts.

-- Benefit from suggestions of others if all your outcomes are predetermined and unshakable.

-- Go wrong if you remember Einstein's exhortation to enrich the lives of others materially, intellectually, or morally.

-- Appreciate the contributions ramrods can make if you regard them as troublemakers.

Chapter 8
Influence &
Manipulation

~~~~~~~~~~~~~~

Overview   In this chapter, four-quadrant correlates are made between the worth of a given project and the need to manipulate others to accept it. Generally speaking, the higher the worth, the easier it is to involve others. The problems and solutions associated with influencing in various quadrants are explored as a means of understanding the gestalt or integrated structures within which influence occurs.

More specific information regarding the foreground and background of influence is found in the gauges by which integrity is assessed. If the team of influencer and influencees agrees on the need for a code of ethics and if they are willing to develop it, they will have a set of groundrules to govern present and future eventualities. A number of questions need to be considered in the shaping of this code.

As the influence team works together, they move through distinct stages. The influencer can expect initial resistance or balking. He overcomes this first barrier by talking about the project and its multiple benefits. He monitors the implementation of the project, looking for and patching cracks in the structural integrity as they occur. At some point, the influencer can walk away from the project, confident that others are so immersed in its worth that they will carry on without him. But the distancing is never total: the influencer maintains a loose but ongoing connection with those who are maintaining the project, even after he has moved on to new projects.

No matter what projects the influencer is engaged in, he will find value in the ROR-Shock Model, which improves upon reality by reifying the ideal or making a concrete reality where only aspirations existed before. Sometimes, in the exploration of reality, the influencer is surprised, perhaps even shocked, by what he learns. For example, he may learn he is more Machiavellian than he realized.

But such knowledge, if approached with an open mindset, allows benefits to be derived for more individuals than the two parties usually involved in seeking Win/Win outcomes. A liberated mindset can lead to Win/Win/Win results.

In her interview, Sherri Malouf further explores the neutrality of certain concepts, other ways to gauge integrity, and the need to use both head and heart as we work in our nestled networks.

Manipulation

Manipulation is unhealthy, for influencer and influencee alike. As shown in the diagram below, the lines indicating manipulation and worth are parallel but diametric in value: the more manipulation you feel you have to use, the less worth your concept typically has (or the less creativity you have found to promote the concept).

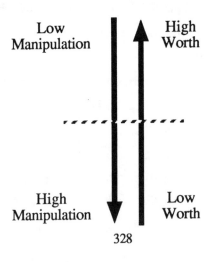

Manipulative influencers are not typically truthful or open in their transactions; they do not tell the whole story; they move others toward ends that are less than honorable or toward results that have been fraudulently or unfairly earned. The word "manipulate" actually has honest origins--the Latin word, *manus*, meaning "hand." (Those who used their hands well or who could handle tools well were said to be manipulative. Even today, this meaning is the first given in most dictionaries for the word "manipulate.")

And of course there are some who learn to handle themselves, others, and situations so skillfully that their actions seem contrived. So polished are they in their presentations, so adept at understanding what motivates people, that they appear to go into automatic pilot in dealing with both expected and unexpected occurrences. After a while, their facility with words seems glib, their smoothness too slick, their sincerity suspect. In the extreme, there are those with an uncanny ability to "psych out" other people, to sense what they want to hear and then deliver it. But such individuals form the ranks of fortunetellers and psychic healers, not the realm in which influencers use integrity as their coin of commerce.

If manipulation seems an easy way out or a quick fix, it very well may be--but not for long. What you lose in reputation and stature will be far more costly than what you gain in expediency. Most people can be exploited once, but will then be distrustful for a long time after.

The overriding goal of influence is working with others to achieve a goal everyone has bought into. When you are the only one supporting the plan, despite repeated efforts, and find yourself using any means to reach the end, you may as well abandon the effort--*if* your intent was to influence with integrity. Influence may not *begin* with everyone in accord regarding the worth of the end product. However, during the process and by the end of the process, everyone participating has opted for involvement and has agreed to the mission and the work required to reach that mission.

Using horizontal arrows to represent these extremes, our diagram would look like this:

| Low involvement | ⟶ | Willing participation |
| High conflict | ⟵ | Low conflict |

If we were to use both sets of describers, the complete diagram would have four quadrants, which we'll label Q1, Q2, Q3, and Q4.

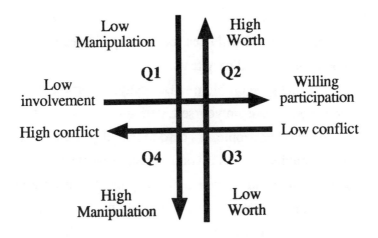

Quadrant Characteristics

Think about some person or group whom you have recently influenced. Then read the four descriptions that follow and determine which one best fits these influencing circumstances.

Q1:   Low manipulation/Low involvement

People who are distinctly non-manipulative may or may not be able influencers. If they are not, they fall into this first quadrant. They inspire little or low involvement on the part of those whom they wish to make part of their mission. Typically, they have intensive commitment to their plan but lack extensive power over others. To be sure, some plans can be executed by a committee of one (if you are trying to influence your supervisor to give you a raise, for example), but more often you will need the synergy of a team to accomplish extraordinary feats.

What's the problem? Basically, the problem is a lack of confidence--in yourself, perhaps in the project, perhaps in other people. It's hard to lead if you are fearful, hard to convince others if you lack enthusiasm or commitment. Confidence may be lagging for other reasons as well: it may be the project is right but the circumstances are wrong, or the mix of personalities is not right. Also, if circumstances are dictating mood--if colleagues, for example, are worried about downsizing--the best and best-intentioned influencers will find confidence or enthusiasm almost impossible to muster. If the timing is wrong, little else will be right.

What's the solution? First consider the possible abandonment of this project. It may be better to reserve your energies for one you feel more strongly about. If abandonment is not the answer, you may have to examine your delivery style. If possible, tape record yourself (at least by audio if not video equipment). Afterwards, with as much detachment as you can garner, critique yourself. Would *you* be willing to do something with or for the person on this tape on the basis of the delivery you are now hearing or watching?

There is another possibility if you feel your influencing is of the Q1 variety. Do some "exit" interviews. After an overture that did not involve or excite your prospective influencees, call them one by one, or meet with them, and simply ask, "What could I have done differently that might have made you more involved?"

Q2:   High worth/Willing participation
The very fact that your project can be described as having high worth may be the reason participation in it is so willingly given. Little outright influencing is needed after presenting your plan to your influencees, for your idea is probably speaking for itself. Typically, in high worth/willing participation situations, the individuals involved have worked together before or know each other well or know you well. Consequently, trust and positive feelings run high.

What's the problem?   There is a danger here, however. It's called groupthink. When the members of a group like each other and the leader, they are less contentious or questioning than they might otherwise be. The unspoken need to conform socially may in fact cause some decisions to be made before their time.

What's the solution?   Ask one person (ideally, the most analytical thinker among you) to deliberately play the role of devil's advocate. He will purposely rain on the collective parade whenever it seems the group is being swept away by their own enthusiasm. This person will ask questions, cite data, get outside opinions--whatever is necessary to ensure final decisions have been subjected to the scrutiny they deserve.

Q3:   Low conflict/Low worth

Properly channeled, conflict may be the best thing that can happen to your influence efforts. But it must be the kind of conflict that is characterized by debate rather than vitriolic observations. If there is low conflict, there is probably low interest. As a group moves from the opening stage of the project (at which they are assembling and getting to know one another) to the conflict stage, questions, challenges, and territoriality issues can and should emerge. Until agendas are uncovered and conflict resolved, the team will not be able to move to the productive stage (at which agreement is reached on operational concerns) and will not ever achieve the accomplishment stage (at which objectives are met). If there is little external conflict, there may be little worth associated with the project. People simply do not care enough to object to it.

What's the problem?   There may be two problems associated with low conflict/low worth.

The lack of conflict may not be a lack of interest at all. Rather, something else may be governing the reactions of those you have chosen to influence. For example, if your position is senior to theirs, they may not be speaking up for fear of jeopardizing their standing.

What's the solution? One way to move the group to debate is to use Delphi deliberations, a group dynamics technique originated by the ancient Greeks. Simply ask those you wish to be involved in your project to anonymously record their thoughts about its worth, about their feelings at the moment, about what you have said so far, et cetera. Then ask them to fold their papers and pass them to you. One at a time, you can read the comments (paraphrasing as necessary) and open each to discussion, and to the conflict that is so healthy to progress.

If the majority continue to evince little faith in the project, you will either have to resell it, repackage it, reject it, or resurrect it later.

Q4:   High manipulation/High conflict

By the time most of us are old enough to enter the workforce, we know when we are being conned and know we do not like it. Only the truly naive can be manipulated without some conflict erupting within them. It may be only a voice whispering inside their heads "This isn't right" or

335

"This is too good to be true." But, almost always, there will be an indication that we are in danger of being duped. (Similarly, the manipulator knows when he is operating in a manipulative fashion.)

The conflict may take any one of several forms: self-doubt, discomfort, worry, stress, fear. Or, it may be expressed in the form of verbal conflict with the manipulator. Suspicion leads some to resort to a more covert means of resolving the conflict within them, such as initiating a background check or using hidden cameras.

What's the problem? If your intuition/common sense/past experience/friends are telling you something is wrong, something probably is. The internal conflict you are experiencing is the best reason to investigate the situation further. Chances are, someone is withholding information you need before making up your mind to commit your time, savings, or heart to this individual.

What's the solution? Stall. Before committing yourself or your funds, ask for more time. Then confer with others to learn more about the potential manipulator and his history. Of course, some issues don't warrant such investments. In these cases, you can simply but firmly ask, "Is there something you're not telling me?" You could also tell the manipulator that you are not comfortable doing what he has asked of you and let that be the end of it.

Integrity Gauges

As we've noted, most people know when they are manipulative and most people know when they are being manipulated. Nonetheless, neither families, schools, nor businesses can operate on the assumption that individuals will recognize manipulation when they use it and when it is being used on them. It is much better to have a clearly articulated set of principles for the ethical conduct of family affairs, school practices, and business operations. Two questions precede the asking of questions that will lead to the formation of ethical guidelines: Can we agree that we need a code of ethics? If you and/or the group with whom you are interacting answers yes, then the next question is: Are we willing to develop that code?

In a sense, the macrocosmic code of ethics is like the microcosmic set of groundrules that governs team meetings. Based on integrity, honor, and respect, the code clearly stipulates what is proper and what will not be tolerated in various circumstances. For many, a gauge of sorts is useful. A number of these are available or can easily be created, gauges that will assist in the decision-making that confronts us on a daily basis. For example, in 1932, businessman Herbert J. Taylor, developed a 4-Way Test for evaluating our intended actions:

Is it the truth?

337

Is it fair to all concerned?

Will it build goodwill and better friendships?

Will it be beneficial to all concerned?

In keeping with such interrogative introspections, these are but a few of the additional questions that can be raised to form the framework within which integrity can drive influence.

Could this harm us in any way?

Could it harm others?

Is it legal?

Does it feel wrong?

If the customer could see us doing this, would he be willing to pay for it?

Would I still do this if news of it were broadcast in tomorrow's newspaper?

Would we be proud to do this with our families watching?

Who will be the primary beneficiary of this action? The secondary beneficiary?

Are there safety/union/OSHA issues we may have overlooked?

What actions would constitute violations of ethical conduct?

What are the consequences of violations?

In what ways might we be, even unknowingly, pressuring others to act unethically?

How do we maintain quality when we have to do more with less?

In different circumstances (transculturally, for example), how might our tolerance limits change?

Should we consider creating hot lines or an ombudsman position?

How and how often should the code be disseminated?

What complex or confusing situations might make our ethical guidelines murky in the eyes of some?

What could cause confidence to be shattered?

Does this action advance our mission?

Is it in keeping with our values?

Would we be proud to say afterwards that we were a part of this action?

What assurances could we give regarding possible outcomes?

Could we be rewarding unethical behavior in any way?

What could we point to in the past that shows we have an ethical track record?

What ethical messages are we sending or failing to send to others?

Do people know what to do or who to turn to if they have concerns about ethical conduct?

If we could develop an intranet message regarding integrity, what would it say?

The Influence Continuum

Assume that you have asked and satisfactorily answered these and other questions about the influence you wish to exert on others. You are convinced that what you want them to do (buy your product, give you a raise, join your team, support your candidacy, et cetera) is a worthwhile pursuit. Now it's time to influence them. You can expect to move through five basic stages: balk, talk, caulk, walk, stalk. For the sake of illustrative convenience, let's assume you are a workplace leader, interested in influencing others to apply more creativity to their problem-solving and decision-making situations.

You agree with Ken Blanchard that the key to leadership is influence not authority. Because you are in a peer rather than superior position, you feel an influence strategy is the only one that will work. Imagine this is your first meeting to explain what you hope others will do.

Balk

You can expect resistance, perhaps even naked rebellion, because your proposal involves change. Most people feel little need to give up a current practice and adopt one that seems to offer little improvement over their existing practice. Be prepared for questions (especially "What's in it for me?"), for challenges ("I'm doing just fine the way I am" or "This is just another management attempt to get us to work harder without paying us more") and for surface agreement that will probably not go deeper without subsequent intervention on your part ("It sounds good. I'll give it a try" or "It sounds good, but let me think it over").

Recommendations for Influencing others during the Balk Stage, at which they don't know (much) about your proposal and probably don't care

1. Lay some groundwork, even if you are not able to spell out many details in advance. Set a climate of expectation in anticipation of the actual unveiling of the proposal.
2. Anticipate resistance and be ready for it; rehearse your responses ahead of the actual meeting.
3. Cite precedents whenever you can. Facts, figures, and benchmarking data from others in comparable circumstances will go a long way toward persuading your influencees of the validity of your idea.

4. Make a dramatic show or powerful presentation, if appropriate. For example, let's say you had trained three of your colleagues from another department to use the very problem-solving technique you want to share with this team. Bring the others to the meeting and ask one of the team members to throw out a problem germane to the workplace. Give everyone, yourself and the three other people as well, five minutes to write anonymous solutions.

Collect the solutions, read them, have the team select the most feasible option, and then ask who wrote it. Ideally, it will be you or one of those trained in your technique. (If not, you can overcome your embarrassment with a lighthearted remark prepared for just this eventuality: "Charlie must have secretly read my notes and used the technique without telling us he was going to.")

Talk

Before you outline your remarks, give serious consideration to this question: What influences me to pay attention? What factors are compelling enough for me to try something I'm not eager to try? What or who persuades me and how? Think through these questions, perhaps even inviting input from others. Then use every effective technique you have (and have analyzed) as you work to persuade others ethically.

To illustrate, seasoned influencers often begin winning over their audience by acknowledging the emotions others may associate with the prospect being presented. One fun way to explore people's reluctance to change involves only an inexpensive purchase on your part. Buy a quart of buttermilk, keep it chilled. Minutes before you start your presentation, place it on the table with cookies and napkins. Tell people to help themselves and then occupy yourself with some papers. Meanwhile, an observer you've planted at the table will note who is willing to try something new and what reasons others give for declining to do so.

Use the observer's comments as a prelude to your remarks, explaining that you fully understand many people prefer to continue doing things the way they've always done them. Next, lead them to the realization that when nothing is ventured, nothing is gained.

Recommendations for Influencing others during the Talk Stage, at which others don't know but are probably willing to listen

1. Use visuals to supplement your mesage. These should constitute not more than half of your presentation. Don't overdo the dependence on numbers, however.

They cannot replace the passionate proposal and the rationale for its execution. (Ideally, your message will be tri-modally delivered: your voice, your verbiage, and your visuals will all be optimized.)

2. Draw a picture with your words. Whether you are using metaphors or simply verbalized pictures, help your prospective followers latch onto the possibilities you envision. A set of architectural blueprints *and* a full-scale, full-color drawing of what the completed project will look like depict the same possibility. Most of us, however, prefer looking at the artistic rather than the technical representation. And so it is with a verbal picture. Especially when you are hoping to inspire or motivate, as opposed to giving a technical briefing, you need to appeal to the head and the imagination and the emotions of your audience.

3. Acknowledge the downside--before others can. There is risk in every venture. By covering up or failing to mention the drawbacks or setbacks that might ensue, you are not only being dishonest but you are leaving yourself open to attack. Presented properly, the negatives may even add to the allure of your proposal by allowing you to cite the need for courage, for example, or the need for people with an adventurous spirit.

4. Make the talk bi-directional. The idea being shaped should be bounced back and forth several times, like a verbal ping-pong on the table of possibilities. Arousing interest means creating collective buy-in, and buy-in means welcoming feedback.

5. First ensure and then assure that the idea you are proposing is both doable and worth doing. Don't worry about aiming slightly higher than existing comfort levels--it's the only way to raise the bar of excellence and keep others aiming high as well.

Caulk

Some people are organizational caulkers; they know how to keep the corporate ship watertight by filling seams or cracks with a soft-at-first substance that, when it hardens, is difficult to crack. Effective influencers are caulkers, in a sense. First, they scrutinize a given entity, such as the plan they hope to effect, and look for weak spots. Then, once the plan or program has been launched, they constantly assess its implementation--solving problems, obtaining further resources, and shoring up a weakening commitment in order to keep the plan afloat.

<u>Recommendations for Influencing others</u>
<u>during the Caulk Stage, at which others are working</u>
<u>to cement ideas into an overall framework</u>

1. Agree upon uniform measurements. Because we have
   an infinite capacity for misunderstanding one another,
   it's especially important for the influencer to establish
   clear and measurable gauges of success. Words alone
   cannot be counted on. For example, two different
   pronunciations of the word "bad" in this sentence--"It's
   not a bad idea"--would lead to either of two
   interpretations: "But it's really not a good idea" or "That
   idea actually has great potential." The quantitative
   measures, although they need not be used exclusively,
   are the ones that will tell us where and if caulking is
   needed.

2. When setbacks occur, remind others of past
   accomplishments. Sometimes the future seems too far
   away, the goal less distinct than it once was, the
   importance of the plan less pressing. The effective
   influencer expects the valleys in the topography of
   implementation. He restores flagging spirits by patching
   up the cracks that may occur along the way.

   Jack Kahn, for example, CEO of Manco Inc., a
   manufacturer of duct tape, spurs his sales staff to ever-
   greater achievement by making promises ("A hairy

346

challenge," *Incentive*, December 1997, page 12). He promised, for example, that if sales quotas were met, he would shave off all his hair. Altered pictures of the non-hirsute executive were plastered throughout the workplace. A new record was set in sales, and as promised the staff shaved the head of their chief executive.

3. Don't let defensiveness plug your ears. You won't be able to caulk if you don't know where the potential leaks may spring up. And you won't know where the leaks are if you refuse to listen to criticism. If you doubt the importance of caulking leaks, figurative or literal, let the following news story convince you. As reported in *USA Today* ("The Chicago flood," April 21, 1992, page 10A), if repairs had been made when leaks in the city's infrastructure were first noted, the cost would have been about $10,000. However, the caulking was not done, and as a result, 250 million gallons of water from the Chicago River spilled into underground pipes and then into the city, causing a loss of $1.5 billion attributable to repairs, lost revenue, and property damage.

4. Use the Five-Why technique for getting at root causes. This method of probing has you continuing to ask

"Why?" until the real causes of problems are uncovered and not the superficial reasons.

Walk

There comes a point at which the leader's thrust recedes and the plan proceeds on the strength of its own momentum. In a sense, he has conceived of an idea, nurtured it through the long period of gestation, helped it get born and continue to grow. Then, as parents inevitably must do with their children, the influencer and influencees part ways. The leader usually moves on to another influence project, secure in the knowledge that his brain-child can now function on its own.

In terms of the change model espoused by Kurt Lewin (Thaw out, Introduce change, Re-freeze), the idea and its correlative change have been implemented. What remains now is the solidification of the plan. In this stage, the idea has been reified, it has become standard operating procedure, it has been made a familiar and permanent landmark in the organizational terrain.

Recommendations for Influencing others during the Walk Stage, at which the influencer can walk away, confident the vision is seen and supported by others

1. As the project draws to a close, think of appropriate ways to recognize those who have joined forces with you. One of the most remembered gestures is a formal letter of commendation, with a copy to the supervisor of those who participated in the project.

2. Bring closure to the collective undertaking by way of a ceremony or celebration of sorts. Not only does hard work on a special project deserve public and lavish praise, but such rituals bespeak the natural ending of one cycle and the beginning of another. People often remember the closing ceremonies with as much intensity as they remember the many months preceding the project's conclusion.

3. Encourage networking among those who have been part of the project. Frequently, all people need is a nudge in the right direction. While you, as the original influencer, need to keep in touch with them, they need to keep in touch with each other as well. Some teams find the initial success so heady an experience that they decide to undertake a second project. Other teams disband after the initial success, but network to keep alive memories of the past and hopes for the future.

4. Keep in mind those who have assisted you in the execution of a new idea as future projects arise. These may be projects of your own or plans being formulated by others. In the latter case, referrals of your recent influencees to future influencers will be appreciated at both levels.

Stalk

Although this word has current negative associations, we use it in the sense of unexpectedly popping in on those who are carrying on with the project you have walked away from.

Recommendations for Influencing others
during the Stalk Stage, during which the influencer
catches others doing the right things right

1. Periodic progress reports will assure you as the influencer that the plan is being executed as you had hoped and that both it and the people putting it into action are able to act independently. You may have walked away from the project by the time this last stage is reached, but you have not walked out of their lives. Establish some means, formal or informal, of staying in touch with those who have worked with you to make your plan a reality.

Your stalking need not take much time or trouble. The contacts can be made on a social level (an annual reunion) or on a communication level (a bi-annual newsletter with updates). But continue to show your interest in the new process or procedure that you have successfully influenced others to undertake.

2. When you make your phone calls or pop in on others, take the knowledge you're acquiring one step farther. After you've witnessed the right things being done right, for example, suggest the organizational newspaper publish a feature article. Or, suggest that a new employee seek advice from those who served on the initial team.

3. Discuss ways of continuously improving on the progress that's been made. Keep a record of the team's suggestions or a log of lessons learned, now that the plan is fully operational. Share these insights with those who may be starting a similar project of their own.

Graphically, the continuum depicting the steps you go through as you influence others to follow your lead would look like this.

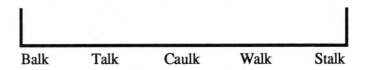

| Balk | Talk | Caulk | Walk | Stalk |

As influencees become more and more committed to the project put forth by the influencer, the effort you have to expend on influencing decreases, as shown in a second continuum line:

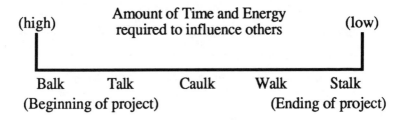

(high)   Amount of Time and Energy required to influence others   (low)

| Balk | Talk | Caulk | Walk | Stalk |
| (Beginning of project) | | | | (Ending of project) |

The five stages were explored within the context of a team situation, when the leader influences others, according to author Vance Packard's definition of leadership: "the art of getting others to want to do something that you are convinced should be done." The stages could apply to a one-on-one scenario as readily as they do to a team setting. In the final stage, however, you would alter your approach somewhat.

To illustrate, if your purpose had been to influence your supervisor to give you a raise, you might have encountered initial resistance or balking. You next would have talked through and talked out the reason for the resistance, and ideally would have been successful in persuading him that you deserved a raise. Next, you would work throughout the appraisal year to make steady improvements in the quality of your work, caulking whatever deficiencies you found in your own performance.

When your supervisor realizes you deserve not only the raise he gave you but future raises as well, then you can relax your influence efforts and in a sense walk away from the need to be convincing. However, you would never walk completely away; as you find yourself succeeding with one thing or another during the year, you would bring these efforts to the attention of your supervisor--in the most professional way possible.

Reality, Openness, Reification: The ROR-Shock Model

Those who engage in principled persuasion take current reality and convert it to a new and improved reality, using openness as their medium. This is a process of reifying or creating something that didn't exist before. Essentially, it asks you to look at present realities; to remain open to the often-hidden opportunities that lie within the present; and then to reify or create a new reality.

Engaging in the process demands numerous skills, some of which you may not even realize you possess. That is why we call the model the ROR-Shock Model: you may be pleasantly surprised, if not sometimes shocked, to learn just how much potential you really have for effecting improvements upon current practices.

Let's begin with a current **reality**. Think of some situation you are now facing--at home, at work, in a relationship, et cetera. The situation should be one that could be made better with proper influence on your part. Briefly describe that situation here. _____

_____

_____

_____

_____

Next, let's gauge your **openness** for taking risks, for trying something new as you plan a strategy for reification, for making the future better than the present. Read the following statements and answer Agree or Disagree, depending on the extent to which you agree with the truth of the statement. Think of the degree to which the statement matches your way of thinking. If you both agree and disagree with a given statement, try to determine which choice you'd agree with just slightly more or less than the other choice. Instead of a 50/50 response, then, you would consider the statement as a choice between 51/49%; you would favor one response slightly more than the other.

(There are no trick questions here. Simply tell if you agree or disagree with the statements.)

☑️   Place a check in the appropriate box to the right of each statement.

	Agree	Disagree
1) We should be adaptable when unforeseen events occur.	☐	☐
2) One change always leaves indentations upon which to build another change.	☐	☐
3) In the beginning, problems are easy to cure but hard to diagnose; with the passage of time, having gone unrecognized and unattended, they become easy to diagnose but hard to cure.	☐	☐
4) A workplace that is used to freedom is more easily managed by its own employees than by any other arrangement.	☐	☐
5) A wise influencer must always tread the path of great men and women and should imitate those who have excelled.	☐	☐
6) People who least rely on luck alone will be the most successful.	☐	☐
7) Success is a combination of opportunity and ability.	☐	☐

8) Most people have no faith in new things until they have been proved by experience.   □   □

9) If you have to beg others to fulfill a mission, you are destined to fail.   □   □

10) If you are respected, you will be secure, honored, and successful.   □   □

11) Things that come easily are hard to maintain. Things that are hard won are easier to maintain.□   □

12) A leader who thinks more about his own interests than about yours, who seeks his own advantage for everything he does, will never be a good leader, for others will never be able to trust him.   □   □

13) In order to keep employees loyal, managers must honor them by sharing both distinctions and duties.

□   □

How Machiavellian Are You?

Because there are thirteen items, if you had seven or more in one category, that is your "majority" category. Which category, Agree or Disagree, is your majority category? _____

Now let's see how open you are to influences that do not represent typical sources of knowledge-acquisition. In all likelihood, you agreed with at least seven of the statements.

Would it "shock" you to learn that these thirteen paraphrased statements are all taken from *The Prince* by Niccolo Macchiavelli? Written 500 years ago, the book has become synonymous with words like "duplicity" and "deceit." And yet, much of what it endorses makes sense for today's leader, manager, and/or influencer.

Does a majority of Agree answers mean you are Machiavellian, in the most negative sense of the word? No, not at all. It means simply that no one thing is 100% "right" or 100% "wrong." Even in *The Prince* there is wisdom from which we can profit. But...if you are not open, you won't be able to spot the worth; your stamp of "worthless" will prevent you from seeing worth in hard realities. If you take no risks into the unpopular or unknown, you will not be able to optimize or reify possibilities that lie hidden in the here and now.

Remember that selling a particular service, product or proposal to others depends on your understanding of the current reality and your ability to remain mentally flexible or open to new ideas. Not until you have achieved these mental states can you create the new reality. It's often true that "if you build it, they will come," but if you don't hear or see the possibilities calling to you, you will never be able to reify them.

Tips for Remaining Open to Possibilities

1) When key events, positive or negative, occur in your life, try to regard them as learning opportunities. Step back and depersonalize the situations, if you can. Regard them as gifts, even the worst of them, gifts that will strengthen you and reify strengths you did not know you had.

2) Develop the comfort you feel in various situations and various cultures. If you allow discomfort to overtake you, you cannot open yourself to the treasures embedded in experiences.

3) Work to form new partnerships, new relationships, new alliances. As they say about insanity, "Only a madman would do the same thing over and over and expect to have different results." To create new realities, you need new thoughts. That's impossible if you aren't having new experiences, if you aren't meeting new people.

4) Deliberately mix concepts, ideas, possibilities that do not seem to go together at all. Ask yourself, for example, what would happen if you combined this with that, or if you changed this thing, or if you eliminated that?

5) Widen the camera angle from which you are viewing the world. Think about things that are happening in the outside world and the impact they might have upon what you are trying to do. Step away from the "brilliance of transient events," as Prussian military strategist Karl von Clausewitz

described them, and think about long-range or short-range consequences that may result from them.

6)   Alter the approach you typically use to solve problems and make decisions. With unprecedented situations, don't always gravitate to your old patterns. Make connections, if you can, between variables you would not typically consider.

Finally, having defined reality and having determined you are receptive to new possibilities, refer back to the reality you described on page 354. Think about the outcome you would like to see evolve from this situation. In other words, if you could be supremely effective in using your influence, how would this situation wind up? What would be the ideal outcome? What would lead to **reification**?

_____

_____

_____

_____

_____

Discuss with other power sellers the steps needed to make this happen.

The Win3 Test

Win/Win Outcomes

You are no doubt familiar with the phrase "win/win" outcomes. It has long been used by upstanding and outstanding influencers to describe agreements that are satisfactory to both parties. When you as influencer, or others as influencees, operate from selfish stances or when compromise cannot be achieved, win/lose or even lose/lose results ensue.

Among the many techniques evinced by those who achieve win/win results, the following are included.

-- *Confident bargaining.* If you are fearful or uncertain about the benefits to be derived, you will exude hesitation, perhaps without even realizing you are doing so. Such revealing self-doubt may make others feel they can take unfair advantage of you. It will help if you start your influence sessions with a statement regarding your belief that the ultimate decisions can be satisfactory to all concerned.

-- *Equitable exchanges.* If you are willing to do "x" now, ensure that others will do "y" tomorrow. An honest, reciprocal balance, established early on, sets the tone for the entire meeting. It may be as small an issue as the meeting room: "Fine. We can meet in your office today but for the next meeting, let's meet in mine."

--   *Astute understanding.* If you can develop a feel for the won't-budge, may-budge, will-budge positions others hold, you can streamline the process of influencing others to accept your own won't-budge, may-budge, and will-budge viewpoints. Even with the won't-budge issues, though, compromise is sometimes possible.

--   *Temporal awareness.* They call it a cooling-off period when labor relations have become heated. We call it an awareness of how and when to use time. The best influencers understand when to be patient, when to suspend discussions, when to push for decisions and when to let time intervene. Sometimes a caucus is called for or a time-out period. Silence itself often serves to promote reflection and ultimate resolution.

Win3 Outcomes

We propose broadening the traditional definition of successful influence; that is, instead of outcomes acceptable to both parties, we encourage consideration of a third party (sometimes an abstract noun) that will benefit from influence exerted by those operating with integrity and those who respond to such influence. For example, you are applying for a job and have followed all the experts' advice on how to land it. You are properly groomed, you've done your homework about the company, your resume is polished, and you have rehearsed the questions you may be asked. If you are successful in your influence, you will be hired. And, of course, you will have a "win" outcome.

Assuming you have influenced with integrity, the other party will have a "win" outcome as well: your employer will have found the best person for the job. This simple example demonstrates the basic premise of influencing or even negotiating with integrity--that results prove beneficial to both the influencer and the influencee.

Now, though, we are asking that a third "win" be considered. Stretch your thinking. Who else or what else might benefit if in fact you are hired for this job? Keeping this third beneficiary in mind may even enhance your chances of getting the job. By identifying the third winner, you may be able to articulate a related goal.

Here's what we mean. Let's say you are eager to be hired because you have some ideas that, if implemented, will improve work processes. Yes, you want a job but you also want a chance to implement the things you have been thinking about. And yes, the employer will benefit.

But the Win3 thinker asks himself if there is another entity that might profit. Assume you got the job. (You won.) Further assume your employer, after a three-month period, has already commended you for the improvements you have made. (He won, too.) Is there a way that your success might benefit others? Who could the third winner be? If you think along internal lines, you might offer to be an SME (subject matter expert) and share your knowledge with other employees working on similar processes.

Or, you could write an article for a trade journal. In this case, the third winner would be the reader, reaping the benefits of your improvements. (Actually, your employer would be a double winner, by way of the positive publicity that would accrue to the organization as your name and company are listed in the author blurb at the end of the article.)

☑ Briefly outline three upcoming influence situations, three occasions when you will attempt to influence others to do something you truly believe should be done. Beneath each description, list the three win-beneficiaries and tell what they will win or how they will benefit.

Situation #1 _____

_____

Winner A: _____ , because_____

_____

Winner B: _____ , because_____

_____

Winner C: _____ , because_____

_____

Situation #2 _____

_____

Winner A: _____ , because_____

_____

Winner B: _____ , because_____

_____

Winner C: _____ , because_____

_____

Situation #3 _____

_____

Winner A: _____ , because_____

_____

Winner B: _____ , because_____

_____

Winner C: _____ , because_____

_____

Preview

Keeping the focus both inward and outward helps ensure your influence is driven by integrity. Passing the Win3 Test means stipulating success for you, for those you seek to influence, and for others who are not directly involved with the give and take of the exchange. In the next chapter, the emphasis on self/others/more-remote others will be explored further, as we consider taking actions that add value on several levels.

You'll read about the benefits employers are seeking, the benefits employees are seeking, and the ways you can influence teams to add value and values to the important work they do. You'll also read about Gil and Tanya Gockley, whose writings and workshops focus on the development of values that enable us to live and work and learn together more respectfully.

INTERVIEW

Sherri Malouf, President,
LMA, Inc., Amherst, New Hampshire

We define words like power and influence as neutral.
Whether such forces are used in a manipulative manner or to
create positive impact depends on how each person uses
power and influence. People don't need a gauge to determine
how ethical their actions are. They know when they are
twisting the truth or disguising it.

There may be some who would profit from a set of
guidelines on the positive use of power and influence. When
I am asked, "How do I know when I am being
manipulative?" I advise people to decide if they are forthright
in telling the other person about the sensitive information in
the situation. Are they open with all the information
surrounding the issue? Clearly, if you are getting someone to
do something and not telling them why, then you are being
manipulative. Another way to look at the whole question is
this: "If the other person had all the facts that you have,
would he still agree to what you are asking him to do?" If the
answer is no, then the action is manipulative.

Each of us has the potential to use any
communication tool in a manipulative way. Most people
know when they have used influence only to suit their own

purposes. Such behavior may work in a one-shot deal, but in the long run, others will not trust you enough to work with you again. The fake friendships, the dishonest work relationships do not hold up under stress. If you want to build genuine alliances, ethical influence provides a basic foundation.

The model we use takes in the big picture. There is a piece of it called "Organizational Street Smarts." To function successfully in organizations, to exert significant influence, we have to know how things work in the organization, we have to recognize office politics and make it work on behalf of the parties involved. We tell people the organization could not function without politics and that they are situated in "nestled networks."

When we understand how we and others fit into certain contexts, we can influence more readily. In developing our personal power, in demonstrating leadership, we have to keep the potential impact of our actions in mind. Awareness of outcome and awareness of our thinking impact how we influence others. For example, if I regard someone as a fool, I talk to him in a way that reflects my impression. And I filter the information I am receiving.

Effective influencers put on a tool belt before they begin their work. The more varied the tools that are in the tool belt, the greater your prospects for success. At LMA, we operate from a heart-centered basis, believing that the best tool is an empathic one: really listening to others, understanding what motivates them. Having discovered our own passionate core, we work with others to discover their own. For too long, businesses have considered the heart a weak or dismissible element of success and so there has been this reliance on the head instead. At LMA, we know the two work in concert.

DO:

-- Let the worth of your idea sell the idea.

-- Gain as much buy-in as you can from those you seek to influence.

-- Exude confidence in yourself, in your project, and in those you hope will be involved with it.

-- Consider using the Delphi technique to uncover reasons for resistance.

-- Establish, if only informally, a code of ethics by which your influence can be guided.

-- Insofar as possible, work with others to develop this code.

-- Lay the groundwork for your plans, if you can, in advance of actually presenting them. You can lessen resistance by doing so.

-- Use the Five-Why technique to unearth possible causes for a given problem.

-- Avoid labels (such as "Machiavellian") that may prevent you from learning to be a more effective influencer. Be open to possibilities so you can derive value even from those situations, words, concepts, or people ordinarily considered negative in their influence.

DON'T:

-- Depend on manipulation to win people over.

-- Ever become too facile with your influence skills. Your glibness may obviate your sincere interest in a given project.

-- Proceed with influence projects about which you feel lukewarm.

-- Automatically assume conflict is a bad thing.

-- Overlook the many questions that should be asked when you influence others.

-- Forget the importance of visuals during the Talk stage of influence.

-- Declare success without having measured it. How can you know you have truly influenced others without some quantification?

-- Fail to keep in periodic touch with those who have executed your plans in the past.

-- Continue to do exactly what you are now doing and expect to see better results in the future. Believing you can do so is one way to define insanity.

-- Be overly influenced by the brilliance of transient events.

YOU WILL:

-- Have less reason to manipulate when the value of your plans speaks for itself.

-- Lose more than you gain when you resort to manipulation.

-- Tarnish your reputation as an influencer if you resort to underhanded tactics. Restoring that reputation in future influence situations may be impossible to do.

-- Almost always be able to stall if you feel you need to investigate something further.

-- Go through various stages in the process of influencing others.

-- Have to offer assurances to your influencees, assurances that your idea is both doable and worth doing.

-- Find both good and bad elements in any reality. Remain open to the ways you can use both to positively reify possibilities.

-- Be occasionally shocked as you learn more about influence. Realize, though, that life is often at its best when things move from the commonplace to the controversial.

YOU WON'T:

-- Be receptive to possibilities if you allow singular meanings to define all words.

-- Be guaranteed the involvement of others just because you are not manipulative.

-- Necessarily be problem-free, even though you are operating in Quadrant 2 (High Worth/High Involvement). The danger of groupthink is especially powerful in these circumstances.

-- Be able to determine the cause of low conflict unless you probe for reasons.

-- Ever experience totally smooth sailing when you launch a new project. Be prepared for setbacks, flaws, and other leaks to be caulked.

-- Grow your business or your career without continually accepting new challenges. You have to walk away when you are no longer needed in one place but are needed in another.

-- Tap all potential unless you find a third beneficiary for Win/Win situations.

Chapter 9
Integrity & Values

~~~~~~~~~~~~~~

Overview   Successful influence effects positive change. Understanding the elements that comprise change enables us to deal more capably with the intervention itself, as well as status that was "quo" before the change, and the status that will become "quo" after the change. While many people fear change, the truth is, as author Bruce Barton points out, when we are through changing we are through.

Continuous improvement means bettering our personal and collective best. As employees become more vocal about the conditions that will enable them to do that, and as employers attempt to create conditions most conducive to betterment, both groups learn more about themselves and one another. On a smaller scale, team members are also seeking the knowledge that enables them to perform more efficiently. Influence is the engine driving accomplishment in all three sets. Integrity is the fuel for that engine.

The interview with Gil and Tanya Gockley reinforces the idea that character determines the extent to which our actions and accomplishments are guided by positive values. Although they focus on the development of these positive traits in children, their words have relevance in settings far beyond the classroom.

The Components of Change

Ever since the Quality movement encapsulated the concept of continuous improvement, employees have been more comfortable with the idea of change. Every team that has ever been formed works to do something different or to do something that has not been done before. Any time a process action team seeks to re-define, re-engineer, re-design, or even mildly improve standard operating procedures, change will ensue. And whenever value is added to an already existing process, some alteration, of necessity, occurs.

Author James Baldwin views change in this way: "Every change involves the breakup of the world as one has always known it." These breakups, however insignificant they may be, are akin to turning-point breakups in that we are being forced to relinquish the old and embrace the new. And so there is always some sense of loss accompanying the transition.

As individuals, as employees, as parents, as friends, as community members, and especially as influencers, we are constantly creating or reacting to change. When we decide that "good enough" really isn't, then we've decided some changes have to be made. Whether we seek to make a difference for ourselves, for our family, or for the department or organization we work in, making improvement means effecting positive change. For this reason, we begin with a list of recommendations for introducing change and enhancing value by making breakups seem natural and acceptable.

1)   *Shun certitude.* Typically, it's not what we know that causes us difficulty. It's what we are certain we know that simply isn't so. Being able to separate unalterable truths from flexible realities is an important skill for those who wish to inspire others to take action.

Take this test to find out if you are relying too much on what you know (or think you know), thus creating a non-receptive or only partially receptive climate for change.

☑ You are not expected to know the exact answer to the following questions, but you can certainly make an educated guess. Simply write a range within which you are fairly certain the correct answer would lie. So, if the question were, "How old was Martin Luther King, Jr. when he died?" you might not know the correct answer, but you could find the reasonably realistic range, such as 35-50, within which the correct answer would probably lie. (King was actually 39 when he died.) Don't "cheat" by making the range too broad. For example, if you said King was between the ages of 1 and 100, you would indeed have the correct range but you would not have a reasonably realistic range.

1. Meetings that are disorganized and poorly run cost American business how much a year? _____

2. How many years ago was December 25 officially recognized as a holy day or holiday to be celebrated?

   _____

3. Thousand-dollar bills, placed one on top of the other, would grow to a height of four inches in order to total $1 million. How high would the pile be if the total were $1 trillion?_____

4. What was the cost of the Congressional investigation into charges that Michael Espy, former Secretary of Agriculture, had illegally accepted bribes?_____

5. How long did the first U.S. satellite stay in space? ___

_____

2)   *Define your stimulus.* What led you to the decision
you have made, a decision to influence others to do something they may know or care nothing about? Determine if
your stimulus was:

___ Personal	___ Professional
___ Spiritual	___ Problem-related
___ Opportunity-related	___ Crisis-related
___ Delegated to you	___ Future-related
___ Passion-related	___ Intuitive
___ Necessity-related	___ Process-related
___ Strategic	___ Research-inspired
___ Other_____	

3)   *Make the mission known.* Having given some
preliminary thought to the origin of your interest in this
particular influence project, you should have little trouble
stating why you want this change to occur. Your private
mission statement, reducible to the back of a business card,
is an ideal core from which to radiate outwards, involving
others and creating webs of power.

4)   *Establish priorities.* To prevent the frustration that accompanies wheel-spinning, ensure that both strategic (long-range) and operational (day-by-day) plans have been stipulated in order to carry out the mission. When steps are not carefully delineated, the vagaries of goals can lead to vagaries of intent on the part of your influencees. Or, if they do comply, they may be doing so without true commitment for they lack an understanding of purpose. One caution here, though: While it is vital that plans be established, the actual means of accomplishing those plans need not be detailed. If we expect our influencees to act with some degree of autonomy, we cannot build fences around them. Doing so creates sheep in a herd and defines the role of influencer as a mere herder of sheep.

5)   *Provide training so influencees can meet expectations.* Even if it's informal, even if it's just an information-studded magazine article, find ways to reinforce the influence you hope to have. It doesn't matter if you are attempting to influence one or one thousand, family or colleagues, volunteers or paid employees. Your word alone cannot carry as much weight as your words plus the words of someone with considerable repute.

6)   *Deal with both the hard and soft sides of the change.*
Overlooking the psychological stress the change will cause
for those engaged in it can spell doom for your project.
Determine what new knowledge is required if others are to
join your cause and provide that information in a way that
invites inclusion. Contemplate the types of fears your
influencees are bound to experience (whether or not they
articulate them) and determine what can be done to alleviate
the problem.

You may be forced to introduce change quickly. For
example, a serious violation or safety problem occurring on
Day 1 may result in a policy change being issued by Day 2.
Realize, though, that the process of adapting to and
internalizing this change may require a much longer period
for those impacted by it.

$\boxed{\sqrt{}}$ Let's take a few minutes to apply the change
considerations to an influence situation facing you. Quickly
note whom you want to influence:_____
to do what:_____
and why this is important to you, to them and to a third
entity (the Win3 Test): _____
Now answer these questions regarding this influence
project.

1) Concerning this situation, what certainties should you reconsider? Which are unalterable? Which should be shunned or replaced? _____

_____

_____

2) What word(s) best defines the stimulus behind your desire to influence others to become involved with your plan? _____

_____

3) State your mission in 25 words or less._____

_____

_____

Tell how you can create webs of power to carry it out.

_____

_____

_____

4) What new information do your influencees need if they are to participate in this project?_____

_____

How will you provide it to them? _____

_____

5) Considering psychological rather than technical information, what can you do to reduce stress, alleviate

fear, and/or create enthusiasm for the changes you are
proposing?_____

_____

(The answers to #1 *Shun certitude* questions appear
in the Appendix. Chances are, as certain as you were that all
your answers fell within the correct range, you missed at
least one. If so, let this serve as a reminder that when
proposing change, it's a wise idea to investigate all
assumptions.)

Values Employers Seek

As Barry Sheehy, author of *Winning the Race for
Value*, asserts: "No organization can perform well...if
employees are demoralized, traumatized, or seething with
anger." Employers are looking for performance. They value
employees concerned about productivity. On the flip side of
the value coin, though, is the recognition that to elicit best
efforts, employers must produce best conditions. Before
they can affirm or awaken certain values in their workforce,
they must develop a sense of cohesion in the workplace.

That cohesion requires us to regard the workplace as
employee-centered. Such a focus, in its most basic thrust,
asks if employees are happy coming to work in the morning,

if they enjoy what they do, the people with whom they work, and the environment in which they work.

A simple analogy will illustrate the importance of this factor. Go back to your high school days. Excluding lunch or study hall, what was your favorite subject?_____ What were your grades in this course? _____ Typically, we do well in those things we enjoy doing. Granted, several possible reasons could explain the enjoyment: We may always have been fascinated by a particular topic, we liked the teacher, our best friend was in the class, we had been hooked by a teacher in the previous year, et cetera. As a rule, though, the work that interests us leads to mastery. Or, as Alfred North Whitehead so aptly framed it, "Romance precedes precision."

Similarly, the reasons high-producers perform as they do are numerous. The more we can learn about those reasons, of course, the more we can provide further input of one kind or another. In short, though, if your influencees enjoy the task you have put before them, chances are they will be committed to that task and give it their repeated "best shots."

It may be true that employees, bottom line, have been hired for what they can do for the organization. (The carpentry equivalent is the recognition that if you buy a drill, it's not because you need a drill. You need holes and the drill is a means to that end. There is a difference, though. By holding the drill as it should be held and using the proper bits, you will get the same-size hole every time. Employees are much more complex.) All other conditions being equal, employees who have been influenced with integrity will perform better than employees who are merely putting in their time in order to draw a paycheck each week.

In a literal sense, the ethical environment is one in which culture has been defined rather than one in which right has been differentiated from wrong. Derived from the Greek *ethos*, the word refers to the defining of attributes, habits, and beliefs germane to a given person or group of people. If we as influencers are to have interpersonal exchanges guided by dialog and not monolog, if we are to develop relationships characterized by harmony and not discord, then we have to re-establish positive morale, restore equilibrium once the trauma has occurred, and replace seething anger with a reason to contribute. Basically, we have to define and build the ideal culture.

Assuming employers have managed to build a culture of confidence, they can rightfully expect certain contributions from employees. And you as influencer, no matter your position, can correctly hope your influencees (no matter their positions) will respond with the same valued traits employers are seeking. We've identified some of the most important.

The P-I-C Three
(Productivity, Innovation, Communication)

Productivity

High-performance employees are doing what they are paid to do. And they are usually doing it faster and with higher quality than those employees not known for their productivity. What makes some employees willing to maximize their potential and others less inclined to do so? The answers will vary, depending on any number of factors. Generally speaking, though, employees who are productive have achieved a balance between input and output.

For example, every workplace has distractions. These distractions take many shapes--stress, noise, and conflicts, to name a few. The highly productive employee has learned to minimize distracting inputs so outputs can be maximized. Whether they use filters or firm resolve, they have determined they will let little interrupt their concentration on the tasks at hand. If time were toothpaste, they would squeeze every possible dollop from it. (They might even cut the tube to scrape out the usable parts hidden therein.)

Such individuals have identified the environmental factors that can make them unproductive; they can pinpoint who and what might prevent them from meeting self-determined goals. Having isolated the barriers, they take steps to deal with them. Such individuals, whether or not they are managers, would probably understand if not concur with this time-driven comment by Jeffrey Cristian, head of an executive search firm: "Restructuring has created managers who have very little time for pleasantries."

Now think about your own workplace. Who or what is causing you to be less productive than you can be?

_____

_____

What can you do about it? _____

_____

☑ Test yourself and others, whether they are employees, teammates or influencees. Decide which of the two possible choices is the better reflection of what you would do if given a choice. (The selections and what they indicate are explained in the Appendix.) As far as your influencees are concerned, you can either ask the same questions of them or select the choices you think they would be most likely to select themselves and then compare your guesses to their actual choices. (Ideally you can do the latter

385

to obtain revealing insights: as well as we think we know some people, the way they see themselves is often at odds with the way *we* see them.)

1. Given a choice, I would rather
   a. be in a library
   b. be at a luncheon.
2. Given an unexpected afternoon off, I would probably spend it
   a. taking a day trip to a favorite nearby town
   b. getting caught up on the files and piles on my desk.
3. Given a choice, I would prefer to
   a. see the works of a well-known artist
   b. read the biography of that same artist.
4. Given a choice of watching a sports event such as figure skating on t.v.,
   a. I'd prefer to see a competition
   b. I'd prefer to see an exhibition or a "show on ice."
5. Given a choice of what to do on a holiday weekend,
   a. I'd opt for coach potato-ism
   b. I'd tackle some of the items on my to-do list.
6. Given a choice of the person I could be seated next to at a dinner party,
   a. I'd choose someone known for her amusing chatter/ gossip

b. I'd choose someone known for her remarkable mind.
7. Given a choice of what to do while waiting for a meeting
    or workshop to begin,
    a. I'd probably write or read something
    b. I'd engage the person beside me in conversation.

A word of caution here: Most influencers strive to find productivity-oriented influencees, especially in undertaking a project. But having all productivity-oriented individuals on your team actually could be counter-productive. Aim for a blend of talents and personalities. If you are attempting to influence others around requests or issues--situations not dependent on teamwork or long timeframes--you will be concerned with factors other than the person's inclination toward productivity.

Attempting to influence your supervisor, for example, to let you assume responsibility for a meaningful issue, you'll need to focus on things other than productivity alone. Among them might be her predisposition toward relinquishing the power-reins, your track record, the right time and place, et cetera.

Innovation
It was Einstein's conviction that "imagination is more important than knowledge." A more contemporary voice,

Tom Peters', asserts "imagination is the only source of real value in the new economy." How do we develop in our influencees the ability to see the big picture, to willingly propose new ideas, to break free from the mental restraints imposed by time-tested tradition?

This incremental process, like all harmonious efforts, depends on a number of conditions: good listening, tact, patience, and time--time for both generating possibilities and exploring their feasibility.

How can you as influencer cultivate a climate of creativity? If you've decided this is an important quality for influencees to possess, you bear some responsibility for creating a climate in which new ideas can flourish. For openers, look around you for idea-toxins: those aspects of the influence process that may in fact be killing ideas still in their embryonic state. The toxins may be excessive pressure, lack of information, fear of ridicule, changing objectives, intimidation, and of course statements that stifle the creative urge. We've all heard these negative comments:

-- "It'll never work."
-- "Just get the job done. We don't pay you to think."
-- "What makes you think your idea will work when everyone else's has failed?"
-- "That's the dumbest thing I've ever heard."

In building an atmosphere of receptivity, you will need to learn what is preventing ideas from being shared. Then, do everything within your power to offer assurances, to make the environment one of acceptance and respect. It will help to have groundrules epitomizing the respect that hallmarks the best brainstorming sessions. For example, "No personal attacks" or "No interrupting" will encourage a full sharing of innovative possibilities.

Consider yourself an employer in this sense of the word: when you influence others, you are making use of their talents to accomplish objectives you have set. "Making use of" is the dictionary definition of *employ*. So, as an employer (a.k.a., an influencer), you serve as an idea-warrior. By this stage in your influence career, you know the importance of rising above the labels:

-- Thomas Edison was considered "too stupid to learn."
-- Bill Wilson, founder of Alcoholics Anonymous, was called a "hopeless" alcoholic.
-- Winston Churchill was labeled "dull."
-- Albert Einstein was told by his headmaster, "Your mere presence offends me."
-- Walt Disney was considered to have no talent when he was in school.

And so, you are willing to take a stand if it means creativity can be nurtured. (As an anonymous sage once observed, "Every great oak was once a nut that stood its ground.")

Additional ideas for stimulating creative thought include the following.

1) *Set aside time for brainwarming as well as brainstorming.* The former activity sets the mood for the brainstorming to follow. Brainwarming is paradoxically relaxed yet fast-paced. Characterized by humor, it nonetheless challenges your group to put on their thinking caps. You may, for example, throw out a word as the theme for the meeting and ask for as many free-association words as they can come up with. The brainwarmers should vary each time you meet, but they should all have this aim in mind: to create an atmosphere so exciting and so accepting that influencees will soon find their feet (and brains) are no longer cold. Rather, they will jump right into the brainstorming.

Not every project, problem, or plan will benefit from creative input. Some tasks, for example, are quantitative in nature and rely upon metrics and cold, hard data for the development of a workable course to follow. Other tasks will benefit from imaginative thought. During the brainstorming period, ensure that all ideas are heard and later reviewed before decisions or priorities are made. Keep in mind Mark Van Doren's advice to "bring ideas in and entertain them royally. One of them may be the king."

2)   *Free thinking from the shackles of stereotypic thinking*. To illustrate, when asked, "How do you get to heaven?" almost every adult you ask will say something like this: "You do good deeds" or "You live by the Golden Rule." Ask a child, though, and you are likely to hear answers like these: "It's easy. You take the God elevator" or "You go to hell and take a left" or "You find a beanstalk and you just keep climbing."

To stimulate this kind of thinking, ask questions like, "If money were no object, what could we accomplish here?" Better yet, use the Force Field Analysis developed by psychologist Kurt Lewin. Essentially, it asks you to list the current state of affairs, and beneath it the ideal state of affairs. In the first column, list all the driving forces that will bring you closer to the ideal state. In the next column, specify the restraining forces that may be preventing you from reaching it.

3)   *Inject novelty into the thinking process*. In order to make fullest uses of the brains you are employing, you need on occasion to push and pull, probe and prod, stimulate and scintillate. Just a little reading in the area of innovative thinking will yield an abundance of ideas. One that often works well is the "force-fit" style of thinking. You set a

structure of some kind and allow a specific amount of time for meeting that challenge. On the next round, your influencees are asked to break their preceding record.

For example, if you were attempting to influence a group to serve as mentors for new hires, you might ask them to list all the benefits they could think of during a three-minute period. Then, you might give them only two and one-half minutes and ask that they come up with a new list, longer if possible, but one that does not contain anything already mentioned on the first list.

4)   *Emphasize the value of diversity.* It would be an unbearably boring world if we all looked alike, thought alike, sounded alike, acted alike. Variety is not only the spice of life; it is the salt and pepper of our workaday fare. Teams that are mixed outperform those that are uniform in their makeup.

Whenever you can, bring in a variety of people with a variety of experience and background, age and gender, race and religion. Further, try to mix thinking styles. Better to combine someone with an analytical thinking style with someone who is known for creativity, than to surround yourself with all convergent or all divergent thinkers. The varying viewpoints can only enhance the final product you produce.

Of course, there will be some situations in which you have no influence over the circumstances. For example, when you appear in small claims court to convince a judge that your case has more merit than your opponent's, you are not concerned with the context of creativity but rather with the content. On such occasions, you will lend diversity to your argument by, for example, bringing in six points, arranged in descending order of importance, instead of repeating the main point over and over.

5)   *When influence attempts are successful, they almost always lead to next steps.* If you've persuaded your boss, for example, to let you attend a conference in London, you would make the obligatory report upon your return. But you could do even more: you could maintain contact with other attendees and prepare a periodic update of post-conference happenings, to be shared with members of your department. Organize a local conference, paralleling the most highly touted aspects of the conference in London. Or, meet with your manager at the end of the year to discuss aspects of your performance that could be traced back to the growth-opportunities provided by your attendance at the London conference.

<u>Communication</u>

Stephen Covey and his associates often use the compass as a symbol to help employees (and other influencees) find the core values or the "true north" principles that will point us in the right direction. If you are seeking good communication with and among your influencees, ideally you will be communicating a similar purity of purpose. First, though, you must define what is motivating you. It is the kind of "irreducible essence" of which Hubert Humphrey spoke: when all else is stripped away, what is it that you stand for? That essence should come through loud and clear when influencees think about what you have asked of them. As they communicate with each other, that essence should also undergird all their behaviors.

Studies have repeatedly shown effective interpersonal exchanges depend on effective communication. But the word "communication" has multiple interpretations. Therefore, it should be broken down into several key components. To assist you in considering the effectiveness of your own communication, review the ten pairs in the following list and select the one term in each pair that you value more highly. In making your selection, ask, "Which of the two am I more likely to use?" or even "Which of the two would I rather use?"

I would rather communicate by...

1. a) arranging information chronologically
   b) putting the most exciting information first
2. a) using comforting words
   b) offering radical, dramatic, challenging thoughts
3. a) supplying familiar terms
   b) exploring unknown possibilities
4. a) stressing a simple set of relationships
   b) acknowledging the many possible cultures
5. a) forming strategic and new alliances
   b) doing what is expected
6. a) expressing myself logically
   b) including multiple, perhaps even contradictory ideas
7. a) using statistics
   b) using personal experiences/accounts
8. a) including data relevant to the task
   b) bringing in information from a variety of sources
9. a) narrowing the scope
   b) extending the known boundaries
10. a) considering possible skepticism
    b) attending to credibility issues

Before we offer recommendations, there is one thing worth noting: the contingency factor. Given the complexities of circumstances, individuals, and goals, any one of these twenty items might be appropriate. Wise use is contingent upon sensitivity to the needs of the moment. Various circumstances demand flexibility from us; to rely repeatedly on the same communication tools is to minimize your effectiveness.

But speaking in a general sense, certain elements in the communication process are effective no matter what the circumstances. You'll find those italicized in the list that follows.

1. a) arranging information chronologically
   b) putting the most exciting information first
2. a) using comforting words
   b) offering radical, dramatic, challenging thoughts
3. a) supplying familiar terms
   b) exploring unknown possibilities
4. a) stressing a simple set of relationships
   b) *acknowledging the many possible cultures*
5. a) *forming strategic and new alliances*
   b) doing what is expected
6. a) expressing myself logically
   b) *including multiple, perhaps even contradictory ideas*
7. a) using statistics
   b) *using personal experiences/accounts*
8. a) including data relevant to the task

b) bringing in information from a variety of sources

9. a) narrowing the scope
   b) extending the known boundaries
10. a) considering possible skepticism
    b) attending to credibility issues

Half of the ten pairs were included as "buffers." That is, because it is difficult sometimes to separate what we do from what we think the experts believe we should do, five of the pairs were inserted to make the identified traits less obvious. How many of your responses match the five that are italicized?

0, 1, or 2 matches: Although you have probably had some successful in influencing others to join the betterment bandwagon from time to time, there is still some room for improvement. To illustrate, while simplicity is a good thing, restricting yourself to a simplistic view may cause you to neglect the multiple possibilities embedded in the various cultures your influence project depends upon. Develop your awareness of such and use the diversity of values and the value of diversity to enrich your undertaking.

3 matches: You're already doing an above-average job of communicating. Nonetheless, if you are the

kind of person who reads self-development books like this one, you are the kind of person who is interested in getting better than you presently are. For the two italicized items you are not employing, select one, and for a period of three months commit to making greater use of that particular tool. Then, for the next three-month period, concentrate on using the other.

<u>4 or 5 matches</u>: You probably have been told many times that you are an outstanding communicator. This many matches confirms that fact. As an influencer, it seems you carefully weigh the conditions in which you are influencing and select the most appropriate medium for your message. In addition, you are apparently a frequent user of the elements employed by the most able communicators.

Outstanding influencers value, and consequently demonstrate, these three traits: productivity, innovation, and communication. Their self-defined drives are aligned with the qualities employers value most. If you are determined both to gain the most from your influencees (in terms of output) and to give the most to them (in terms of input), you'll make certain your influence exchanges reflect the P-I-C Three.

Values Employees See and Seek

Those who represent the management of an organization have a dual burden. Their actions are viewed not only as extensions of their own character, but also as extensions of the organizational character. When managers act in a way to destroy the trust employees value so deeply, faith in the organization as a whole erodes. Each of us wants to be proud of the corporate body that employs us. If you doubt the power associated with pride, call to mind the televised reports of cities and citizens following the winning of championship sports pennants.

Employees watch what managers do. Consequently, when there is incongruence between what is espoused and what is actually done, faith and pride and trust begin to crack. According to a survey of 200 companies ("Workers Distrust Top Executives, Study Shows," *Benefits & Compensation Solutions*, November 1997, page 8), it takes about seven months for trust to be built but less than half that time for it to be lost. To build or regain trust, leaders should:

	Column A	Column B
° Maintain integrity	_____	_____
° Openly communicate their vision and values		
	_____	_____

° Show respect for employees as equal partners

_____ _____

° Focus on shared goals more than personal agendas

_____ _____

° Do the right thing regardless of personal risk

_____ _____

° Listen with an open mind   _____ _____
° Demonstrate caring compassion _____ _____
° Keep confidences.   _____ _____

☑ For a moment, replace the term *manager* with the word *influencer* and the word *employees* with the word *influencees*. Now return mentally to the last situation in which you influenced someone to do something you felt had considerable value. In column B, write a number from 1 to 5 (1= possibly true of me, 5=definitely true of me) to reflect the degree to which these actions are true of your influence efforts. Then, cover the second column (or make a copy of this page and fold it over) and ask one of the influencees from this situation to evaluate you in Column A by applying the same scale of 1 - 5 to these eight traits.

From the very beginning of an influencer/influencee relationship, promises are made, even if they are not articulated, by way of the hope that is inspired. As influencer, you have an obligation to keep that hope alive, to keep employees motivated or peers inspired or influencees believing in the possibilities they glimpsed in your initial request for their contributions. To keep the attitudes you've helped create at the motivated-performance level and not the marginal-performance level, you need to provide ongoing support.

That support may come in the form of providing your influencees:

-- clearly stated objectives
-- feedback
-- coaching or championing
-- recognition
-- sufficient tools and resources for accomplishing the task to which they have committed themselves
-- responsibility with authority
-- an environment in which stress is minimized.

In addition to doing the right things, influencers must allow employees to voice their opinions on the value and morality of organizational practices. That is the position taken by authors Dawn-Marie Driscoll, W. Michael Hoffman, and Edward S. Petry, writing in *The Ethical Edge*. They posit a scenario in which employees are encouraged to speak up and speak out. Such a policy not only encourages joint decision-making regarding values, but may also prevent lawsuits from being filed or judgments being awarded to defendants who actually do file. The authors assert organizations that do not encourage discussion and perhaps even disagreement are putting themselves at risk.

☑ Think about the last time you attempted to influence another person(s).

Quickly outline the circumstances here: _____

_____

_____

Did you encounter resistance to your proposal?_____
If not, what factors were instrumental in the ready acceptance of your idea? _____

_____

_____

_____

If there was resistance, how did you feel when you heard it?

_____

_____

Did you respond defensively? (Try to recall your exact words.) _____

_____

_____

Did you try to cut off/overcome the opposition or did you listen carefully and allow the feedback to influence you? (Try to recall what was said on both sides.) _____

_____

_____

_____

Once the opposing viewpoints were explored, how did the discussion impact the outcome?_____

_____

_____

Answer either of these two questions:
1) How was the outcome better than it would have been without the disagreement?
2) What do you *wish* the disagreement had led to?

_____

_____

_____

Exerting Influence on Teams
Virtual Teams

Virtual reality has created virtual offices in which virtual teams work. Sometimes, team members are working in the actual office or in their nearby home office. At other times, they are geographically dispersed. Influencing those whom you cannot see requires new tools.

To be sure, many of the traditional influence techniques will work no matter where your influencees are located. Other techniques, though, have evolved specifically for these e-situations.

--   *Regular meetings are vital.* When conference rooms won't work, conferencing will. This modern-day kind of meeting can be accomplished through telephone, videoconference, e-mail, and chatting in electronic rooms. Your e-influence can be just as powerful as your in-person influence, but it requires a bit more organization to influence in these technologically advanced times.

--   *Develop esprit for the corps.* Especially with influencees who are not in close physical proximity, an ongoing theme or competition or celebration will substitute for the closeness enjoyed by those who work together in the most literal sense. For example, you could start each of your e-mail postings with a provocative question and announce the winning answers in the next day's mail. Flexiplaces allow us to be productive, no matter where we are. They also, however, create a sense of isolation. Effective influencers are sensitive to this possibility and take deliberate steps to overcome it.

-- *Redefine your role.* Whether you are a manager for dispersed employees or an influencer working with a team of influencees located in various sites, the stereotypic definition of "leader" must undergo some revision. In the past, the chain of command clearly designated how decisions would be made, how work would be delegated, how employees would be supervised. However, today's influencer-- assuming she has made clear the objective toward which influencees are working--recedes into the background as the project itself assumes greater importance. Thanks to the push toward empowerment, employees are handling more of their own problems, turning to supervisors only as necessary.

Clearly, this kind of independence is healthy and productive. But it can lead to serious problems if deadlines and duties are not clearly spelled out. As influencer of a team that is spread out, you will probably have to explore new ways of ensuring assigned tasks are being completed without seeming to micromanage. Because you can no longer stop by someone's workplace and ask, "How's it going?" while you actually *see* how it's going, you'll need to communicate in ways that are sensitive, supportive, and supervisory--all at the same time. Your span of control is being replaced by a span of communications.

Traditional Teams

No matter what kind of team you are heading as influencer--self-directed work team, virtual team, cross-functional team, process-improvement team, project-assigned team--certain ingredients are required in the recipe for success. The first letter of each ingredient, when combined with the other letters, spells the word *opus*. And, if your influence has the effect you intend it to have, you will create a new reality, an output or opus that simply did not exist before. The next time your team meets, think O-P-U-S.

Objective:

The objective of your initial and subsequent meetings should be listed at the top of the agenda. The agenda ideally should be sent out several days ahead of the meeting, so attendees can gather their thoughts about the issue or assignment and have time to gather relevant materials. Allude to the objective several times during the course of the meeting.

(Even if you are only meeting with one person, attempting to influence her, for example, to consider you for an upcoming project, you should have an outline with time allocations indicated, so she knows what to anticipate If you think the chances of your proposal being accepted are less than 50%, do not submit the agenda ahead of the actual meeting. Otherwise, the individual may have made up her mind before you have even had a chance to present your case.)

Participation

Remind your influencees of the importance of each person's contribution and ensure the comfort level is high enough so ideas can flow freely. The word "participation" also implies an exchange. Therefore, listening to one another is as important as presenting our own thoughts. Participation requires some sacrifice, as a rule, so you should recognize the time and effort others are expending on your behalf.

We recommend another kind of participation: the rotation of various roles that make meetings run smoothly. For example, the same person should not always be asked to serve as scribe (no matter how neat her handwriting is). The time monitor (who should use the time allocations you have listed beside each agenda item to move discussions along) and the topic monitor (who reminds the group when they are bringing in irrelevant issues) should be different in each session.

As milestones are met and mini-successes realized, plan celebrations to encourage further participation in the project. And give thought to including those who will be impacted, however remotely, by the implementation of the plan or idea you and your influencees are executing. Inviting their participation early in the project will help ensure acceptance later on.

Utility

Ideally, long before the influence project is underway, you will have ascertained the utility of the idea you are presenting. Its usefulness should be apparent for all concerned--you, the influencees, and the larger community in which the plan is being executed.

(You may be surprised to learn the word utility has this definition: "the greatest happiness of the greatest number." Always try to maximize the impact of the work you and others are putting into a project.)

Further, to help guarantee your plan will be used, make the verbiage surrounding it user-friendly. No matter how worthy an undertaking you have chosen, if others cannot understand its value, they will probably make very little use of it. (Even with a one-on-one request, make it easy for the potential "buyer" to purchase or agree to the idea or product you are trying to sell.)

Synthesis

You'll have to work hard initially to achieve synthesis, which literally means working together or having unanimity of thought concerning a given proposition. (A set of groundrules that each participant has agreed to will go a long way toward establishing cohesion.) Until you have ironed out the inevitable intellectual, emotional, and psychological wrinkles that appear at the beginning of an influence undertaking, you cannot achieve synthesis.

Once all influencees, however, have "bought into" the idea you are advancing, you will be sharing a like mind. Periodically, of course, some differences of opinion may emerge, but having overcome the widest gaps at the beginning, these smaller divisions are usually fairly easy to reconcile. The same process should be used to center the team each time differing viewpoints are expressed. They should never be squelched. Keep in mind, however, that spending too much time airing grievances could sabotage your project.

Preview   In our final chapter, we shall explore both vision and visibility--the former as an aim to which we commit part or all of our lives, and the latter as a natural consequence of vision-attainment. We'll also present

Kimberly Hyland, whose influpreneurial spirit uses both in the work she does with youngsters.

INTERVIEW

Dr. Gil and Tanya Gockley, Authors:
Loving is Natural, Parenting is not:
creating a value-centered family,
Rochester, New York

In terms of values, we feel employers are looking for people who can work together, who are team players, and who are willing to take a stand on some issues but not every issue. (Doing so means compromise cannot occur.) A willingness to compromise, to collaborate, to truly listen to opposing viewpoints--these are the traits that lead to synergistic results. We really believe that schools need to help children develop a sense of character, and to become productive members of several communities--their families, their schools, their communities, and ultimately their workplaces.

Our ValueSkills® is an identification of the inner qualities that lead to outer manifestations of harmony and cooperation in those various settings of which we all are part. Among those qualities are patience, enthusiasm, and basic consideration for others. We regard these as base boundaries for developing respect and responsibility in our relationships and obligations.

We have precedents, of course, for doing unto others as we would have them do unto us. In the contemporary roles we play, we have a right to expect whatever we demonstrate. So, if an organization expects employees to evince honesty and collaborative behavior, then the organization must treat employees with those same qualities. We tend to have returned to us whatever traits we are modeling. Consequently, we are earning on a daily basis the right to be treated as we wish to be treated.

Over the years, we have come to view character according to this definition: Character is what you do when there is no audience. We de-emphasize the manipulative aspects of our everyday actions, those actions for which we hope to receive reward or to avoid punishment. Character is an intrinsic aspect of our being; it guides us to do what is right whether or not an audience is watching.

Whether we are working in school, at home, or on the job, each of us is an integral piece of that particular puzzle-picture. When one of us fails to contribute, the picture simply cannot be viewed as an integrated whole.

DO:

-- Recognize the constancy and inevitability of change.

-- Make the mission known to all concerned.

-- Look for ways to develop cohesion.

-- Set aside time for brainwarming and brainstorming.

-- Define and be defined by your irreducible essence.

-- Form strategic alliances to help extend your influence.

-- Include information from a variety of sources to dislodge the mental plaque that can form around thinking.

-- Recognize the power of pride as a motivational force.

-- Build trust by demonstrating care and compassion.

-- Invite participation and discussion regarding ethical practices.

-- Follow the O-P-U-S plan in working with traditional teams.

-- Realize people expect to receive what they have demonstrated.

-- Encourage influencees to value intrinsic rewards.

DON'T:

-- Overlook the sense of loss that accompanies change, even positive change.

-- Forget to involve influencees in the setting of priorities.

-- Begin your influence efforts without first establishing a culture of confidence.

-- Hesitate to break free from stereotypic thinking.
-- Think that uniform perspectives will yield best outcomes. Entertain contradictory views.
-- Think your words or actions go unnoticed. Let there be congruence between them.
-- Avoid risk when striving to do the right thing.
-- Fail to make special provisions for virtual teams.
-- Assume the objective is clear or remembered.
-- Neglect synthesizing efforts after initial consensus has been achieved.

YOU WILL:

-- Have to shun certitude or at least revisit strongly held beliefs in order to make serious improvement.

-- Be a more effective influencer if you are dealing with both the hard and soft sides of change.

-- Have to lessen or eliminate distractions if you want influencees to be productive.

-- Need innovative thinking if good ideas are to become good practices.

-- Be able to enhance output by valuing diversity of thought and of thinkers.

-- Have a more receptive audience if you share personal experiences with them.

-- Be regarded warily if promises are not kept.

-- Need regular telemeetings for those located in off-site workplaces.

-- Have to make special overtures to develop esprit de corps with virtual teams.

-- Need full participation if the value of each person's contribution is to be realized.

YOU WON'T:

-- Be able to express your objective clearly without defining the stimulus that prompted you to take action.

-- Find high performance where employees are demoralized.
-- Have a culture of creativity if idea-toxins are permeating the atmosphere.
-- Complete the influence cycle unless you take the next steps following the acceptance of your proposal by an influencee.
-- Maximize your influence efforts without acknowledging the many possible cultures the plan could impact.
-- Succeed in your influence endeavor without providing support to influencees.
-- Be able to function as you normally do when you are influencing a remote team. Re-definition of your role will be required.
-- Successfully put your plan into effect without considering utility and user-friendliness.

Chapter 10
Influence, Vision &
Visibility
~~~~~~~~~~~~~~~

Overview   Having worked through considerations of
manipulation and Machiavellianism, we can give some
thought in this chapter to the visibility that naturally accrues
to expert influencers, as they make their visions concrete
realities. We'll explore the long-term outcomes attainable by
visionary influencers, as well as the promise and pitfalls of
self-promotion. Finally, the entrepreneurial spirit, typified in
the behavior of influencers, will be explored. In the final
interview, you'll meet Kimberly Hyland, who portrays her
vision in incremental steps and who, in so doing, has
brought distinction to the community in which she lives and
works.

Long-Term Outcomes

Influencers can be equated with trailblazers, with pioneers, with those who look into the future and make the present road lead there. "Do not go where the path may lead," Ralph Waldo Emerson wrote, "go instead where there is no path and leave a trail." This is what influencers do, they fashion new paths. They help us take part in the shaping of the future. They use influence to help others see their vision and achieve long-term gains.

While influence circumstances will vary--not every idea you have is geared toward long-term results, not every proposal will be made to a whole group of prospects--the following vision-related blueprint will apply to virtually any situation in which you hope to capture present interest and future commitment.

1. Look to the unknown, the unseen, the undone.

Good ideas abound. Moving good to great, however, and fleeting to fixed, requires work. Think of an idea you would like to implement--at home, at work, in a volunteer setting, in a relationship--but an idea destined to have long-term results. This should not be a transient idea, such as influencing team members to design a survey one way or the other.

Instead, it is an idea with longevity, one that will become a permanent fixture on the familial or organizational terrain, if not forever, at least for a good while. This idea, when implemented, should become standard operating procedure for those involved, or should become an annual event, or even the stuff of which legends are made. It should make a difference, an important difference, in the way you and others think or act or believe.

You should look ahead and actually envision what this future state would be like. Think of the long-term benefits for both present influencees and future beneficiaries. Then, use the Force Field Analysis to explore possibilities.

☑   Describe the current state or present conditions that you hope to improve. If you can, gather data related to these circumstances. _____

_____

_____

_____

_____

Now describe the idealized state. In other words, tell what the ideal circumstances would be. What long-term consequences do you wish to occur? Be as specific as possible, including as many details as possible. _____

_____

_____

_____

_____

    Numerous aspects of the present circumstances can help you achieve the idealized state. They may be individuals, groups, organizations, equipment, or intangibles like past successes, a can-do spirit, a genuine concern for one another, et cetera. Explore the many elements that can help you reach the long-term outcome you envision and list them here.

1. _____

2. _____

3. _____

4. _____

5. _____

6. _____

7. _____

    Now it's time to realistically consider those individuals, environmental factors, or other things that may be preventing you from reaching this idealized future. Who or what is a barrier? List those persons or things.

1. _____

2. _____

3. _____

4. _____

5. _____

6. _____

7. _____

2. Develop your hook

If you can detach yourself from the excitement you feel for your idea, if you can look at it dispassionately, state why another person would want to agree with it and/or you. What could possibly be so enticing that it would make others willingly give up something--time, money, effort, or perhaps even power? What distinguishes this proposal from the present way of doing things or viewing things? What makes it unique? What can it give them that they don't already have? What can it tell them that they don't already know? What long-term benefits will it have for them or for the unit (familial or professional) in which they function?

Your "hook" represents the best thing (from the perspective of other people) about the idea you are putting forth. Without a hook, you'll have little hope of reeling them in.

☑   Write your hook here in 25 words or less, citing one distant or long-term beneficial result._____

_____

_____

_____

_____

3. Sharpen your hook

Dull hooks simply don't grab. You may have a truly unique selling point, but if it is not expressed in terms that attract, you may not be able to persuade others of its real worth. One shortcut to creating memorable hooks is to study junk mail you receive and make a list of the terms used by professional ad writers. Then use some of those terms to refine your own hook.

☑ Here are 54 such terms. Circle ten you think might work in expressing your own hook more vividly.

avoid costly...	win/winner/winning	discover
guarantee	enrich/enhance	can afford
important	immediate results	quality
you won't regret	lower	free
limited	potential	reduce
If you are serious...	timesaving	at last
capture	performance	dedicated
you'll receive	big savings	proven
show you how	profit with	no obligation

your very own	and much more	need...?
100%	no muss, no fuss, no...	revive
features	faster	increase
satisfaction	risk-free	valuable
complete	stimulating	unique
no more...	only	stop
deliver	unlimited	also available
learn how	fully secured	maximize
	you can afford it	

Of the ten you encircled, use at least three in rewriting your hook, keeping it to a statement of 25 words or less and again citing at least one long-term benefit.

_____

_____

_____

4 . Deliver a 1-2-3 punch

Your vision was the starting point. You used it to develop a hook and then revised that hook to make it as convincing as possible for the influencee(s) who will be hearing or reading your words. Next, you want to broaden that 25-word scope by fleshing out with details the skeletal outline you provided in the hook. When possible, limit those details to three main points, the 1-2-3 punch. (Turn back to the Force Field Analysis, page 419, to get some ideas.) And, take some verbal risks in presenting them. There should be confidence in your message. You should be making strong statements, not understatements, at this point.

☑ Proceed now to describe the three main points of your proposal, citing advantages, precedents, anticipated savings, ease of implementation, trends, technological advances, future concerns, reductions in cost or time, urgency, statistics, forecasts--anything that explains to your influencee why your idea should or must be carried out.

1. _____

_____

_____

2. _____

_____

_____

3. _____

_____

_____

Lay your proposal aside for a while. Let new influences, insights, and stimuli penetrate your consciousness. Then return to it and tighten the verbal nuts and bolts. Make the images sharper, the points more pointed, the facts more prominent.

5. Hint at possibilities for the future.

Certain aspects of your vision are indelibly etched in your mind's eye. Other aspects, however, are less clearly "seen." With the long-range projections that are flexible, invite your influencees to make projections of their own, to speculate, to dream. There are possibilities you've not yet conceived, ramifications you've not yet considered, paths you might never have thought of exploring. If your idea is to be truly far-reaching and firmly entrenched in the future, new tributaries will grow from the main stream you are exploring.

A long-term project, for example, might be the formation of a national professional organization, one that holds an annual conference. Spin-offs of this successful project, though, might be regional conferences or the publication of proceedings from these conferences. Often, these derivative projects or products can only evolve "in the moment," but it is a moment that has been prepared for carefully. Through these events, your influence will be truly long-lasting.

☑   Considering the vision you have delineated, what are some possibilities that might open up from the realization of it? (The proposal-presentation should not delve into these possibilities, but it should allude to them. One of these glimpses of the future may be enough to capture the imagination and the commitment of an influencee who has been lukewarm up until now.) _____

_____

_____

6. Ask for what you need.

End your spoken or written presentation with an unequivocal request. What exactly do you want from your influencees? What are they supposed to do? To what extent should they be involved? You can allude to the elements of your action plan, you can allude to the value they will derive, you can allude to future possibilities, but above all else, tell them in no uncertain terms what you need. Now is not the time for meekness, hedging, or half-hearted overtures.

☑   One mark of a successful influencer is the ability to align what he has with what he needs. Think of the people who will be on your team as you work to make your vision a new reality. List each person here and briefly note what

talents and/or traits he brings to the table. (For the time
being, leave the Task lines blank.)

Person	Talent/Trait	Task
_____	_____ _____	_____
		_____
_____	_____ _____	_____
		_____
_____	_____ _____	_____
		_____
_____	_____ _____	_____
		_____
_____	_____ _____	_____
		_____
_____	_____ _____	_____
		_____
_____	_____ _____	_____
		_____

7. Develop an action plan.

Assuming you honestly wish to make your vision an
improvement upon current reality, you will need a plan that
includes both long-range and short-range goals. And, it
should subscribe to the ancient Roman exhortation to *divide
et impera* (divide and rule). Pick up a calendar and proceed

with the final step in making your vision a reality that many can share.

☑   As you think in terms of executing your vision, divide the work into five chronological segments.

1. What would have to be done within the next year if this plan is to become a reality by then? _____

_____

_____

2. What would have to be done in the next nine months?

_____

_____

_____

3. What would have to be done in the next six months?

_____

_____

_____

4. What would have to be done in the next three months?

_____

_____

_____

5. What would have to be done in the next month?

_____

_____

_____

Divide and rule again. If you look only at the next month,

1. What should be done tomorrow and for the next six days? _____

_____

_____

2. What should be done in Week 2? _____

_____

3. What should be done in Week 3 _____

_____

4. What should be done in Week 4? _____

_____

Go back now to Step 5, "Ask for what you need." For each line in the Task column, write one thing that has to be done in the next four weeks and one thing that has to be done in the next year. Match talents/traits with tasks for each person on your influencee list.

Self-Promotion
Leading Edge or Bleeding Edge

If you have succeeded in making your long-term vision attractive, if you have put your action plan into effect, you have exposed it and yourself to public attention. You cannot influence without having others notice you--perhaps for the first time or perhaps in a different light. You've lifted the bushel, so to speak, from your light, and have made it and yourself available for all to see. Like many other situations associated with influence, however, visibility is a double-edged sword. With one edge, it can cut through the group identification and make you stand out as a singular entity. Yet with the other edge, the very attention you will be receiving may create further problems for you.

One sharp example should suffice. The mayor of New York City, Rudolph Giuliani, has rightfully sought credit (for himself and his party) for a number of achievements occurring during his term of office. But as a public figure, particularly one who trumpets vision-attainment, he lays himself open for good-natured kidding (if not outright criticism). *New York* magazine ran ads on the sides of city buses, calling itself "possibly the only good thing in New York Rudy hasn't taken credit for."

If you were the Big Apple's big cheese, so to speak, would you respond at all (yes or no)? _____ If you answered yes, how would you respond (with humor or with hostility)? _____ The mayor promptly ordered the magazine to remove all its ads, claiming his privacy and civil rights had been abused. The magazine found the order worthy of settlement in the courts and sued. The brouhaha was brought before two federal courts, but essentially the mayor was advised to expect a certain amount of public ridicule by virtue of being a public figure.

A little bit of humor in this scenario probably would have gone a long way. Giuliani could have said, for example, "It's the reference to me that makes the ad such a good one!" By contrast, think about the ridicule so often showered on former vice president Dan Quayle, author of statements such as the following:

- "Republicans understand the importance of bondage between a mother and child."
- "The loss of life will be irreplaceable." (speaking about California earthquakes)
- "Sometimes cameras and television are good to people, and sometimes they aren't. I don't know if it's the way you say it or how you look."
- "I stand by all the misstatements that I've made."

As a rule, Quayle shrugged off the fun that was poked at him; he didn't threaten lawsuits when his intelligence was questioned or when his gaffes were collected into books. Thus, he influenced public opinion to regard him benignly. Rather than add more fuel to the satire-fires, he presented himself as an even more likeable figure. Self-promotion, an inevitable component of influence--whether it's direct or indirect, intended or inadvertent--can be done well or poorly. Whatever decisions are made regarding reactions, the influencer will be exerting further influence.

Promote to the Hilt

If influence is a sword with double edges, self-promotion is the hilt or handle of that sword. Whether or not you *intend* to promote yourself as you promote your ideas, the two promotions are inseparable. Focusing influencees' attention on your proposal means focusing their attention on yourself as well. Power does not flow to invisible people. By virtue of creating new realities for yourself and your influencees, you not only increase your personal power but you also acquire visibility.

The Seven Habits of Highly Effective Influencers

Follow these recommendations in order to exert greater influence and thus increase the likelihood that your vision will be seen and supported by a wide array of potential influencees.

1)   *Stop thinking of self-promotion as underhanded or shameful.* Instead, regard it as an effective means of communicating what you can do for others who could benefit from your ideas. Let them know you are serious about moving forward with your vision. Welcome their input.

Even if the self-promotion is not done for job-related reasons, it is nonetheless necessary in order to influence others to learn about and then subscribe to the proposals you may be making. Yes, you will wind up looking good if the vision is realized. However, if you are influencing with integrity, looking good will not be your primary objective. Achieving Win/Win/Win outcomes will be. Think of promoting your idea first and yourself second and do away with guilt.

2)   *Widen your networks.* They say the person with the fattest rolodex wins. By extension, the influencer with the widest network wins too. While your initial group of influencees may purposely be small, the number of people who should be advised or kept apprised will probably be large.

Mathematicians tell us that as the number of units in a network grows arithmetically, the worth of the network increases exponentially. There are many resources you can tap as you seek endorsement for your plan. As author

Harvey Mackay maintains, "The person to your left, to your right, in front of you, or behind you at this very moment is someone who can potentially make a real difference in your life."

Even if your influence is a one-on-one endeavor--you want to run for president of a professional association, for example, and are hoping to influence the current president so he will endorse you--your network of advisors can assist in helping you formulate your plan. It doesn't matter that the members of this network are not part of the association. Sometimes an outsider's viewpoint is more cogent than an insider's. As your network grows, so do your influence and your visibility. Unlike the minimalist fashion philosophy that asserts less is more, in influencing, more is more.

3)   *Let your expertise do the walking.* As the ads for yellow pages used to tell us, when we let our fingers do the work, we save time and trouble. Letting your reputation and your credentials precede you will help immensely as you work to win others over to your way of thinking. You can present your expertise, of course, in a way that is even- or that is heavy-handed. To avoid the latter, subordinate the credentials to the import of the idea. A simple example follows.

"I have eleven years' experience working on fundraisers like this. We've always come out ahead."

Less offensive would be a statement like this:

"In the eleven years I've spent on fundraisers like this one, monies raised always exceeded expenditures. If we find the right corporate sponsor, we're bound to come out ahead."

The emphasis is not on "I" but rather on the fundraising strategy. But the "I" is in there. The person unused to or uncomfortable with self-promotion would omit the reference altogether, thus denying the influencee the opportunity to assess the worth of the idea on the basis of the influencer's background.

4)   *Look for the dumb*. And then set about improving upon it. There is no such thing as a perfect organization, a perfect family, a perfect relationship, a perfect job, a perfect person. The prospect of making improvements (and of learning in the process) keeps us young, no matter what our age. There are some dumb things going on in your personal or professional environment. Finding those things is the starting point of many an excellent vision. Even if you already have your vision planned out, you can still look for dumb practices and show how your plan can alleviate some of them. Such correlating brings your vision down to earth

and lends it an immediacy and relevancy it would not otherwise have.

5)   *Speak up. Write up. Act up.* Take every opportunity you can to make others aware of who you are and what you can offer to them. Even the simplest of verbal gestures can lead to Win/Win/Win outcomes. For example, you're at a social gathering and you introduce yourself this way, "Hi. I'm Pat. I run a small business downtown." If the other person is a sensitive listener, he will ask you what kind of business it is. But he might not, thereby missing a possible connection.

By contrast, if you say, "I run a typing service that specializes in resume preparation," you've uttered four additional words, but you may have answered an unspoken need the other person has. Horn-tooting can be done blaringly or blithely, but it must be done if you are to promote your idea and yourself. Get into the habit of optimizing chance encounters (on airplanes, in elevators, at social events) by succinctly but revealingly telling who you are and what you can do for people. When possible, demonstrate what you can do. The hands-on experience is an irresistible one for most people.

Another excellent means of gaining visibility for your vision is to do some writing--for your organizational news-letter, for your local newspaper, for a trade journal. Even if you are not paid for your efforts, you are widening your sphere of influence and gaining visibility for your vision. Consider making a presentation at a professional conference, one of the best ways to build a name for yourself. Simply put, the more pebbles you drop into the pond of possibility, the more ripples you will create and the more far-reaching your influence will be.

6)   *Gain experience in safe circumstances.* Especially with proposals that are far-reaching or costly, you will need as much practice as you can get before the actual delivery. Gain that practice in places and with people that are accepting. In general terms, you will want to learn how to control your nerves, your pace, and even your audience.

More specifically, you will need to ascertain which parts of your proposal seem to confuse others, which parts you see the audience nodding in agreement with, which parts are not as well-received as you thought they'd be. With an audience of friends and family, you can develop both the general and the specific honing.

For the general development, address non-threatening groups, if only for a few minutes. Speak up at the next PTA meeting, for example. Or volunteer to speak to your child's class at school. To rehearse delivering the specific elements of your proposal, present it to someone familiar with the circumstances but who does not represent the actual decision-making body. If the proposal is lengthy or complicated, break it down into four main parts and present one part to each of four groups of colleagues. Ask for honest feedback and avoid being defensive as you hear it. Instead, listen and make notes.

7) *Promote others as well.* It's no secret that the spokesperson of a team is typically the person associated with the team's success. By the time your vision has been executed, you will have already received quite a bit of attention. It's time to step aside and share the spotlight. You can still promote yourself, but make the spotlight's circle big enough to include several others.

To illustrate, if you were accepting an award or being honored for the triumphant implementation of your vision (the establishment of a daycare center at the work site), you might say, "Lest you think this brainchild of mine was nurtured by a single parent, let me assure you a whole village was involved here. The person who handled the financial end of it was...." Then, after you have acknowledged the skills of those who worked behind the scenes, you could go on to accept the accolades on behalf of the whole team.

The Entrepreneurial Spirit

Influpreneuring is a special word we've coined for the influencer who wants to make a difference at work. We all know that entrepreneurs are businesspeople whose love of independence is powerful enough to propel them into starting their own businesses. Intrapreneurs, a term coined by author Gifford Pinchot, are businesspeople who have an entrepreneurial spirit but who have opted to remain within the corporate confines. They run their own small area of the organization as if it were their own business; they serve as internal entrepreneurs.

Influpreneurs can be either inside or outside a large bureaucratic structure. They are leaders, visionaries, idea people who can take a good idea and run with it. Their ideas may be as broad and encompassing as the formation of a whole new company, or as narrow yet effective as proposing a new ad campaign and persuading others to adopt it.

What distinguishes the influpreneur from his corporation-ensconced counterpart is usually the size of his proposal: Entrepreneurs and intrapreneurs typically operate on a grand scale. Influpreneurs may as well, but we would define influpreneurs more narrowly as those who make suggestions and convince others to follow them, whether or not they are initially willing to do so. (As Harry Truman so aptly defined it, "What makes leadership is the ability to get people to do what they don't want to do and like it.")

Further, the influpreneur may or may not be a businessperson. The youngster who presents an idea to other children on the playground and influences them to participate in it can rightfully be considered an influpreneur. But always, after persuading others to follow a particular course of action, the influpreneur works with them until that course of action is complete and an amelioration of one sort or another results.

☑ By now, you have no doubt proven you have what it takes to influence with integrity. But this is our last chance to assess where you are so you'll know where you have to go in order to maximize your talents. Don't agonize over the following statements.

Instead, read them and react quickly by encircling the number that most closely applies to you and your typical way of thinking/behaving. Use 0 to indicate "not at all applicable" and 5 to reflect statements that are "very applicable" to you.

	Not at all					Very
1. I have a clear vision of an improvement I'd like to make.	0	1	2	3	4	5
2. I think of myself as a leader.	0	1	2	3	4	5

3. I have good persuasion skills.   0   1   2   3   4   5

4. I ask for help when I need it.   0   1   2   3   4   5

5. I take pride in what I do.   0   1   2   3   4   5

6. My feelings are not easily hurt.   0   1   2   3   4   5

7. I am future-oriented.   0   1   2   3   4   5

8. I am comfortable talking about my accomplishments.

                                   0   1   2   3   4   5

9. I am a risk-taker.   0   1   2   3   4   5

10. I am secure enough to give credit where it is due.

                                   0   1   2   3   4   5

Total: _____

Skip ahead to the Interview with Kim Hyland--if you scored 40 points or more. If your score was less than that, read the following recommendations for developing your influpreneurial skills.

1. **Vision**   While we worked extensively in this chapter on having one particular vision-project, you will need many more to keep your mind and spirit vital in the years ahead. As you read the newspaper every day for the next ten days, keep a log of the articles that had the greatest impact on you. You need not analyze why, but you should make note of what the article was about.

441

On the eleventh day, go back and review your notes. You'll probably find a pattern beginning to emerge. Or, you may find one particular story that moved you, that caused something within your soul to resonate. These patterns and stirrings mark the beginning of a vision project. Something you read troubled you or inspired you. At first, it just whispered to you. Then the volume grows. Soon, an influence project will emerge from these (in)sights and sounds.

2.   **Leadership**   You may want to start by reading some magazines and books about leadership. But all the reading in the world cannot compensate for the experience of actually leading others toward a commonly supported goal. To develop your skills in this regard, start off small. Undertake a project of short duration or little complexity. Persuade a small group to join you and work together until the goal has been met. Only then will you know the frustration and simultaneous thrill of taking an idea to fruition through collective efforts.

Continue to set these self-challenges, each time assuming more responsibility, each time profiting from the mistakes or missteps of the preceding effort.

3.   **Persuasion**   We recommend two ways of enhancing these particular communication skills. 1) Make note of the most effective persuaders you encounter in a

442

typical day (including those you see on television or hear on the radio). Determine exactly what it is these remarkable speakers say that convinces others their words are worth listening to and, even more impressive, worth following.

2) Keep a log detailing the outcomes of your persuasion efforts each day. Stop when you have seen a 50% increase in the success rate. At the end of the first week, you may find you were successful in 10 out of 30 persuasion attempts. When you reach 15 out of 30, you can relax a bit.

4. **Help**   Sometimes influencers incorrectly feel they must have all the answers if they are leading others. Nothing could be farther from the truth. First, you never will have all the answers. Pretending you can will only weaken the strength of your influence. Secondly, by not obtaining help from those qualified to give it, you will weaken the strength of your plan. It needs nurturing by the very best minds and spirits. In denying your idea access to a wide array of talents, you may be sabotaging your own success.

5. **Pride**   Influpreneurs take pride and give pride in the concept to which they have committed some part of their lives. Yes, they believe in it but they want others to believe in it as well. Thus, they speak passionately about their undertaking. If you are keeping your pride to yourself, set a goal to tell at least one person a day--in the briefest of

terms unless circumstances dictate otherwise--about this plan of yours. The next week, try to update the original five, again briefly, but tell five new people. Take it one week further: update ten and find five new listeners.

6. **Tough skin**   Growing a thick emotional hide is facilitated by two practices: self-talk and absurdizing. Self-talk means reminding yourself, whenever you are subjected to criticism, that you will emerge from the incident stronger, perhaps not at first, but stronger in the long run for having endured it and having learned to cope with it. Too, the criticism may have merit and, if it does, your plan can only be strengthened by it.

When you self-talk, you also remind yourself that no matter how brutal the criticism may be, the very fact that you are alive to hear it puts you one step ahead of the game. Your good health, after all, is more important than anything else in the world. This attack or negative commentary is only words, and in time you won't even remember or care about the words. Keep everything in perspective.

The second practice, absurdizing, will thicken your hide by making you used to hearing zingers and stingers. Invite a number of people who truly care about you to bombard you at unexpected times with absurdly critical comments. Get used to shrugging them aside with comments that protect your self-image while, at the same time, defusing a (pretended) conflict situation.

7. **Future** Read a book such as Daniel Burris' *Technotrends*. Let it point you in the direction of what you must do to prepare for the future so you can wisely influence others. Keep a file of trends and predictions and periodically update your vision(s) on the basis of what you are learning.

8. **Achievements** Ilise Benun, who edits a newsletter titled *The Art of Self Promotion*, advises adding a twist to overly familiar words to deepen their significance or to arouse interest in those you hope to influence. She gives the example of the New Jersey attorney who practices "Hoboken law." She also recommends using stories to promote your ideas, products, or services. The stories should reflect personality, facts and figures, anecdotes, and details that reveal.

Certainly, your achievements should be cited. But a long listing of accomplishments is not only boring, it suggests an inward concentration rather than an outward concern for others. Bring some creativity to the cataloging of your achievements.

9. **Risk** You can increase your risk-tolerance by putting into action a plan of increasingly larger risks. We are not referring to anything that would jeopardize

life, limb, or career. Rather, for one full month, sets goals such as, "Today I will start a conversation with a complete stranger" or "At the meeting this afternoon, I will offer one idea." When you can, have a friend or colleague critique your attempts.

10.   **Credit**   Ronald Reagan was rumored to have on his desk in the White House a sign that read, "It's amazing how much can get done if no one cares who gets the credit." This is a cohesion-building attitude for a team. Help create it by taking deliberate measures to recognize the influencees who are working to create a new organizational reality. (Also consider recognizing others who are involved in a less direct way.) Few achievements are ever made without collective contributions.

INTERVIEW

**Kimberly J. Hyland, Band Director,
Oneonta Middle School, Oneonta, New York**

One of the barriers I encounter when I attempt to influence students is their understandable lack of long-range vision. None of us can see into the future, but children, given their lack of experience, are much more myopic than the rest of us. So, I begin the school year by telling them what I hope we can do by the springtime, the levels at which I hope they will perform. The end of the year is very far away in their minds so I try to set mini-goals, attainable at incremental stages. This philosophy, I think, works equally well with adults. Dramatic breakthroughs are rare and difficult to achieve; goal-breakdowns, though, are more common and more reachable.

Other parallels exist, I think, between students and employees. We're all learners, for openers. And often our initial motivation for that learning is a grade, a reward, a way to be better so we can look better and get the prize--be it a report card letter or a promotion. In time, though, the initial purpose gets subjugated to the sheer pleasure of learning something new, the excitement of seeing progress being made. In my case, students can look back and compare what they sounded like a month ago or a marking period ago to the way they sound now. They realize, for example, they can play scales now that they couldn't play then. Success with all the weekly and monthly goals culminates in a grand final performance.

Using the theory that initial, extrinsic rewards recede in importance as intrinsic rewards take over, I decided to enter the band in the Fiesta-val Competition. The trick to getting any middle school student to do something is to promise them a trip to an amusement park. I enticed them in the beginning with this promise, knowing that the excitement of participating in a nation-wide competition and meeting other young musicians would soon become the real reward.

The quality of performance in these competitions is at such a high level that middle schools typically are not included. But we applied nonetheless and were accepted. Apart from the value of the experience, I knew the event would help improve skills, for the judges do a critique of the performance. Our students actually wound up placing first in their division and also won the championship trophy for first place for any concert performance group.

Influencing others toward a love of music is easy for me (although getting 65 youngsters to perform as an ensemble is not). Each day, I tell myself that whatever we do has to be guided by music. The community has been tremendously supportive of our efforts and this inspires me too. It was a good feeling to be able to thank them for their fundraising by bringing distinction to our small town.

I cannot ever remember my life without music in it. Its influence has been profound, so profound that I regard Plato's quotation as a guiding principle--"If you want to educate someone, educate three parts of them: physical education for their body, mathematics and logic for their mind, and music for their soul." I fear education of the soul is being ignored in too many places.

DO:

-- Regard yourself as a trailblazer whenever you influence others to rally around a common cause.

-- Sharpen your hook by using words that appear in advertisements.

-- Align needs with the talents and expertise of those you influence.

-- Regard self-promotion as a neutral concept. It can be used ethically or deceptively. But in promoting any good idea you have, you inevitably promote yourself.

-- Ask for help when you need it.

-- Be attuned to ordinary circumstances that can be converted to extraordinary opportunities for promoting your plans.

-- Regard yourself as an influpreneur even if you cannot work as an entrepreneur or an intrapreneur.

-- Think of ways to bring novelty to overused words. Also, use stories to reflect your personality.

-- Set mini-goals.

-- Explore both intrinsic and extrinsic goals for your influencees.

DON'T:

-- Overlook the possibilities of having a long-term impact on the present.

-- Have too many points in the body of your proposal. We recommend the 1-2-3 punch.
-- Think you can do it all. Distribute work and credit equitably.
-- Assume your network is as wide as it should be.
-- Undertake a big project if leadership is new to you. Start small and improve gradually. Keep a log of lessons learned so each new attempt is better than the one before.
-- Hesitate to speak "pridefully." Genuine passion on your part can enthrall others.
-- Give a long list of your achievements when you self-promote. Find creative ways to express and not simply impress.

YOU WILL:

-- Find the Force Field Analysis a valuable tool for planning your strategy.

-- Often be able to make your message more focused if you set it aside for a while and then return to it for revisions.

-- Need an action plan, broken down into long- and short-range steps.

-- With some effort, learn to subordinate expertise so you can include it without sounding as if you are bragging.

-- Get better at self-promoting than you already are if you continue to practice in safe circumstances.

-- Be called to new visions periodically by reading the newspaper and noting what captivates you.

-- Learn from effective persuaders you see and hear around you. But, you will have to analyze their techniques to discover what works. Then, you'll have to try out those techniques for yourself.

-- Need to develop a tough hide by self-talking and absurdizing.

-- Discover that moderate risk-taking can catapult you and your idea into a prominent position.

YOU WON'T

-- Influence effectively without a hook that intrigues/attracts/interests your audience.

-- Spark imaginations if everything is specified. Allude to future possibilities but don't delineate every detail.

-- Be as likely to harm yourself with the sharp edge of the sword of influence if you can put things in perspective. Laugh at yourself from time to time.

-- Be able to escape visibility if you are influencing.

-- Find the "dumb" without looking for it. It abounds in every environment.

-- Know what effect your persuasive efforts are having unless you are keeping track.

-- Regret reading a book about the future and using the information to periodically calibrate your visions.

-- Achieve in isolation and you should not accept credit in isolation. Expand the circle of deserved recognition to your influencees.

-- Always have agreement or acceptance in the beginning of a project. But you can influence others to like what they initially resisted. Accomplishing this is the mark of a true leader, at least according to Harry Truman.

Appendix

~~~~~~~~~~~~~~

Studying the cases in which others have been
involved is an excellent way to learn. The following
scenarios are based on real-work occurrences. Influence was
required to turn these problem people/problem situations
around. As you read these scenarios, decide what you would
do and record your answer. Then discuss your choice with a
colleague or friend whose opinion you respect. After
learning what she would have done, compare the relative
merits of each choice according to the rationales that guided
both you and your colleague. Then, turn to the end of the
Appendix to learn what the panel of experts selected as the
option most likely to succeed.

Case Study #1

Linda is a relatively new trainer, whose inexperience
is overshadowed by her competence. During the first few
minutes of her introductory remarks, she notices one
participant reading the newspaper, turning the pages loudly,

and clearly ignoring everything she is saying. At the first break, she takes him aside and essentially asks him to participate. His response, delivered in the politest of terms, is quite honest.

He tells her he does not want to be there but has to be, as the class is mandatory. Then he assures her, "You just go ahead and do your thing. I'll stay out of your way and do my thing. [He showed her a stack of reading at this point that he intended to catch up on.] They just won't be the same things."

How do you think Linda should respond?_____

_____

How might a man respond in these circumstances?_____

_____

A minister? _____

_____

A parent? _____

_____

An experienced trainer? _____

_____

Other? _____

_____

Considering these positions and any others you feel would be appropriate, select one and give Linda the persona of this individual. What is the most influential statement she could make, using what language? (Write here the actual words you think she should use as she speaks in the voice of the person whose identity you've selected for her.)

_____

_____

_____

_____

How does your reply match or differ from that of your colleague? _____

_____

How does it match or differ from that of the panel of experts (reported at the end of the Appendix section)? _____

_____

_____

Case Studies (#2A, B, and C) from Chapter 4

#2 A   You have failed to meet a commitment.

Ineffective: I won't be able to ship the materials to you next week as I had promised.

More effective: Sam, as you know, we have always shipped your materials on time, ever since we began working together six years ago.

But...there's a first time for everything, as they say. And next week's shipment will be delayed by four days. Our line operator is in the hospital with two broken arms and as hard as we've tried to play catch up here, we're still running four days behind schedule.

To make it up to you, though, we're going to extend the payment terms an additional 30 days for this particular order.

What the Experts Had To Say About Case Study #2A

Our panel acknowledged the fact that the more effective version is also more wordy. However, the length was justified, the panel felt, on several counts:

1)   The influencer subtly reminded Sam of the company's excellent track record up to this point.

2)   The influencer offered an explanation, which most people appreciate having.

3)   To compensate for the inconvenience, the company is offering an apology via extended credit terms, on a one-time-only basis.

#2B   You, as team leader, have learned the team's proposal has been rejected.

Ineffective: Well, guys, just as we expected, our brilliant leaders have failed to see the merit of our proposal. Poof! All that hard work down the old toilet.

More effective: We feared our proposal stood only a 50/50 chance of being accepted. The odds, it seems, were against us. However, the committee has recommended several ways the proposal can be strengthened. This team is realistic enough to know there's more we can do. And I think we're optimistic enough to know we can meet the highest standards. I say let's examine their recommendations, and if we can commit the time, let's go for it.

What the Experts Had To Say About Case Study #2B

The original message was sarcastic ("our brilliant leaders"). It was also negative and pessimistic. Further, it set up an us-versus-them dichotomy. The more effective message acknowledges the team's fear going into the situation. But it does much more: it offers hope. First, by providing an analysis of where and how the proposal failed. Second, by calling upon the pride of team members (there is an indirect admission that the proposal was not their very best work) and by reminding them that they can do much more. A can-do spirit clearly comes through in the last sentence, along with a realistic observation about the commitment required.

#2C   Senior management, in a cost-cutting mode, has decided that neither the annual Christmas bonus nor the annual Christmas party will be given this year.

Ineffective: You can call me Scrooge if you like, but there'll be no ho-ho-ho's around here this year. We can't afford the Christmas bonus nor the usual Christmas party.

More effective: You may have heard some rumors about the Christmas bonus. You may also have heard that Franklin, Inc., our chief competitor, has just laid off 400 employees. That is not a rumor. Our company fortunately is in a fairly solid position. Our jobs are secure, at least for the foreseeable future. While we will not receive our Christmas bonus this year, we are really much better off than those who have lost their jobs just prior to the holiday.

As for the Christmas party, the company is trimming expenses and so we will not have the extravaganza to which we've grown accustomed. But we are still free to plan a pot-luck party of our own. And, if we can just get Harold to put on a Santa costume, we should have as much fun as we've always had.

What the Experts Had To Say About Case Study #2C

From time to time, we all need to be reminded how fortunate we are to have what we have. To forestall the predictable gripes, the influencer wisely addresses the rumor by alluding to a non-rumor: the fact that comparable employees have actually lost their jobs. He is honest-- acknowledging that their jobs are protected for a while at least, and that the company is indeed in a cost-cutting mode. But he offers a solution--they can plan their own party--and uses humor at the end to lift spirits to the holiday-level.

Case Studies (#3A, B, and C) from Chapter 5

#3A   The association president wrote an apology to the human rights caucus. In part, he distanced himself from the offending speaker by noting the association cannot control the speech of the hundreds of speakers whom they hire each year. He did assure the caucus that they had taken some preventive measures, however.

The association leader has admitted they probably will not rebook this particular speaker. And he has stated that future speakers will be "strongly reminded" of the need to be politically sensitive to people of varying backgrounds and ethnic origin.

#3B   The attorney acknowledged the receipt of many similar requests, all of which had to be denied, no matter their worth, creativity, or originality. He then acknowledged the important purpose behind the request but restated the policy of refusing permission for the use of the corporate trademark. In the next paragraph, he explained the reason for that policy. He concluded with an expression of regret along with a wish for success to the speaker.

#3C   The president took a strong stand. He assured employees the company was contesting the citations. In addition, he used the word "alleged" violations, thus reinforcing the concept of innocent until proven guilty. He perhaps attempted to garner sympathy by noting the company was only given 15 working days to respond. Next, he alluded to the company's history of compliance, and assured his audience the company fully intended to cooperate with the federal agency "to ensure the safety and health" of all employees.

He next restates the company's strong objections to the characterization of the alleged violations as "willful." The bulletin concludes with an assurance that the company is working with OSHA officials to reach a satisfactory resolution to carry out their action plan for these concerns. The final sentence is a promise to keep the workforce informed.

Answers to Chapter 5 quiz

1-e; 2-d (spoken to Al Gore, who had decided to make fewer campaign appearances in some states than in others) 3-i; 4-f; 5-b (said to his wife as he danced with Imelda Marcos); 6-h; 7-a; 8-g; 9-c

Answer to Chapter 6 sentence revision

Middlebrook secretaries distrust Meadowbrook secretaries. (There really is no need to say "currently" or "presently" as a substitute for "at the present time." The very fact that present tense is used means the situation is occurring at the present time.)

Other sentences to be revised.

1.   If the proposal is rejected by your office, clear and logical reasons must be submitted in sufficient detail to permit transmittal to the proposer without editing or revision being needed.
(Can you reduce it to ten words?)

_____

_____

2.   It is the purpose of this article to report on the state of the parks in this state, which are the subject of controversy between environmentalists and some government officials because of the way the parks are being handled, and because of the widespread and complex problems that seem to be the result of a lack of foresight. (Can you reduce it to 15 words?)

_____

_____

3.   A useful purpose can be accomplished if discussions are held between you, the supervisor, and the person who made the proposal, for such discussion can be used to convey the company's interest in both the proposal of the given employee and in the employee himself or herself. (Can you reduce it to 12 words?)

Answers to Chapter 9 quizzes

Shun Certitude

1.   According to author Thomas A. Kayser, the time wasted in meetings costs American businesses in excess of $37 million a year.

2.   Just about 1650 years ago, Pope Julius I officially set December 25 as the date to celebrate.
the birth of Christ. At that time, 350 A.D., he was the recognized religious leader of the Roman Empire.

3.   A stack of $1,000 bills would reach 76 miles before it amounted to $1 trillion.

4.   The cost of the investigation was more than $11,000,000. Mr. Espy was subsequently cleared of all charges.

5.   The first U.S. satellite was in space for 12 years, from 1958 to 1970.

Productivity

1-a;   2-b;   3-b;   4-a;   5-b;   6-b;   7-a

Individuals with a majority of the above answers tend to be more task-oriented than those who did not have a majority. Extreme task-orientation for an influencer, however, can be as damaging as limited task-orientation. If you concentrate only on the job to be done without considering the feelings or needs of those doing it, your influence will be minimal. Further, you may be promoting apathy or worse yet, rebellion. Remember that accomplishments are not achieved in a vacuum; they are made because others have agreed to be influenced by you. You owe them more than mere task-completion.

What the Experts Had To Say About Case Study #1

The panel agreed on the approach: Linda would have to assume control of this situation or else other participants would be disrupted. Panelists decided Linda should speak on an Adult-to-Adult level, but that if this approach did not work, she should assume the Parent-to-Child approach. The dialog would sound like this as she moves from the first to the second mode and then back to the first again.

<u>Participant</u>:   Just go ahead and do what you have to do. I won't bother you if you won't bother me.

<u>Linda</u>:   That's not going to work, John. I'm hired to teach the entire class, and that means everyone has to be involved, engage in the assignments, and work as a

466

member of the team. I'm certain you have a lot of experience that would be valuable to the others.

Participant: I do. However, it's a waste of my time to share it.

Linda: I invite you again to be a participating member of this class. If you cannot, then you will have to leave.

Participant: Are you threatening me?

Linda: No, I'm merely stating the chain of events here and re-stating my obligation to the firm. I'm being paid to teach. I cannot teach if you refuse to learn. Please put aside this stack of magazines and join us. Again, I'm confident you can contribute to our discussions. I'm equally confident that you don't know everything there is to know about this subject. However, if you refuse to participate, then you'll have to leave. I'll be happy to call your supervisor to explain why I've told you to return to work. Think about it. If you decide to stay, you're certainly welcome. If you decide to leave, you should do so before the others return from break.

Bibliography

~~~~~~~~~~~~~~~

Augustine, Norman, *Augustine's Travels* (New York: AMACOM), 1998.

Benun, Ilise, editor, *The Art of Self Promotion* (P.O. Box 23, Hoboken, NJ 07030).

Bick, Julie, *All I Really Need to Know about Businesss I Learned at Microsoft* (New York: Simon & Schuster Pocketbooks), 1997.

Blanchard, Ken, *Gung ho!* (New York: William Morrow), 1998.

Burris, Daniel, *Technotrends* (New York: HarperCollins), 1993.

Caroselli, Marlene, *The Language of Leadership* (Amerherst: HRD Press), 1990.

Cohen, Herb, *You Can Negotiate Anything* (Secaucus, NJ: L. Stuart Publishers), 1980.

DiZazzo, Raymond, *Saying the right thing: the 4 secrets of powerful communications* (Naperville, IL: Sourcebooks, Inc.), 1997.

Driscoll, Dawn-Marie, W. Michael Hoffman, and Edward
S. Petry, *The Ethical Edge: Tales of Organizations that
Have Faced Moral Crises* (Portland, Oregon: Master
Media Ltd.), 1997.

Fisher, Roger and William Ury, *Getting to Yes* (Boston:
Houghton Mifflin), 1981.

Giacalone, Robert and Jerald Greenberg, *AntiSocial
Behavior in Organizations* (Thousand Oaks, CA: Sage
Publications), 1996.

Gockley, Gil and Tanya, *Loving is Natural, Parenting is not:
creating a value-centered family* (Rochester, NY:
Coleman Press), 1997.

Goleman, Daniel, *Emotional Intelligence* (New York:
Bantam Books), 1995.

Gunning, Robert, *How to Take the Fog Out of Writing*
(Santa Barbara, CA: Gunning-Mueller Clear Writing
Institute), 1985.

Handy, Charles, *The Gods of Management* (New York:
Oxford University Press), 1995.

Hurt, Floyd, *Rousing Creativity* (Charlottesville, VA: Probe
Press, Inc.), 1996.

Jackson, Tim, *Inside Intel* (New York: Dutton), 1997.

Jandt, Fred and Paul Gillette, *Win-Win Negotiating* (New
York: Wiley & Sons), 1985.

Kayser, Thomas, *Mining Group Gold* (New York: Publishers Group), 1995.

Macchiavelli, Niccolo, *The Prince* (New York: Everyman's Library), 1958.

Mackay, Harvey, *Dig Your Well Before You're Thirsty* (New York, Doubleday), 1996.

McGregor, Douglas, *The Human Side of Enterprise* (New York: McGraw-Hill), 1960.

Nierenberg, Gerard, *Negotiating the Big Sale* (Homewood, IL: Business One Irwin), 1992.

Pinchot, Gifford, *Intrapreneuring* (New York: Harper and Row), 1985.

Sheehy, Barry, *Winning the Race for Value* (New York: AMACOM Books), 1996.

Spence, Gerry, *How To Argue and Win Every Time* (New York: St. Martin's Press), 1996.

Index

~~~~~~~~~~~~~~

Gates, Melinda 238
Gennaro, Joseph 126
Gillette, Paul 63
Giuliani, Rudolph 430
Gladstone, William 164
Gockley, Gil & Tanya 411
Goethe, Wolfgang von 222
Good news/Bad news Technique 151
Gunning, Robert 116

H
Haig, Alexander 85, 196
Handy, Charles 38, 136
Hart, Gary 196
Hart, Kitty Carlisle 122
Having pre-determined outcomes 309
Hayakawa, S.I. 222
HeartMath, LLC 228
Help 443
Hiding negative information 302
High manipulation/high conflict 335
High worth/willing participation 333
Hoboken law 445
Hogan, John 87
Honesty 206 ff.
Humor, self-deprecating 220
Humphrey, Hubert 394
Hurt, Floyd 318
Hyland, Kim 447

I
Iacocca, Lee 146, 199, 244
Improvements 57. 244
Influence Continuum 340
Influpreneuring 439
Information pressure 238
Innovation 387
Inquire 295, 298

P

Q

R

W

Y